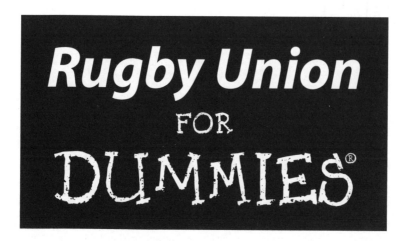

Rugby Union FOR DUMMIES®

by Nick Cain and Greg Growden

JOHN WILEY & SONS, LTD

Rugby Union For Dummies®

Published by
John Wiley & Sons, Ltd
The Atrium
Southern Gate
Chichester
West Sussex
PO19 8SQ
England

Email (for orders and customer service enquires): cs-books@wiley.co.uk

Visit our Home Page on www.wiley.co.uk or www.wiley.com

About the Author

Nick Cain has been a rugby writer for *The Sunday Times* since 1995 and before that he edited *Rugby World* for eight years. He has covered rugby union all over the globe, including four World Cups – he is about to embark on his fifth in Australia in 2003 – and four Lions tours.

He had a chequered playing career punctuated by such diversions as travelling, working on farms and in demolition in New Zealand, and as a fledgling journalist for an English language newspaper in the military junta Argentina of the early 1980s. He played rugby for Manchester University, Ponsonby (New Zealand) and Belgrano (Argentina) before grinding to a halt with Wasps thirds a decade ago.

Greg Growden is one of Australia's best-known sports writers. He began writing about rugby union in 1981, and since 1987 has been the chief rugby writer for the *Sydney Morning Herald* and *Sun-Herald* newspapers.

Greg has written for numerous international newspapers, including *The Guardian* and the *New Zealand Herald*. He is also a regular on New Zealand television rugby shows.

Greg's other books include *A Wayward Genius: the Fleetwood Smith Story* and *Gold, Mud, Guts, The Incredible Tom Richards: Footballer, War Hero, Olympian*.

Dedication

Dedication? Well, one thing's for sure: not everyone who picks up a copy of *Rugby Union For Dummies* is going to have the dedication, in terms of hours of practice and self-analysis, that it takes to become the next Jonny Wilkinson. Hopefully, though, whatever your aspirations as far as this great game is concerned, you will find something in these pages to help you meet them.

As for my own dedication, I would like to thank my better half, Gill. Her patience, sunny disposition and unstinting support, despite the fact that she must sometimes feel like a rugby widow, are priceless. Thanks also to my son, Hugo, and daughter, Ella, who never complained as their dad yet again disappeared to "The Shed at the End of the Garden" to work (at least they didn't jump for joy in front of me). A dedication too to my mother, Marion, and late father, Tony, for their faith in their sometimes wayward offspring.

- Nick Cain

Author's Acknowledgments

I had invaluable assistance along the way, not least from Stephen Jones, my colleague at *The Sunday Times*. Stephen is not only one of the finest writers on the game, and a fount of knowledge on anything to do with it, he is also a stalwart friend. To John Griffiths (the best statistician in rugby union), Alan Pearey (at *Rugby World*), and Justin O'Regan (at *Planet-Rugby*), your help was much appreciated. Lastly, thanks to the team at Wiley & Sons – Jason Dunne (Executive Editor), Daniel Mersey (Project Editor) and Samantha Clapp (Editorial Assistant) – for their courtesy and unflappable approach to the project.

- Nick Cain

Publisher's Acknowledgments

We're proud of this book; please send us your comments through our Dummies online registration form located at `www.dummies.com/register/`.

Some of the people who helped bring this book to market include the following:

Acquisitions, Editorial, and Media Development

Executive Editor: Jason Dunne

Acquisitions Editors: Jane Ogilvie, Lesley Beumont

Project Editors: Daniel Mersey, Liz Goodman,

Developmental Editors: Kristen Hammond, Jon Underwood

Technical Reviewer: Alan "Jock" Hossack

Editorial Manager: Peter Storer

Editorial Assistant: Samantha Clapp

Proofreadrer: Jenny Scepanovic

Cover photo: Pictor International/Alamy

Production

Project Coordinator:

Layout and Graphics: Brian Drumm, Joyce Haughey, Michael Kruzil, Barry Offringa, Julie Trippetti, Mary Gillot Virgin, Shae Lynn Wilson, Melanee Wolven

Proofreaders: John Greenough, Susan Moritz, Dwight Ramsey, Charles Spencer

Cartoons: Ed McLachan

Illustrator: Paul Lennon

Indexer: Keyword Editorial Services (Michael Wyatt)

Special Help: Jan Withers

Photo credits: Fig 6-3, © Sport the Library/Action Photos Rugby Union; Fig 6-5, © Getty Images/John Gichigi; Fig 6-8, © Getty Images/Jaimie McDonald; Fig 6-9, © Sport the Library/Tom Putt; Fig 6-11, © Newspix/Mark Evans; Fig 7-4, © Getty Images/Daniel Berehulak; Fig 8-1, © Getty Images/John Gichigi; Fig 8-2, © Getty Images/Clive Brunskill; Fig 9-3, © Newspix/Mark Evans; Fig 11-1, © Newspix; Fig 11-2, © Sport the Library; Fig 12-1, © Newspix/Pat Hannagan; Fig 12-2, © Sport the Library/Photosport Rugby Union; Fig 13-2, © Sport the Library; Fig 13-3, © Sport the Library; Fig 13-4, © Sport the Library; Fig 18-1, © Sport the Library; Fig 18-2, © Sport the Library.

Publishing and Editorial for Consumer Dummies

Diane Graves Steele, Vice President and Publisher, Consumer Dummies

Joyce Pepple, Acquisitions Director, Consumer Dummies

Kristin A Cocks, Product Development Director, Consumer Dummies

Michael Spring, Vice President and Publisher, Travel

Brice Gosnell, Publishing Director, Travel

Suzanne Jannetta, Editorial Director, Travel

Publishing for Technology Dummies

Andy Cummings, Vice President and Publisher, Dummies Technology/General User

Composition Services

Gerry Fahey, Vice President of Production Services

Debbie Stailey, Director of Composition Services

Contents at a Glance

Table of Contents

Introduction

. . . .

Congratulations! You have *Rugby Union for Dummies* in your hands, an edition written specially for Britons who are keen to find out all they can about one of the most exciting of sporting codes. With this book, we aim to satisfy your curiosity, fill the gaps in your knowledge and show you that rugby is a whole new exciting world waiting to be explored.

Thousands of people around the world are passionate about rugby union, and nowhere more than in the British Isles, where the game originated. For the uninitiated, rugby union may seem like a game from another planet where the inhabitants speak a strange language and talk about things called scrums, rucks, mauls and lineouts. All these strange words, the laws that govern the game, the positions of the players on the field and what they are supposed to do can easily overwhelm the beginner.

We wrote this book so that rugby union beginners can get to know the game quickly and easily, without ever feeling overwhelmed or intimidated. Before long, you find you are an expert on the game, the most innovative and fascinating of football codes, a code that is forever evolving.

About This Book

Our simple aim in writing this book is to provide you with everything you want to know about rugby. All the information is here. You don't have to read this book right through from page one to the end though in order to make the most of it.

Each chapter covers a rugby topic in itself, so you can easily dip into those chapters where we talk about the bits of the game that you don't quite understand. When you are watching a game on television, for example, and a referee's signal confuses you, just turn to the chapter that explains the referee's signals and the basic laws that govern the game.

If you want to become a player, you can easily navigate your way to the sections of most interest to you, and also take advantage of the handy hints throughout the book. Whether you want to become a referee, a club official, or simply a spectator, a chapter has been written with you in mind.

No matter where you sit on the rugby totem pole, whether you are an outright beginner or a self-adjudged expert, *Rugby Union for Dummies* has something that you find interesting.

How to Use This Book

To make it easier for you, *Rugby Union for Dummies* follows certain conventions. For example, to make it easier for you, every time we use a new term or an important phrase, it is in italics and its meaning is explained.

We explain everything very, very clearly, and not in language full of rugby gobbledegook. For a quick reminder of the meanings of certain terms, you can always turn to the glossary at the back of the book.

Don't be restricted by the order in which the contents of this book appear. Flip through it, maybe starting with the chapter on the laws, where we explain the most important rules of the game. Check out the diagrams, drawings and photos, which make it easy for you to immediately understand the most important aspects of the game.

You may find that in a discussion of a particular aspect of rugby in one chapter, we refer to another aspect of the game. Whenever that happens, we tell you which chapter to turn to for more information about that other aspect. For example, when we talk about tactics, we mention player positions and tell you which chapter to turn to for more detailed information on positions.

Foolish Assumptions

Don't feel intimidated if you know nothing about rugby union. Even some players have difficulty remembering things like the laws, so never worry that you are a rugby dummy – we certainly don't think you are! Before long, you are going to feel like an expert.

You may have been watching a game and asked

- Why are all those players grabbing each other around the waist and then charging at each other like stampeding rhinos?
- Why does the referee keep waving his arms around?
- Why are the players standing in a straight line and jumping for the ball?

> ✔ Why is a hooker called a hooker?
>
> ✔ What is a ruck and what is a maul?

This book answers these questions, and many, many more. Our assumption is that you basically know nothing – and we go from there.

How This Book is Organised

This book is organised into six parts according to the famous *For Dummies* design. Each part focuses on an important part of the world of rugby union.

Part 1: Rugby: Roots, Boots and All

If you are totally new to rugby, this part sets the scene for you. We describe the history of the game, how it all comes together on the field, and how the popularity of rugby circles the planet. We also explain what all those lines on the pitch mean and how the scoring system works. This part ends with handy hints on how to kit yourself up for a game of rugby and how to take precautions to minimise the risk of injury.

Part II: Getting Down and Dirty

A really important chapter starts this part. We give you detailed information on the positions the players occupy and their roles. Then we introduce you to the most important laws that govern the game as well as to the officials who control the game. This part helps you to improve your skills on the field, and explains rucks, mauls, scrums and lineouts. It then moves on to an explanation of tactics before describing some of the best ways in which to get fit and stay fit for rugby. You can also find out about coaching and how to get involved in it.

Part III: Welcome to Planet Rugby

This part tells you all about the competitions, the tournaments, the teams, the players and the fields on which they play. We describe the World Cup, international rugby competitions like the Six Nations, and the most important national competitions. This part also talks about the rugby scene in the UK and Ireland and tells you how you can get involved in your local club, whether you are interested in coaching, playing, or just soaking up the atmosphere.

Part IV: Following the Game: The Informed Fan

If you are a fan, this part is for you. We guide you to the best sources of rugby information whether they are on the screen, in the newspapers or on the radio. This part also has some great hints on getting the most out of being a spectator.

Part V: The Part of Tens

The part without which no *For Dummies* book would be complete. This part is packed full of fascinating bits of information that you can store away and draw on whenever you feel like impressing all those around you at the rugby club. It contains our take on the greatest rugby highs, as well as rugby trivia that is funny as well as interesting.

Part VI: Appendixes

This part contains three really useful collections of information – the winners of a whole range of rugby competitions, a glossary of rugby terms, and a list of key rugby organisations with contact details.

Icons Used in This Book

To help your navigation through this book, keep an eye out for the icons, the little pictures that sit in the margin. They guide you to particular types of information. This list tells you what the icons in this book mean.

This icon highlights tips and snippets of advice that can help you, whether you aim to become a better player, a better coach, a better spectator – or all three.

Paragraphs with this icon attached contain information that is especially useful to remember.

You won't see this icon very often, but, when you do, take heed, because it indicates areas that may cause concern.

This icon indicates a technical discussion is under way. You can skip this information if you want to, because it isn't necessary for an understanding of the basics. If you do read it, though, your rugby expertise goes up a few notches.

Whenever you see this icon, you find an explanation of rugby terms that helps you understand just what is going on in the game.

Paragraphs that sport this icon contain descriptions of outstanding rugby players, the players who are the big names in the game.

Where to Go from Here

Here you are, ready to go. What direction you go in depends on your needs. Have a good look at the table of contents because it's very detailed and gives you an excellent overview of the book and the way in which it is structured.

For the beginner, the best place to start is at the beginning! But if you want to immerse yourself in the laws of the game, head for that chapter. Perhaps you have a particular interest in the best British players, in which case, turn to the Part of Tens. Wherever you go – enjoy!

Part I
Rugby: Roots, Boots and All

Evolution of Rugby Man

In this part . . .

To make you feel comfortable about everything rugby union, this part provides an introduction to the game, how it began, and what it is all about. For those new to rugby union, we provide you with a comprehensive rundown of the whys and wherefores of the game.

In this part of the book, we give you an outline of the beginnings of the game of rugby union and describe how it has become one of the most widely played and most loved sports on the globe. We explain the basic aims of the game, what is required to win and the scoring system, the field on which the game is played, and what goes on during a game. And, last but not least, you find out what gear you need to have when you turn up for that first rugby training session.

Chapter 1

Rudimentary Rugby

- -

In This Chapter

▶ Discovering the origins of rugby: The legend lives on

▶ Making sense of what's happening on the field

▶ Understanding the basics of the game

▶ Enjoying the view from the sidelines

▶ Going global: rugby from coast to coast and pole to pole

- -

*W*hy do hundreds of thousands of fans around the world follow 15 players and an oval ball on a field of grass as if the world would end if they missed one pass or kick? Because they are hooked on rugby union, a game of passion which is full of action, excitement, beauty, unpredictable movements and drama. When played by the best exponents of the game on earth, rugby union satisfies the soul like nothing else.

The Game They Play in Heaven

Rugby union buffs are a pretty serious bunch. They treat their game as if it is played only on the most sacred of turf. That's why rugby enthusiasts are among the most passionate, most one-eyed, most vehement (and sometimes most single-minded) of people when they start talking about their favourite subject, especially if they are in a tired and emotional state. Rugby fans firmly believe that rugby is "the game they play in heaven", a tag that first appeared in the 1980s and which perhaps gives the game more respectability than it deserves.

Rugby is sports heaven to fans because it has so many elements that make it exciting for players and spectators alike: fast running, towering kicking and fearless tackling. And always the sense of danger, especially when huge bodies start crashing into each other – a classic example of irresistible forces meeting immoveable objects. This chapter gives you a taste of what rugby is all about.

What's in a Name?

Some people use the word *football* to describe any game that involves kicking a ball around. Although sometimes called *rugby football* by the purists (the Victorians used this term to differentiate it from its cousin, *association football*), rugby union allows players to actually carry and pass the ball by hand, as well as kick it (unlike modern soccer, which really is limited to kicking and heading the ball). So the word "football" is a bit misleading for this sport.

The game gets its name from Rugby, a town in England's Midlands, where it was first played at Rugby School. The legend goes that in 1823 a schoolboy by the name of William Webb Ellis first picked the ball up in the middle of a football game and ran with it, thereby breaking the old rules and setting a precedent for the entirely distinct game of rugby (see the nearby sidebar "Rugby Union, legendary stuff" on how this romantic myth grew). What is certain is that the game was developed at Rugby School, where they even have a plaque set in the school wall admitting to it – thousands of fans have had their photograph taken standing next to this plaque.

The game developed when students from Rugby took the sport to other schools, and from there it was taken up by university undergraduates at Cambridge and Oxford. Gradually, after many rough and tumble years, it was refined into a game suitable for the "plucky sort of chaps" who played a significant role in the development of the British Empire.

Rugby quickly spread throughout the English-speaking world. The first national union was established in England when the Rugby Football Union was formed in 1871, although clubs had existed as early as 1839 at Cambridge University. The first club established in the southern hemisphere was in Australia, at the University of Sydney in the 1860s. Rugby union is now played all over the world, from large countries such as France and Japan, to minnows like Barbados, Guam and Kazakhstan.

Breaking up: amateur rugby union and professional rugby league

Many people still believe that rugby union and rugby league is the same game. Not so. Rugby union is vastly different to rugby league, even though league derives from the union game.

Rugby league came about when players and officials became disillusioned with the attitude of the Rugby Football Union (RFU), the English national union that, in the 19th century, effectively ruled the sport, and decided to break away and form their own code. RFU officials were determined to keep their game strictly for amateurs (see sidebar "League splits from Union").

And, up until the 1990s, so it was – rugby union was a strictly amateur game. The rugby union authorities in both hemispheres were very strict in ensuring that the game was a totally amateur sport, due to their belief that staying amateur was the only way to guarantee that the game remained strictly a leisure pursuit rather than a means of making a living. Any player who was discovered to have been paid was barred from the code.

Rugby league has always been a professional game where players are openly paid. Over the years, rugby union players have signed for rugby league clubs, lured by big contracts, actions which at the time meant they were barred from their former sport. Since the mid-1990s, however, rugby union is also professional and players are allowed to play openly for both codes.

Noting the differences between the two codes

Even though the league game is derived from rugby union, the two rugby *codes* have different laws and vary in the number of players in a team – rugby union has 15 and rugby league has 13.

Some of the main differences between the two codes are as follows:

- ✔ Rugby union has lineouts; rugby league doesn't.
- ✔ Rugby union has unlimited tackles, whereas rugby league has six tackles, after which the ball is handed to the opposition.
- ✔ In rugby union, a tackled player must let go of the ball, whereas in league, a tackled player can retain possession.

Getting It Together on the Field

Rugby is played with an oval ball on a field, usually grass, about 100 metres long and 70 metres wide (the dimensions of the field are explained in Chapter 2). You don't need an enormous amount of equipment to play rugby – a jersey, shorts, socks, boots and a ball which you can obtain from any good sports store are enough to get you started, as we explain in Chapter 3.

Rugby Union, legendary stuff

William Webb Ellis, a schoolboy at Rugby School in England in 1823, is regarded by many as the father of rugby, having supposedly been the first person to pick up a ball in a football game and run with it, rugby style. His role as the game's originator has, however, been questioned by eminent historians, who believe the game actually got into its stride well before William Webb Ellis got bored with booting the ball about, soccer-style.

The Webb Ellis legend was created 50 years after the alleged event took place – and by someone who wasn't even at the school at the time when young William made his alleged historic run. To complicate matters, Webb Ellis was dead by the time the story gathered pace so he couldn't confirm or deny it.

The legend has been described as an elaborate hoax concocted by the school's old boys in order to make Rugby School rules the undisputed, official laws of the game of rugby.

Myth or reality, the World Cup revolves around the presentation of the William Webb Ellis Trophy, a fine example of the goldsmith's art, which is awarded to the winners (We discuss the trophy further in the chapter on the World Cup, Chapter 12). If you take a close look at the trophy, you see that perched on top of it is a miniature ball – a round football, much like the one Webb Ellis is reputed to have picked up – supported by garlands.

Each team has 15 players divided into forwards and backs. These players have specific roles on the rugby pitch – roles which we explore in more detail in Chapter 4. Essentially, the forwards win the ball while the backs score the points required for victory. The aim of each team is to score the most number of points, either through tries or goals.

A team must therefore win possession of the ball and attack with the ball in the hope of beating the opposition's defence players. The tussle between a team's attacking players and their opponent's defending players provides the drama that makes rugby special.

Aiming to score

The basic aim of rugby is to score a *try*, which is worth five points. A try is scored when the attacking team crosses the opposition's *goal line* (sometimes called the *tryline*) and puts the ball on the ground. The attacking team then has the chance to kick a *conversion*, by kicking the ball between the H-shaped *goalposts*, thereby adding another two points. (We go into detail in Chapter 2 about the scoring and points system.)

A game of rugby is supposed to last for 80 minutes, split into two halves of 40 minutes each. But the referee can, and often does, add extra time if play has been stopped while a player receives treatment for an injury. The winning team is the one with the most points at the end of the match.

The laws for getting the ball to the point of scoring are pretty straightforward; the most important laws can be narrowed down to just five. They're mostly commonsense rules governing such things as where players need to stand to be in the game, how they pass the ball, foul play and tackling. One of the most important people on the pitch is the referee, who is assisted by two touch judges, and between them they ensure the game is played fairly and properly. (We tell you all about the laws and the officials who regulate the game on the pitch in Chapter 5, where you can also find a handy checklist of the referee's signals.)

Rugby union certainly cannot be accused of stagnating. The game is one of the few that is ever changing, thanks to its laws being regularly updated.

Shaping up to play

Because rugby caters for all shapes and sizes, everyone can find a spot in the team. But that doesn't mean you can simply amble onto a rugby field and success automatically follows. A rugby player needs certain basic skills, most importantly, coordination and the ability to run in a straight line at a reasonable speed.

A rugby player must also be able to catch a ball with relative ease, hold onto it without dropping it for several seconds, and not be scared witless if someone built like the Incredible Hulk looms in front. (Turn to Chapter 6 for more information on the skills you need in order to play a mean game of rugby.)

While learning how to tackle may be intimidating at first, with practice it comes easily. The breakdown is another aspect of the game that may at first intimidate the newcomer, but once you understand the basics, you can take your place in a scrum, ruck or maul with confidence. Chapter 7 has all the details about the breakdown.

The sight of rugby players soaring to catch the ball is unforgettable and we devote an entire chapter, Chapter 8, to the lineout, a form of play unique to rugby union that calls for split-second timing and strength.

Rugby teams spend many hours on the training field improving their skills and strategies. We are fortunate in Britain and Ireland in that there are plenty of open spaces in which to practice. As most rugby matches are played on grass, all you need to do is visit your local playing fields and you're ready to go. The more time you spend with a rugby ball in your hands, the better your skills are when you actually start playing this wonderful game. We tell you all about the best training exercises, warm-up routines and fitness food in Chapter 10.

If you can drag a friend along to practice with you, so much the better – passing the ball to yourself isn't much fun.

Coaching and those tantalising tactics

In addition to being a physically demanding sport, rugby also requires considerable brain power. A team's players spend hours with their coach improving their training techniques and developing the skills and strategies they need to improve their chances of winning. The combination of skills and clever strategy make rugby the exciting game it is. (We discuss the tactics that teams bring into play to crush their opponents in Chapter 9.)

One of the great pleasures of being a spectator at a superb game of rugby is to watch the way one team can psych out another on the pitch. Whether a team is on the attack or forced back on the defensive, many of the moves they make have been rehearsed many times before.

The team's director is the coach, whose sole aim is to ensure that on the Big Day, his team's performance is as good as it gets. The coach's role is pivotal to the success of a team: He improves the performance of each individual player as well as that of the team as a unit.

The coach decides what tactics a team uses during a game, and determines which player is best in which position. The coach may decide whether the team tries out some special attacking moves or whether certain defensive tactics are likely to upset the opposition.

Even at Age Grade level, there's nothing like coaching your budding little Jonny Wilkinson to a winning season. (We devote Chapter 11 to a discussion of all aspects of the coach's role, and especially the joys of coaching juniors.)

Rugby on the Home Field and World Stage

Some rugby fans start off cheering for cousin Freddy at the occasional Saturday match, then, next thing you know, they've joined the local club and wouldn't miss a game for anything. The addiction progresses to following a Zurich Premiership, Celtic League or Heineken Cup team and engaging in passionate debates about who is likely to win the Six Nations . Or the World Cup.

Rugby union is now one of the most popular team sports in the world, having spread across many continents. Although rugby is a long way behind football as the ultimate world game, its influence around the globe is growing stronger every year.

For the addicted rugby fan, the numerous tournaments and competitions only serve to feed their addiction. In Part III of this book, we describe how players can progress up the rugby-playing ladder and, if they're good enough, the club, provincial and international teams they can play for.

Home is where your grassroots are

Rugby union's grassroots are the clubs where keen youngsters are introduced to the game and encouraged to develop their talents and enthusiasm. Local club rugby caters for so many levels of skill and proficiency that it's not surprising that people have strong ties with the club system. Chapter 15 tells you how to get involved in your local club, which is sure to welcome you whether you are a youngster, an oldster, a woman, a potential player or a social member.

League splits from Union

On August 29, 1895, 22 clubs in northern England decided to break away from the RFU , exasperated by repeated refusals by the ruling body to allow them to compensate players for money lost by taking time off work to play rugby football. The clubs met and conspired at the Mitre Hotel in Leeds, where they organised themselves into what they called the Northern Football Union, which eventually became the Rugby League in 1922.

The newly formed breakaway body set about looking at ways of attracting spectators to the game. Within three years, the game was professional, and with this new professionalism came a new set of laws and a reduction in players from 15 to 13.

The "Great Schism", as it became known, also occurred in Australia. The NSW Rugby League was founded on August 8, 1907 at Bateman's Hotel in George Street, Sydney. This meeting was held under great secrecy because Dally Messenger, Australia's best rugby union player, was intimately involved. Players in the new league competition were paid, with Messenger being paid what was then the vast sum of £180 to turn professional.

Until relatively recently, relations between the two codes have not been exactly warm. For the next century, rugby union regarded itself as the clean and pure amateur code, and rugby league the low-brow professional alternative.

If you prefer to watch your rugby on television, the Heineken Cup (Europe-wide), the Zurich Premiership (England), and the Celtic League (Scotland, Wales, Ireland) are made for it. Supporters of rugby in the northern hemisphere have been electrified by these competitions. Each of the Six Nations countries also have their own domestic rugby competitions and rivalries, which are played out in front of stadiums bursting at the seams. (You can find all the details of these great northern hemisphere competitions, including the teams that participate, in Chapter 14.)

Around the globe: The A to Z of rugby

Players from more than 120 countries represent their country at rugby union tournaments. The game's ruling body, *the International Rugby Board*, boasts 96 member countries from Andorra to Zimbabwe.

In between Andorra and Zimbabwe are the rugby-playing nations of Barbados, Botswana, Cameroon, Chile, Colombia, Croatia, Georgia, Guam, India, Kazakhstan, Kenya, Latvia, Lithuania, Madagascar, Moldova, Nieu Island, Peru, Russia, Senegal, Slovenia, Swaziland, and Vanuatu – to name just a few.

In some countries, such as New Zealand, Fiji, Tonga and Western Samoa, rugby is the national sport and is treated almost as a religion. Even on the wild and windswept plains of Canada, you can find burly locals kicking a rugby ball around.

Playing the world stage

The growth of major tournaments, has ensured that rugby has a prominent international identity. The most important of these is the World Cup, first held in New Zealand and Australia in 1987, which involved 16 nations competing in a tournament whose future success was uncertain.

Thankfully for rugby, the World Cup concept took off after that first tournament, which was enlivened by an outstanding inaugural winning side in New Zealand, and several outstanding games, in particular the Australia versus France semi-final which took place in a now-forgotten suburban ground in Sydney. (Chapter 12 is full of more such fascinating information about the World Cup.) What impressed most rugby fans at the first World Cup was the realisation that rugby had spread itself across the globe, with enough competitive countries to make it work. Since the 1991 tournament in the British Isles and France awakened rugby to its true potential, the Rugby World Cup has grown to the extent that it now requires extensive qualification matches before the 20 teams that actually compete in the tournament are determined. The 1991, 1995 and 1999 World Cup have all been major international extravaganzas.

The two halves of planet rugby have their own major tournaments, which are held annually. The Six Nations in Europe is the oldest and greatest of these, while the Tri-Nations has become the southern hemisphere's flagship rugby event. Also fiercely contested are trophies like the Calcutta Cup (England v Scotland), and the Bledisloe Cup, where the contestants are Australia and New Zealand. Turn to Chapter 13 for details of these major tournaments, other great rugby rivalries and the famous playing fields on which the winners are decided.

Raising rugby's profile at the Sevens

Sevens rugby, rugby union's version of one-day cricket, has also had a significant impact on the international flavour of the game. The advent of the Hong Kong Sevens tournament in the 1980s encouraged numerous lesser-known countries to try their hand at the game, which is played on a normal-size field but involves only seven players on each side. Sevens rugby is very exciting because tries are relatively easy to score and the focus is entirely on attack.

For years, countries not known for rugby union skills would play in the Hong Kong Sevens, where the emphasis was on the enjoyment provided by the game. It was an ideal way to be introduced to the game, and convinced many to return home and set about trying to improve the standard of rugby in their country.

Seven-a-side rugby was played at the Commonwealth Games in 1998, the first time rugby had been played at this international event. (Chapter 13 has more information about the Sevens tournament and the Commonwealth Games, as well as an interesting titbit about rugby as an Olympic sport.)

Nowadays countries previously regarded as Sevens novelties are becoming viable rugby nations. The game is slowly establishing itself in Asia. Japan, in particular, has progressed markedly, with local businesses willing to pay exorbitant sums for players. Keen to win honour and prestige, Japanese companies are anxious to have a strong team that can beat every other company side.

Cheering from Rugby Cloud Nine

Rugby is a physical contact sport. When played properly, it is an exciting, edge-of-the-seat spectacle that gets the spectators' blood pumping and their adrenaline rushing. Fair warning: You may need to ask your doctor if it's okay to become a rugby fan because the thrills and spills can make it a real roller-coaster ride.

If toughing it out on the pitch doesn't appeal to you, you can have just as much fun watching rugby as playing it. The life of a sideline dweller is often very satisfying, and certainly less fraught than that of the grunt-and-groan merchants on the pitch.

Newspapers, radio, television, videos, sports magazines galore, and even – surprise surprise – books are covering rugby to a greater extent and in greater depth every day to satisfy the rugby fan's insatiable appetite for all things rugby. Chapter 16 is your media guide to getting the most out of the rugby that's televised, and Chapter 17 is all about the best rugby Web sites, the plethora of print media that awaits you at your local newsagents and in the bookstores, and the radio stations to tune into to listen to commentaries on the game.

Of course, for soaking up all the atmosphere, you can't beat being there. Cheering your team on from the stands is the ultimate high. All you need to succeed as a first-rate barracker is a bit of bluff, a bit of cunning and the willingness to learn a few specific terms so that those around you believe that despite your pasty, unathletic appearance, you are actually a walking, talking encyclopaedia of the game.

Like most sports, rugby has its fair share of unusual and unique terms to describe the action unfolding in front of you. To help you talk the talk of the rugby veteran, turn to Chapter 18, which is also a mine of information on how to become a knowledgeable spectator.

Showing Off Your Rugby Knowledge

Everyone likes a Top Ten list, and we're no different. Part V of this book is packed full of fascinating bits of information that you can store away and draw on whenever you feel like impressing all those around you at the rugby. Something for everyone!

For our take on the greatest British players, go to Chapter 19; for the greatest highs in the game, go to Chapter 20; and if you want a really good laugh, Chapter 21 is full of rugby trivia.

By the way, if at any stage you need a quick refresher on terms like *scrum*, *binding*, *blindside, prop* and *hooker*, you can find a glossary at the end of this book that explains these arcane terms. Don't worry: You are in no danger of drowning in rugby-speak!

Chapter 2

The Aim of the Game

*Y*ou've probably heard great tales about the camaraderie of rugby. How players are members of exclusive clubs, whose prime aims are world peace and the brotherhood of man. Don't be fooled. Like a lot of things in the sphere of rugby, it's just a lot of hot air. No matter what level of rugby you play, the aim of the game is to win, and that can trigger all sorts of weird emotions. World peace and brotherly love go out of the window when players are determined that their team is going to win.

In this chapter, we describe the field of play and then outline the ways in which you can score points and the time allowed for the game. Then we briefly describe the positions of the players and the various movements on and off the field.

Getting the Measure of the Field

Rugby is played on a grass field, although sand and clay are permitted, provided they are not dangerous. A permanently hard surface, such as asphalt and cement, is prohibited. The place where rugby is played is variously referred to as the field of play, the playing field, the rugby field and the pitch, but they all mean the same – the battlefield, which is shown in Figure 2-1.

The players do battle in the following areas:

- **The field of play:** The area that is in the centre of the ground is the *field of play*, which measures no more than 100 metres long by no more than 70 metres wide.

- **The playing area:** Encompassing the *in-goal* areas as well as the field of play is the *playing area*. The playing area is defined by posts flying flags; the posts are at least 1.2 metres in height.

- **The in-goal areas:** At each end of the playing area are the in-goal areas, which must be between 10 and 22 metres in length and 70 metres in width.

The playing area has numerous lines marked on it, of which the most important are the following:

- **10 metre line:** Two 10 metre lines are marked on the field of play, which are situated 10 metres either side of the *halfway line*. When a team kicks off, the ball must cross this line for play to continue – in other words, the ball must be kicked at least 10 metres towards the opposing team to allow play to start. If the ball does not travel 10 metres, a *scrum* is formed in the middle of the field, with the non-offending team getting the *scrum feed* or *put-in*.

- **22 metre line:** The field of play has two lines 22 metres out from each *tryline*. Goal kickers attempt to take conversions near these lines.

- **Dead ball line:** The line beyond the in-goal area at each end of the field is called the *dead ball line*. Once the ball goes over this line it is out of play.

- **Halfway line:** The *halfway line* marks the centre of the field and is where the game starts. The game is also restarted at the halfway line after successful tries or penalty goals.

- **Sideline:** The two lines marked along the length of the field are called the sidelines. A ball is described as going *into touch* when it crosses either *sideline* and goes out of the field of play. The sideline is also called the *touch line*.

- **Touch line:** The touch line is the same line as the sideline.

- **Goal-line (Tryline):** The line at either end of the field of play which a player must cross for his team to successfully score a try is called a tryline.

Finally, the target, the goalposts. Goalposts are situated at each end of the playing area and must be 5.6 metres apart with a *crossbar*, the transverse bar between the goalposts that's three metres from the ground. The minimum height of the goalposts is 3.4 metres. As a safety precaution, the goalposts are usually covered with padding to stop players suffering serious injury if they crash into them.

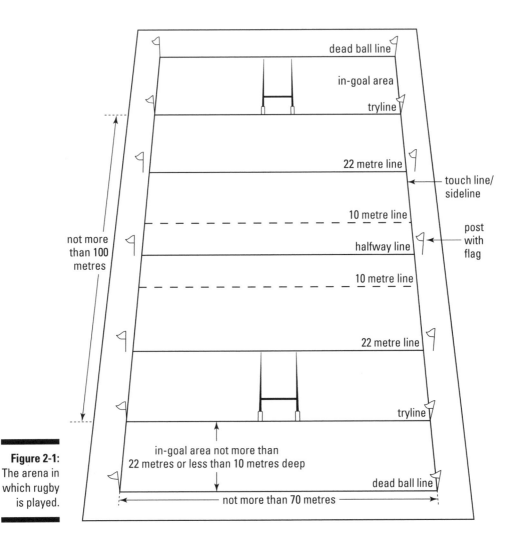

Figure 2-1:
The arena in
which rugby
is played.

Understanding the Scoring System

A rugby scoreboard can be very confusing to the uninitiated. Maybe it's not as bewildering as the scoreboards at a cricket ground, but it still appears pretty arcane. It's even harder to keep track of the score if you don't know what each individual point-scoring activity is worth.

A team can put points on the scoreboard in only a few ways. Once you know what they are, your enjoyment of the game really takes off as you understand what's at stake on the field.

Scoring a try

The most advantageous way to rack up the points is by scoring a *try*. A try is scored when the attacking team manages to cross the defending team's try-line and puts the ball on the ground in their in-goal area. A try is the *pièce de resistance* of rugby – similar to scoring a goal in football or hitting a six in cricket. If a try is scored, the referee raises his arm and blows his whistle.

A try is worth five points, which is the most number of points you can score at once.

Fouling up: Penalty tries

A *penalty try* is awarded if the referee believes the defending team deliberately fouled the attacking team in order to prevent them completing a move that would inevitably have led to a try being scored – "beyond reasonable doubt" is the official phrase. If a penalty try is awarded, the referee runs to a spot beneath the crossbar at the centre of the goalposts and indicates he has awarded the attacking team a penalty try by raising his arm and blowing his whistle. As with a normal try, the attacking team is allowed a conversion kick and the chance to add further points to the score.

A penalty try is worth exactly the same as a normal try – five points.

Taking a conversion

Once a try or penalty try is scored, the attacking team has the chance to add a further two points to the scoreboard by kicking a *conversion*. The referee stands at the spot where the try was scored, and points the *goal kicker*, a member of the attacking team, to where exactly on the field of play he can take the conversion. The goal kicker must take it in a direct line down the field from where the try was scored. If the try was scored near the sideline, the goal kicker must take his conversion kick near the sideline. (Figure 2-1 shows the sideline.) Usually, the goal kicker places the ball 20–30 metres from the goalposts, a distance with which he feels comfortable.

Making sense of the scoring system

In the modern era, having an outstanding goal kicker in your team is of paramount importance. The reason why goal kickers are immensely valuable is because their skills are so often called upon during the game because one player or another has committed any one of the several thousand indiscretions that attract a penalty. And, the rules being the rules, the game is held up for yet another kick at goal – worth three points.

You can't blame the players for this situation. Because a successful penalty kick is so highly valued, a team can easily outscore their opposition in the try department, but still lose the match because they haven't kicked enough penalties.

While the points system has worked reasonably well for some years, many close to the game, including international officials and players, think that in its current form it may have outlived its usefulness. The fact that two penalty goals are worth more than one try is controversial – if the essence of rugby is to score tries, many argue that tries should be better rewarded. Either a try should be worth more, or the value of a penalty goal reduced.

If teams are to be discouraged from constantly breaking the rules or playing dirty, it is logical that penalty goals should attract a substantial value. The problem lies in the fact that, unfortunately, too many referees award too many unnecessary penalties, often giving teams a leg-up they do not deserve.

One solution is to increase the score for a try to six points, making a converted try worth eight points, rather than seven. Supporters of this idea argue that this would be more equitable. Then at least an unconverted try would be worth the same as two penalty goals. A small step, but one that might be worth experimenting with.

The goal kicker places the ball on either a specially constructed *kicking tee* or on a patch of sand. A kicking tee is a small plastic gizmo that's placed on the ground and holds the football upright (it's described in more detail in Chapter 3).

Once he has placed the ball to his satisfaction, the goal kicker steps back, checks the wind direction, cleans the mud from his boots, coughs nervously and then runs in (as shown in Figure 2-2). The goal kicker tries to kick the ball so that it passes between the goalposts at a point above the crossbar.

The defending team, who must stand on or behind the goal line as the kicker prepares to take the conversion, is allowed to rush the kicker as soon as he begins his run at the ball.

Figure 2-2:
Running in
to take a
conversion.

If the goal kicker successfully converts the try, another two points are added to the total. Thus, a "converted" try is worth seven points: five for the try plus two for the conversion. If the goal kicker misses, the team only gets five points for the try – and the kicker gets a heap of abuse from his team.

Drop-kicking a drop goal

A *drop goal* (also called a *field goal or drop kick)* is slightly different in nature to a conversion. With a conversion, a player places the ball on a kicking tee or pile of sand, steps back and then runs up to the ball before kicking it between the goalposts. A drop goal involves a player releasing the ball from his hands and trying to kick it just as it hits the ground, as shown in Figure 2-3. (We discuss the drop kick further in Chapter 6.)

Scoring a drop goal is a clever manoeuvre which requires a lot of skill. Because it's such a specialised skill, field goals are rare – they take perfect timing and lots of practice to get right. If the kicker gets it right, and the ball passes between the goalposts and above the crossbar, his team scores three points.

Breaking the laws: Penalty goals

If the referee considers that a team has broken one of the laws of the game, he can award the other side a *penalty kick.* This means that the other team is given an advantage at the expense of the other. The referee indicates the award of a penalty by blowing his whistle and raising his arm in the direction of the team to whom the penalty has been awarded. The captain of the team to whom the penalty has been awarded then has to make a decision.

The captain can opt for a kick at goal. If he chooses this option, the goal kicker places the ball on the spot where the penalty occurred and tries to kick the ball through the goalposts in similar fashion to a conversion. If the penalty spot is too close to the goalposts, the referee directs the goal kicker to the area where he can kick from; he is allowed to take his shot from any spot in a straight line down the pitch, and at any distance. The defending team is not allowed to rush the kicker when a penalty is awarded.

Figure 2-3:
Scoring a drop goal with a drop kick requires a lot of skill.

A successful *penalty goal* is worth three points.

Doing time

Play is divided into two halves of 40 minutes each so players have 80 minutes to prove themselves. But the referee has the power to add extra minutes to make up for time lost through injuries or delays in the taking of those never-ending penalty shots at goal.

The referee's use of the time clock is sometimes open to serious misinterpretation. If the first half seems much longer than the second half, it probably is. Not many games start on time because usually someone is late – perhaps a player or an official, or even the referee.

Often, the official time clock is not visible, because many grounds, particularly at the lower levels of the game, do not have such expensive apparatus. The official time clock at these grounds is the referee's own wrist watch. Unfortunately, referees sometimes forget to adjust their watches to compensate for injuries or delays in the game.

Top of the Table

League Tables are used in most sports and are a way of finding out how a team is progressing in a competition.

Table 2-1 is an example of a competition table showing how four teams are rating in the competition after two rounds. The teams are the Warriors, the Mongrels, the Waybacks and the Misfits. A team earns four points for a win, two for a draw and nothing for a loss. Bonus points are given to a team that scores four or more tries in a game, or loses by seven points or less.

Table 2-1					A League Table			
Team	*P*	*W*	*D*	*L*	*For*	*Against*	*Bonus Pts*	*Pts*
Warriors	2	2	—	—	60	10	2	10
Mongrels	2	1	—	1	35	30	1	5
Waybacks	2	1	—	1	30	35	—	4
Misfits	2	—	—	2	10	60	—	0

Key

P = games played

W = wins

D = draws

L = losses

For = the number of points a team has scored

Against = the number of points a team has scored against them

Bonus Pts = the number of bonus points a team has accumulated

Pts = the team's overall number of points

Teams such as those that participate in the Zurich Premiership in England (and the Tri-Nations and Super 12 tournaments in the southern hemisphere) use the bonus point system to provide teams with further incentives during a game. (See Chapter 14 for details of the Zurich Premiership.)

Introducing the Players

One of the reasons why the game is so popular is that rugby is one of the few sports that caters for all sorts of body shapes and sizes. A photograph of a rugby team often looks as if one specimen of every human body type has been assembled at the same spot, at the same time, to provide an illustration for an anthropological study.

Team photos are proof that everyone can get along. Within every team, the tall, the small, the fat, the skinny, the lanky and the cranky can all find a position that suits them.

Taking up position

Each *squad* – the group of players who make up a rugby team – comprises 22 players, including the 15 players who start the match and the seven reserves. The starting 15 take to the pitch at the commencement of the game, and the seven reserves sit on the sideline for use in case of injury and tactical changes.

While most of the positions involve specialised skills, that doesn't mean players are stuck in the same position for the rest of their rugby lives. You have scope to move about, especially if your body shape changes with age. (Each position and each player's role in that position are described in detail and with diagrams in Chapter 4.)

The 15 players who start the game comprise eight forwards and seven backs: The forwards have the prime role of winning the ball and the backs have the duty of doing something positive with it, like scoring the tries needed for victory. An old adage says the forwards decide who wins a match and the backs decide by how much.

Playing by the rules

A match is started by a *kick-off*, which is taken at the centre of the halfway line (see Figure 2-1). Unlike football, where the kick-off is aimed at a team-mate, in rugby the team kicking off does so towards its opponents. Here are the basic rules of rugby, which are covered in detail in Chapter 5.

- ✔ After the kick-off, any player who is on-side may take the ball and run with it.
- ✔ Any player may throw the ball or kick the ball.
- ✔ Any player may give the ball to another player.
- ✔ Any player may tackle, hold or shove an opponent holding the ball.
- ✔ Any player may fall on the ball.
- ✔ Any player may take part in a scrum, ruck, maul or lineout.
- ✔ Any player may ground the ball in an in-goal area.
- ✔ Whatever a player does must be in accordance with the laws of the game.

Going on and off the field

In this section, we talk about the action both on and off the rugby pitch. While 15 of the 22 players start the game, there's often a hive of activity on the sidelines as the game develops. Coaches can replace players who are injured, make tactical changes to combat a threat posed by the opposition, or simply take off a player who is tiring or having a "bad rugby day".

In addition, players who have transgressed the rules of rugby have to be called in off the pitch – sometimes for only a short period of time but at other times, for the rest of the game. And then there are those who get carried off on a stretcher . . .

Bringing on the reserves

Players who don't start the game but come on as replacements are called *reserves*. The reserves sit near the field of play and are used by the coach to replace one of the players on the field.

Sensational and scurrilous scores

The New Zealand All Blacks have developed a habit of beating opponents by big margins. In 1974, they belted South Australia by 111 points, prompting one Adelaide newspaper to use the headline: "New Zealand 117–6. South Australia to bat tomorrow".

In 1962, the Northern NSW team were beaten by the All Blacks 103–0 in Quirindi, with New Zealand scoring 22 tries. The All Blacks also went crazy in a 1995 World Cup game when they slaughtered Japan 145–17 in Bloemfontein.

But the record for the highest number of points scored by a winning team in an international game belongs to Hong Kong, who defeated Singapore 164–0 in 1994 in Kuala Lumpur. It was a busy day for Hong Kong's Ashley Billington, who finished with 10 tries and 50 points.

Tries were sometimes not the be-all and end-all in rugby as Sydney club Parramatta discovered in the late 1890s. Playing Richmond, Parramatta annihilated their opponents by scoring 22 tries to nil. Impressive stuff, but they still lost the game because at that time the team that kicked the most goals was declared the winner – and there were no kickers in the Parramatta side. With five minutes remaining, Richmond slotted the only goal of the match to win the game.

The first team to score 100 points in a Test was Wales in a World Cup qualifying match against Portugal in Lisbon in 1994. The final score was 102–11.

Each reserve now has a basic designated role. Wearing the shirt numbers 16 to 22, they are as follows:

- ✔ reserve hooker, 16
- ✔ reserve prop, 17
- ✔ reserve forwards (usually one second-rower, and one back-rower), 18 and 19
- ✔ reserve scrum-half, 20
- ✔ reserve backline players (usually both can cover several positions), 21 and 22

Of the seven back-up players who sit on the *reserve bench* (the name given to the place where the reserves sit), three are specialist positions – those of the hooker, prop and halfback – because specialist positions require specialist back-up. In the case of a scrum, an injured prop must be replaced by another prop, and not by someone filling in, because of the dangers of a scrum collapsing through someone not having the required technique, strength or experience.

Replacements – from macho to much(o)

The reserve bench has changed dramatically over the years. Once upon a time, rugby was considered the ultimate macho experience and the use of reserves intensely frowned upon. For some years teams were not allowed to use reserves, with injured players going through the pain barrier not to let their side down. Staying on the field until the final whistle was a matter of honour, before they were rushed off to the nearest hospital (or cemetery!).

However, with the replacement issue becoming inextricably linked with player safety, attitudes have mellowed. As a result, replacements for injured players were first allowed in 1968, with two permitted from a reserve bench of four. Although the bench numbers increased to six, the number of replacements you could use remained at two, until the introduction of tactical substitutions in 1996 (five could be used from a six man bench). This led to the arrival of the seven man bench in 1998, with all of them available as tactical substitutes or injury replacements. This effectively turned rugby union from a 15-man game to a 22-man game.

Officials are deeply concerned about the risk of serious injury to front-rowers if a scrum is incorrectly set, or injury to someone who doesn't have the ability to withstand the pressure coming through from the opposition. Safety levels have been very much improved on several counts, with one of the most noticeable effects being the increase in the number of people sitting on the reserve bench.

Clever use of the reserve bench can often mean the difference between winning and losing a match, particularly if it's going right down to the wire. With the faster and fitter game of rugby being played these days, the reserve bench has become a vital part of any coach's arsenal.

Ringing the changes

Bringing on players from the reserve bench to replace those coming off the field is called the *interchange system*, although it is usually known as *bringing a player off the bench*. The use of tactical interchange, or substitutions, is only a recent rugby phenomenon. It was borrowed from British and Australian rugby league competitions and has been introduced to rugby union where it has been in place since 1996.

The interchange system means that fresh players are often brought in as "impact performers", usually in the second half, to try to take advantage of a tiring opposition. This does not mean that a team gets an unfair advantage, as the opposition also has the chance to use fresh legs whenever required.

Coaches can be imaginative in this area and, through astute use of their tactical replacements, get an advantage over the opposition.

What is not acceptable is a constant interchanging of the same players, or in other words, repeated swaps. A player is allowed to come on for another at any time of the game, with the original replacement allowed to return to the field only if the man who replaced him is injured.

But not everyone is in favour of having seven reserves. There are some, particularly in the game in the northern hemisphere, who believe that the interchange system deprives the game of its attritional qualities. For instance, a prop can eventually wear down his opposite number in the scrum, only to find his hard work goes unrewarded because the opposing side can bring on a new prop. Teams in the southern hemisphere believe it has helped speed up the game, but there is a strong counter-argument that, with both teams able to bring on fresh legs, gaps in tiring defences are closed down rather than opened up.

Cooling it in the sin bin

In another bid to speed up the game, and to stop teams resorting to endless professional fouls to upset and slow down the opposition, the *sin bin* has been introduced. This is not a fiery pit that naughty players are tossed into – it usually comprises a couple of plastic chairs on the sideline.

If a player commits repeated breaches of the law, the referee can send him to the sin bin for a period of ten minutes, after which time he can resume his place on the field. Usually the referee gives the player one warning, but if he continues to be caught offside, to illegally obstruct the opposition from getting to the ball or grab the ball when he shouldn't, he's likely to spend ten minutes cooling his heels. He is not allowed any contact with team-mates until his time is up.

To indicate that a player is being sent to the sin bin, the referee produces a yellow card from his pocket and shows it to the player and the crowd. When a player is sent to the sin bin, the number of players on his team on the pitch is reduced to 14. The coach cannot replace a player who is sent to the sin bin.

Controversial red cards

Thankfully, not many English, Welsh, Irish and Scots players have faced an early bath having been sent off. Among the most controversial was the dismissal involving the burly England prop Mike Burton in the infamous "Battle of Ballymore" against Australia in Brisbane in 1975 (see Chapter 7 for more about this famous game).

Strangely, the sin bin hasn't really stopped players from offending. Each season, there seem to be more and more players directed to the sin bin; some appear to actually enjoy having a mid-match breather. However, a player who's been sent to the sin bin can expect a dressing-down from his coach if, because of his stupidity, the team's been forced to defend without him for ten minutes and the opposition has scored.

Being sent off

Being sent to the sin bin is not the same as being sent off. When a player is sent off he is banned from the rest of the game and cannot be replaced. This is usually if he shows malicious intent and is caught openly kicking, punching, gouging or attempting to maim an opponent. If the referee produces a red card from his pocket, that means the player is sent off and must go straight to the *dressing room* – and probably face a judiciary meeting the next morning.

Bleeding all the way to the blood bin

As with all other high-level contact sports, rugby uses the *blood bin rule*. The rugby law book says that any player who has an open or bleeding wound must leave the field of play until the bleeding is controlled and the wound is dressed. The referee stops play as soon as he sees a player is bleeding or has been alerted to the fact by his touch judges.

A team is allowed to make a replacement for a bleeding player. The term *blood bin* does not refer to any specific place; it usually means either the dressing room or a place on the sidelines where the team's medical staff can stitch up wounds or stop the bleeding.

The bloodied hero

One example of a player who became famous for being eternally blood-splattered was former Wallaby hooker Chris Handy (who later became a television commentator). During the first test between Australia and New Zealand in Sydney in 1980, Handy was hit by a right-hander from giant All Black lock Andy Haden.

As Handy recalled in the book, *Well I'll be Ruggered*, the copious bleeding made him appear to be some sort of legendary tough guy, even though he maintains that the only reason he looked so bloody was because he wasn't very good at fighting!

Handy said that when the trainer came onto the pitch to fix up his facial wounds, he pushed him away. The next day, every Sydney newspaper carried graphic photographs of Handy's blood-splattered face.

As you might expect, it's not unknown for some teams to try and take advantage of the "blood bin" rule by using the pellets of fake blood available in theatrical shops. Another ploy involves an old professional wrestling trick, where a player got a quick nick with a razor blade and immediately sported a bleeding wound. These ploys have been especially handy to teams who believe a player requires a short rest from the game.

Unlike wrestlers, who had the razor blade tucked away in their shorts, the usual trick for a player who needed to be replaced was to collapse suddenly as if hit by a sniper. The trainer, with fake blood pellets or razor strategically placed in a large towel, would rush over to the player and start mopping his brow – like magic, blood would flow. The trainer, trying to look aghast, would summon the referee and encourage him to send the bleeder to the sidelines.

This kind of behaviour crosses the line – it's underhand and brings the game into disrepute. It doesn't exactly enhance a player's looks either. Teams do weird things to achieve their objectives.

Chapter 3

Grab Your Rugby Gear

*O*ne of the main advantages of rugby is that most of the gear you require is often supplied by the club you play for, and the cost is covered by your club subscription. Club subscriptions vary from level to level but they shouldn't break the bank. As most clubs are eager to attract members and players, they do all they can to convince you to join them. But even if your club looks after you in the equipment department, it's still a good idea to buy a few items before you tackle the big boys.

In this chapter, we describe the gear that you need to pack into the kitbag, as well as some extra items that you may consider worthwhile. Then we discuss the important issue of personal safety while playing rugby and the precautions you can take to protect yourself on the pitch.

Getting It Together: The Essentials

Rugby is one of those sports that doesn't require you to purchase and lug around a great deal of equipment in order to play – no clubs, bats, rackets, sticks or animals are involved. And don't feel that you have to buy the top-of-the-range gear; what's important is that what you buy is right for you.

A strong yet lightweight sports bag is essential to carry your rugby kit around in. The bag should be big enough to hold a rugby jersey, socks, shorts, boots, ball and towel – maybe even a change of clothing. Try and find a bag that has separate pockets and has a compartment, either on the outside or the inside, where you can stuff your muddy socks and shorts. Even when all your kit is in the bag, it should still have plenty of room for extra equipment, such as a law book.

Make sure you get the latest edition of the law book; a new edition usually comes out each season. You should be able to pick up the latest edition for free, especially if you pester your club officials long enough (The laws of the game are covered in Chapter 5.) An adequate sports bag can set you back about £20 – even cheaper at sale time.

Having a ball

A rugby ball is the first item any aspiring rugby player buys. Rugby clubs usually have an abundance of balls but it's still a smart idea for you to have your own. Experienced players recommend you have a ball in your hands as often as possible so you can practice your kicking, passing, catching and handling skills.

A rugby ball is oval and not round. It can be made of leather, but these days most are made of strong synthetic material and consist of four panels. Some balls have dimpled surfaces to make them easier to grip when playing in wet conditions.

What's really important is that the dimensions of the ball are right. Getting a ball that's smaller than the one actually used in the game is alright for practising handling, but it's far better to get used to a ball that is exactly the same as the kind you are going to be playing with during a match.

Any reputable sports shops can help you find a ball that is right for your age and size. You don't have to take a tape measure when you go shopping for a ball; the staff in the store usually know the correct sizes. The rugby ball used by kids is slightly smaller than the one used by adults. Whatever your age, though, it's important that you train with the same size ball that you play with in a game.

The dimensions of a rugby ball are as follows:

- **Length:** 280–300 millimetres
- **Circumference (end-to-end):** 760–790 millimetres
- **Circumference (width):** 580–620 millimetres
- **Weight:** 400–440 grams
- **Air pressure:** either 0.67–0.70 kilos per square centimetre, or 9½–10 pounds per square inch

Air pressure is important. Make sure that your ball has some give in it, enough for your fingers to be able to make a small dent. This is important because a softer ball is easier to handle, mark and pass, and is therefore good for training purposes.

While a *match ball* is usually pumped-up until the skin is tight, a *training ball* doesn't have to be so firm. A match ball is the bees-knees, top-of-the-line, highest-quality ball there is on the shelves (which figures). A training ball is good enough and authentic enough to practice with and is virtually the same as a match ball at half the price.

Rugby balls range in price from £7 to £40. Most balls around the £10 mark fit the bill and can give you years of pleasure. Don't bother buying a match ball. While a training ball is of an inferior quality to a match ball and is usually made of a synthetic material, it's perfectly fine for your needs and is much cheaper than a match ball.

Looking after your feet

Of all your rugby equipment the gear which is probably the most important is the gear on your feet. A perfectly good day can be ruined by a pair of socks that have slid right down the back of your brother-in-law's old rugby boots and are scrunched up painfully under your instep.

Booting up

The best place to buy boots is at a reputable sports shop where experienced staff can recommend the right kind of boot for you, based on your age and the level of the game you're involved in. Boots don't have to be made of leather, nor is it essential to have leather uppers, although most high quality boots do.

The first rule of "boot law" is to make certain that your feet fit snugly, to avoid the pain of blisters. Boots should also be comfortable, compact, protect your feet and have the required traction on the pitch.

Make sure you inspect the soles of the boots. Usually at least six studs are required on the sole of each boot; the studs must be circular and securely fastened. Although rugby boots range widely in price, you can find good reliable brands that start at £30. While a lot of rugby gear is available at fairly low prices, please don't economise in the boot department – cheap can be nasty, and nasty means blisters or worse.

The case of the missing boots

One of the most celebrated cases of Mislaid Boot Syndrome happened on the New Zealand tour of South Africa in 1960, when All Black full-back Don Clarke arrived at the ground to discover something important missing from his kitbag. Not having enough time before kick-off to go back to the team's hotel and get Clarke's boots, officials rushed into the dressing room to find a spare pair. Luckily, superstitious team-mate Kel Tremain always carried a second pair of boots in his bag. These boots didn't look too impressive when they were hauled out of Tremain's bag – battered, worn and scarred, they had definitely seen better days.

Clarke ran onto the pitch wearing Tremain's boots and within a few minutes put them to the test when New Zealand was awarded a penalty goal. As Clarke kicked the ball, there was a loud "ka-boom" sound as the boot exploded on impact with the ball. Bits of leather flew everywhere and Clarke, who was one of the great goalkickers, never forgot his boots again.

When you buy a new pair of boots, walk around in them for a while to get used to them before trying them out at a training session or during a match. Nothing is worse than playing or training with blistered feet – it can turn you off the game fast – even faster than an Lions winger.

When heading off to the game, always, always, remember to check your kit bag to ensure that your boots are in there. The embarrassment of showing up without your boots can scar your psyche for life, and playing barefoot in a game of rugby can scar some essential bodily parts, too. Don't laugh – it happens more often than you think, even at international level.

Socking it to them

Depending on the club you play with, you may be supplied with rugby socks to ensure you are wearing the right club colours. If not, the club can tell you where to buy the right socks. When buying socks, ensure they stretch right up to your knee, enabling you to roll the top back over to just below the knee.

Make certain that each sock has an elasticated band near the top so that it stays up during the match. To have your socks dangling around your ankles is not a recommended fashion statement. If your socks have a propensity to sink to half-mast, get a couple of short lengths of bootlace and tie a piece around each sock just below the knee and then fold the top of the sock over. Don't tie it too tightly or you'll impede the flow of blood to your legs which could give you cramp.

What the socks are made of is not overly important; most players wear socks made of synthetic fibres. Socks are not expensive and the type that are OK for players at club level are available at sports shops starting at about £3 a pair. If you are considering socks made of natural fibres, bear in mind that woollen socks can get very heavy when wet. You may prefer a mix of natural fibres and synthetic – naturally, the better the quality, the higher the price.

Selecting jerseys and shorts

Rugby jerseys are usually supplied by the club you play for. But be warned – don't expect this jersey to be a perfect fit because you are probably the 4,000th person to wear it. Your battle-scarred garment is likely to stand up on its own due to its starch content and be covered in stains from ancient muddy battles of yore.

Although jerseys are provided, new players usually have to obtain their own shorts. The shorts you choose are determined by the club you play for, and your club can tell you what colour to get. There may even be two different colours, for games at home and for away trips.

Make sure the shorts you buy are comfortable and not too tight. If anything, the shorts should be bigger rather than smaller. If shorts are too tight, they can easily get ripped off in a contact sport like rugby...and your mother wouldn't want you showing your undies to the crowd, even if they are clean.

I also recommend that you buy shorts with a lace inserted in the waistband that can be tied into a knot in front to ensure they don't fall down around your knees during a match. It is hard enough tackling an opponent without your efforts being impeded by a pair of shorts heading south.

Rugby shorts range between £5 and £10 in price and can be found in sports shops and well-stocked department stores.

Kicking in with a kicking tee

Over the last few years, the introduction of a kicking tee has made life a lot easier for goal kickers. This small plastic apparatus is placed on the ground and holds the rugby ball upright, as shown in Figure 3-1. A kicking tee holds a ball in the same way as a golf tee holds a golf ball when a golfer prepares to hit a drive. In rugby, it's used when a team attempts to kick a conversion or a penalty goal (the scoring system is explained in Chapter 2).

Figure 3-1:
Placing the
ball at the
correct
angle on the
kicking tee.

Kicking tees are quicker and less messy than the old method of kicking off a patch of sand, or the kicker creating a launch-pad by hacking away at the pitch with the heel of his boot: With sand you had to wait until someone arrived with a sand bucket, wait for the goal kicker to build a sandcastle, be satisfied with his work, place the ball on top of his castle – and then, at last, actually kick it.

Different goal kickers like to place the ball on the kicking tee at different angles, depending on their kicking style – the kicking tee caters for all the different variations.

It's not imperative for every player in the team to own a kicking tee, especially if you have no interest in goal kicking. However, if you want to kick for goal, it is a 'must have' on your shopping list. You won't use your own tee in a game because clubs have piles of them, but for practice, a kicking tee is vital. Your club may even let you have one of their spares, particularly if you start kicking match-winning penalties or conversions.

It is not compulsory to use a kicking tee, as some players still prefer sand. Try both and see what you are most comfortable with. Kicking tees are cheap, usually costing between £4 and £8, and can be found in most sports shops.

Knowing what's barred on the pitch

You need to take note of things that are just not allowed on the rugby pitch. Players cannot wear or take onto the pitch:

- anything contaminated with blood
- anything sharp or abrasive
- anything containing buckles, clips, rings, hinges, zippers, screws or bolts
- jewellery, such as rings or earrings
- communication devices, just in case you're thinking of tucking two-way radios into your rugby boots!
- shorts with padding sewn into them

In addition, players are not allowed to have one stud at the toe on the soles of their boots. Nor are players allowed to wear gloves onto the pitch, other than the fingerless variety (We talk about gloves in the section on protective equipment later in this chapter).

Referees usually inspect both teams before the game to ensure players are not trying to sneak on anything they shouldn't. The referee and the touch judges have the authority to inspect any player's clothing and boot studs.

The rugby catwalk

The increase in rugby sponsorship has had a major impact on how teams look. Most sides now take the pitch with the name of the latest whiz-bang business venture splashed across the front of their jerseys. Some jerseys are works of art that Salvador Dali would be proud of. And some, like those of several of the Zurich Premiership teams, look like the aftermath of a playschool painting session.

Unfortunately, as a player, you have little say in the matter of the design or colours of the jersey you play in because the club colours are the club colours.

If you want to be fashionable (but hopefully not at the expense of comfort on the pitch), you need to know what's in and what's not. One season, big Bombay bloomers may be in, but the next season, it's back to hip-hugging, skin-tight shorts so popular in the 1970s. So at a training session, make a careful note of what your team-mates are wearing before you decide to go big or tight on your next excursion to the sports shop.

What you select from the trusty wardrobe to wear off the pitch really depends on whether you see yourself as a clothes horse. There are still a few clubs around in leafy suburbs where the garb resembles a Paris Fashion Show, but, as a general rule, Rugby Union is a sport with an egalitarian outlook and any social snobbery that used to exist has been relegated to the dim and distant past. So, whatever you wear, you will be made welcome.

Protecting Your Assets

Did we mention that rugby is a physical sport? The only guaranteed way to avoid injury during your rugby career is to take to the pitch in a suit of armour. We don't recommend this for several reasons: Armour is heavy and expensive, and if it rains, you've got little chance of showing off your fancy footwork when you're rusted solid.

But despite the inevitable knocks, you are unlikely to spend much time wishing you'd never picked up this book in the first place. In Chapter 10, we explain how to avoid injuring yourself on a rugby pitch and one of the best ways to do that is to don some protective clothing.

Wearing protective equipment

Rugby players can wear shoulder pads or protective vests. Figure 3-2 shows a player wearing shoulder pads; the pads are attached at the back with velcro straps. Before you buy shoulder pads make sure that they comply with the *International Rugby Board* (IRB) rulings.

The IRB allows for pads made of soft, thin material to be incorporated into an undergarment or jersey, provided the pads cover the shoulder and collarbone only. No part of the pads can be thicker than one centimetre when uncompressed, or have a density of more than 45 kilograms per cubic metre.

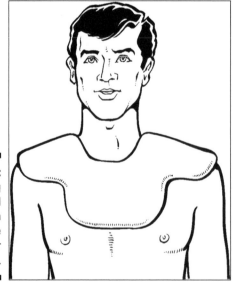

Figure 3-2:
Shouldering
the load
with
protective
shoulder
pads.

Don't buy pads which are not IRB approved. When buying shoulder pads or vests, which are around the £30 mark, it says on the packaging whether they are approved by the IRB. Women are also allowed to wear chest pads made of soft, thin material, as long as no part of the pad is thicker than one centimetre when uncompressed.

Other pieces of protective equipment that you may consider include:

- ✓ **Shin guards:** These look like small shields and are inserted under your socks to lessen the blow if your shins are accidentally kicked by a hefty opposition boot. Made of light plastic, they are quite inexpensive.

- ✓ **Headgear:** A lot of male and female forwards wear headgear for safety reasons, and you should not hesitate to buy a headguard if it makes you feel more comfortable on the pitch. As with shoulder and chest pads, headguards must be made of soft and thin material, with no part of the headgear thicker than one centimetre when uncompressed. Good, comfortable, safe brands can be purchased for between £20 and £50.

- ✓ **Mouthguards:** Nearly all leading players wear mouthguards, which are custom-made by dentists, to protect the teeth from wayward knees elbows, boots or bodies. Unless you want a grin like chipped crockery, mouthguards are an essential investment. Some shops stock cheap hot-water mould mouthguards for a few quid but it's far better to get one specially moulded to your mouth. So, make sure you talk to your dentist next time you are in for a check-up.

- ✓ **Gloves:** Players are allowed to wear fingerless gloves or mitts but it's only recommended for more experienced player. Because of the cold weather, gloves are especially popular in New Zealand and Europe where they claim to be able to help players grip damp, muddy balls. Some top players swear by them, but they are usually the ones endorsing the product.

Avoiding serious injury

While shoulder pads, headguards and shin guards offer some protection if you are hit in a certain spot, they do not guarantee a totally pain-free existence.

The best way to avoid serious injury is to play hard and at full pace: "The half-hearted are the first to get hurt" is an old adage. Your club can show you how to take other precautions, such as tackling properly and falling properly.

Rugby administrators are increasingly vigilant when it comes to safety, instituting numerous laws to protect those on the pitch from serious injury. The referee is on the side of the player and should stop any action that looks dangerous and/or risky where a player could get hurt.

Do not hesitate to use any form of protection allowed by the International Rugby Board if you feel it helps. If the likes of Martin Johnson do, then you can hardly be called soft! But remember that wearing protective gear should not encourage you into coming back from injury too soon. There is no substitute for giving injuries time to heal completely.

Shopping for the best gear

There are several specialist rugby outfitters in the British Isles, and they advertise in magazines like *Rugby World* and web-sites like *Planet-Rugby* (you can read more about these in Chapter 17). However, rugby novices can reliably go to any large sports shop and get virtually everything they need to at least look like a rugby player. Go to a store that stocks a large range and has trained staff.

The quality of most gear is determined by the price, but don't be afraid to shop around. Most sports shops have a sale when they sell their stock at reduced prices. Find out when these sales are on – they usually occur in the off-season when the stores are trying to get rid of old or excess stock in anticipation of the new season's stuff. So the best time to buy your gear is not the day before the start of the new season, but several months before, when you may be able to snap up some bargains.

Don't be misled into buying something that doesn't seem quite right, doesn't fit comfortably, or is too big or small. There is nothing worse than using gear which is the wrong shape or size as it's then basically useless. Be finicky, take your time, and only buy what you want and what is right for you. You need to see and try the gear to know whether it is right for you.

Only buy equipment over the internet or from catalogues if you know your exact size and exactly what you want, and if you know it can be changed easily and efficiently.

Part II
Getting Down and Dirty

In this part . . .

Now that you have a basic knowledge of rugby, it is time to get serious and know exactly what is required to play the game.

In this part, we start off by explaining the various playing positions, and what skills you need to be a star. Having covered what you do, we move on to how you do it without getting on the wrong side of the referee – we delve into the all-important laws that govern rugby. We also explain in detail the skills you need to acquire in order to excel on the field.

Forward play, in particular rucks, mauls and scrums, are explained in this part. We also give a detailed description of lineouts, and analyse the tactical moves you need to make to outwit your opponents. Getting physically fit for rugby is also important, and we give you advice on how to stay taut, trim and terrific. And for those of you who want to be a coach, this part describes the steps you will need to take to embark on this very rewarding occupation.

Chapter 4

Location, Location, Location: Positions on the Pitch

*F*orget the Charge of the Light Brigade. When 30 strapping rugby players all take the field at once, there's a rush of beef to rival the greatest cattle stampede. To the rugby-watching novice, it can look like total confusion. But do not despair, rugby union has a major advantage over a lot of other sports – the number on each player's back actually does mean something.

In this chapter, we help you sort out which number goes with which playing position and what that position is trying to do in the game.

Counting Forwards and Backs

A team comprises eight forwards and seven backs. The forwards (known collectively as the *pack*) have the prime role of winning the ball, and the backs have the responsibility of doing something positive with it, in particular, scoring the tries required for victory. (For details on the scoring system, see Chapter 2.) Figure 4-1 shows the forwards and backs in typical attacking formation.

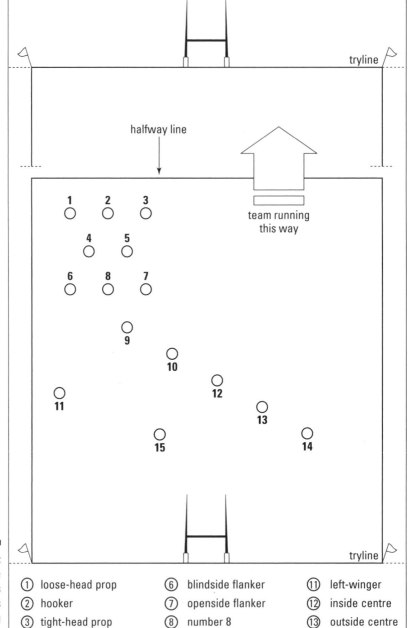

Figure 4-1:
The
forwards
and backs
getting
ready to
attack.

① loose-head prop

② hooker

③ tight-head prop

④ lock (second row)

⑤ lock (second row)

⑥ blindside flanker

⑦ openside flanker

⑧ number 8

⑨ scrum-half

⑩ fly-half

⑪ left-winger

⑫ inside centre

⑬ outside centre

⑭ right-winger

⑮ fullback

Unlike games like cricket, where the introduction of numbers defies logic, or Australian Rules football, where the player's numbers are totally meaningless from a positional viewpoint, rugby union uses jersey numbers to help everyone crack the code. In this regard, rugby is spectator friendly. On the field, the players who start the game are numbered from 1 to 15, with the reserves being numbered from 16 to 22. (For more information on reserve players, see Chapter 2.)

Jersey numbers indicate the position each player occupies on the field. Numbers also allow spectators, players and coaches to identify who is to blame if something goes horribly wrong – or who to cheer when something wonderful happens. Once you are clear about the designated role and responsibilities of the player in each position, you can start to appreciate whether he's a brute or a ballerina.

Before long, you find yourself nodding sagely when the show-offs in the crowd start babbling on about how "the blindside is seagulling", the "tight-head is too loose" and "the hooker is on the burst".

Getting In Tight with the Tight Five

The tight five are the five forwards who form the core of the *scrum*, a set formation of players who *bind together* to compete for the ball after an infringement occurs. At this stage of the game, you often hear the phrase *packing down,* which means a scrum is about to be set.

The tight five's main function is to keep the scrum solid and functional, in the hope that when the ball is placed in the scrum it ends up on their side. When a scrum is called for, the tight five join together first, followed by the three back-rowers (see "The Back Row of Forwards" a bit further on in this chapter). As shown in Figure 4-2, all eight forwards bind together and face their opponents. Both units then come together shoulder to shoulder, creating a tunnel in the middle. The ball is thrown into this tunnel and both teams compete to win it.

Picture those wildlife documentaries where two huge rhinos come together and head butt each other for supremacy of the herd and you've got some idea of what goes on when a scrum is formed. Sadly, no-one knows *exactly* what goes on in the scrum because only the foolhardy stick their heads into that tunnel of darkness. (For more information on scrums, turn to Chapter 7.)

The fact is, you never really know what is going on in forward play because sometimes the forwards don't even know themselves. Understanding the plays can be a little easier if you take the tight five positions one by one, and define them.

Figure 4-2:
Forming a
scrum,
ready to
compete for
the ball.

Facing off in the front row

The tight five are the three front row players (the "front-row") and the two locks (second row) who stand behind them. The front row players are easy to pick: the loose-head prop wears the number 1 jersey; the hooker wears number 2; and the tight-head prop wears number 3. Don't panic – we explain these weird names in the next few paragraphs. (If you are uncertain about the location of these players, have another look at Figure 4-1.)

With their large, sometimes roly-poly, physiques, the front-row may look a bit Neanderthal. Which doesn't worry them at all, far from it. They get great enjoyment at the setting of a scrum by charging into the opposition front row, an activity which is punctuated by porcine grunts, screams of pain and other unmentionable noises.

That's the way they like it, because they believe they are the three most important rugby players on the field and, in some respects, they are right. They provide the concrete base to the structure of any team. If the front-row are weak or off their game, the team is at risk of collapsing.

Propping up: tight-heads and loose-heads

The words "loose" and "tight" in the terms *loose-head prop* and *tight-head prop* simply describe how the props sit in the actual formation of the scrum. The scrum-half (more about him later in this chapter, but enough to say here that he's the team organiser) puts the ball into the scrum. Because of the alignment of the scrum, the loose-head prop has his head outside the scrum and can see what the others are doing. The tight-head prop, however, sticks his head on the inside of the opposition's loose-head prop. (We talk more about scrums in Chapter 7.)

Figure 4-3 shows the scrum-half putting the ball in at the scrum, and the hooker being supported by his loose-head prop and his tight-head prop. For those of you who are fascinated by the origin of words – yes, it does come from the fact that these two players "prop up" the scrum.

Figure 4-3: The scrum-half putting the ball in at the scrum.

Tight-heads and loose-heads have exactly the same aim, though their techniques are different. They are specialised positions, where the tight-head is the anchor of the scrum, requiring enormous strength to keep the scrum straight and intact, while the loose-head is more the technician, using different tricks to give his team an advantage, either in getting the ball away from the scrum, or disrupting the opposition scrum platform.

Don't get too concerned if it takes some time to tell the difference between a tight-head and a loose-head prop. One very well-known international lock admitted at the end of his career that he didn't have the faintest idea which one of his front row team-mates was the tight-head or loose-head prop. "They all look the same to me – big and ugly," was his excuse. He wasn't kidding. But a few years later he came up with the best way to remember exactly who is who: "The loose-head is on the left-hand side of the scrum. The tight-head is on the right-hand side of the scrum. The way to remember this is that 'tight' rhymes with 'right'."

Highlighting the hooker

In between the two props is the *hooker*. He is the most outgoing of the three and is seen a lot more around the field because his responsibilities are more wide-ranging. Apart from having the important duty at the scrum of winning the ball, he also has a crucial role at every *lineout*. (A lineout is how play is restarted when the ball has been taken out over the sideline or kicked into touch; we discuss lineouts in detail in Chapter 8.)

At the scrum, the hooker is supported by his two props, placing him in the middle of the scrum tunnel between the two opposing packs. When the scrum-half feeds the ball in between the feet of the two opposing front rows, the hooker is required to "strike" at the ball, hooking or heeling it back behind the feet of the players in his second row and back row so that his side regains possession.

The hooker must also be right on his game at every lineout, because he has the tough task of throwing the ball in and making certain that it is right on target to one of his lineout jumpers. To do this correctly, the hooker must have the nerve and skill of a professional darts player, but without the 20 pints of best bitter that lubricate practitioners of that less-physical game.

Hookers can make or break their reputation on their ability as a lineout thrower. For example, while Phil Kearns is now regarded as one of Australia's greatest hookers, for some time he had to overcome the stigma of being only an average lineout thrower, which led to the nickname "Lightning" (as in "lightning does not strike in the same place twice"). Angered by what he perceived to be a slur, Kearns spent hours and hours on the training field practising his throwing. The expertise he built up and demonstrated led to the nickname being dropped.

The hooker is looked upon as one of the true leaders of the forward pack. The demands made on him are many and it can be a difficult position to play, as it involves a combination of power and stamina – as well as blistering pace. This is because hookers are often relied upon to make quick charges at the opposition's *tryline* in a bid to score. In these situations, their bulk is important in breaking through tackles. And big hookers, like England's Steve Thompson, are often sighted at the end of a backline attack, where they are waiting for a pass from one of their centres or wingers, where brute strength and a quick step can get them over the tryline. (We discuss centres and wingers later in this chapter; the tryline is shown in Figure 4-1.)

Towering over the second row

The locks, who wear jersey numbers 4 and 5, are the giants of the scrum circus. These two (who may look as if they got lost on the way to a basketball game) are usually the players the rest of the pack try to lift through the clouds to catch the ball thrown-in by the hooker. Also, because of their height, if they are not the key jumper, they often become responsible for lifting a lighter man skywards. More often than not, locks wear headguards or have tape wrapped around their heads. Some like to think this is to stop the opposition from grabbing hold of their ears and ripping them off as trophies. Another reason for the tape is that it stops the sweat that pours off the locks' brows from dripping into their eyes. The real reason for the tape, however, is it makes them look like real tough guys...

Locks are the workhorses of the pack. They *bind-on* behind the front row; this requires them to grasp onto the bodies of the props using an underarm grip between the props' legs, holding the waistbands of the props' shorts, while the other arm is used to bind onto the lock adjacent to them. They are known as the "engine-room of the scrum" because they have to provide the required push to ensure that the scrum stays stable, doesn't collapse, and is not pushed back by the opposition. Sometimes you see locks who aren't eight feet tall, probably due to the fact that the blatant lifting of players in the lineout has made the presence of genuine giants somewhat redundant, but it's still rare. The general requirement is that you have to be tall and won't snap in two when pressure is applied in the scrum.

A truly great lock is almost superhuman. While they may have a physique that at first sight doesn't look as if it belongs on a rugby pitch, they need to be an outstanding ball player and have tremendous agility. Passengers need not apply.

It's a hard position, but at least you're seen. However, the disadvantage of being highly visible is that nothing a lock does during a game goes unnoticed. So any mistakes are highlighted – but so too are the glittering moments.

Stirring It: The Back Row of Forwards

The *back row*, consisting of the players in jersey numbers 6, 7, and 8, often like to call themselves "The Three Musketeers" because they are ferocious competitors and usually up to a lot of mischief.

If back-rowers do it right and get away with a few cheeky manoeuvres during the game, victory is usually inevitable. An excellent back-row combination is vital for a successful team, especially because the three players are involved in so much of the game, creating numerous opportunities and thwarting so many of the opposition's tactics.

Holding firm with the number 8

The player who holds the scrum together is the number 8 who, surprise, surprise, wears the number 8 jersey. This position usually goes to the most skilful forward because so much of the match happens around him; he is often the first to receive the ball from scrums, lineouts and in open play. He is usually sighted all over the field, and has to make his presence felt.

From any scrum, the number 8, working in tandem with the scrum-half and fly-half (we explain the roles of the scrum-half and the fly-half later in this chapter), decides how the team attacks or defends the next play. If his team is attacking, and the ball arrives at his feet after it has been heeled back by the hooker, he must decide whether he runs with it himself, passes it to his scrum-half, or leaves it for him to pick-up.

A good number 8 always knows exactly what the opposition are up to and seizes any opportunity to take the ball forward himself if he believes he can expose a defensive weakness by making a quick run from near the scrum. He basically has to be everywhere and anywhere, always thinking and always near the ball, especially when there is a breakdown in play.

England number 8 Lawrence Dallaglio is the perfect example of how someone should conduct themselves in this position. His vision and work-rate is outstanding, which means that in many matches he leads the tackle count statistics and is among the players who have touched the ball most in the match. Dallaglio can ill-afford to make mistakes and get lost on the field because he is usually the player who inspires confidence in the rest of the team through outright feats of courage and skill.

Foraging with the flankers

The number 8 is joined in a life of crime by two flankers, also known as *wing-forwards*. Number 7 is the *"openside" flanker* and number 6 the *"blindside" flanker*.

The terms *"openside"* and *"blindside"* refer to where the players are situated when a scrum is set. More often than not, a scrum is set on one side of the field and the openside flanker joins the scrum on the side where there is the greater amount of space. The blindside flanker joins the other side of the scrum, which is closest to the sideline. As the flankers are perched on the "flanks" of the scrum, it means they can switch from one side of the scrum to the other if tactics dictate it.

Patrolling the openside

As the openside flanker has to patrol a greater amount of field, he is usually the smaller and speedier of the two. His prime aim is to be first to the ball wherever it is on the pitch. He has to be the first to the ruck and maul, where he acts as a feverish scavenger, trying to wrestle the ball out of the opposition's hands, or ensuring that his own team takes the ball into the breakdown area and that they come out with it so they can continue attacking. (We discuss the niceties of rucks, mauls and scrums in Chapter 7.)

What openside flankers get away with at the bottom of rucks and mauls is often unsightly and ugly – a bit like ferrets on a trail. For example, they fight and tussle for the ball, trying to wrestle it out from a tangle of arms and legs. But if they are good enough to get away with it without upsetting the referee, they are worth their weight in gold. It is not surprising that openside flankers so often win best and fairest awards because if they are good, they are in full view of everyone for virtually every second of the game.

Toughing it on the blindside

The blindside flanker has to be just as industrious. Along with the number 8, he is usually the second or third to arrive at the breakdown to assist the openside flanker in his sneaky work. He also has to be an outstanding defender, particularly as many opposing teams attempt to attack down the blindside from a scrum. The blindside flanker has to be always mindful of this and be ready to cut off this option immediately with a devastating tackle. Usually, he is also required to be the third major lineout jumper. And, like the number 8, the blindside flanker is also required to be one of the real hard men in the team, particularly if the match starts to involve a bit of push and shove.

Not surprisingly, flankers are usually the first to be sent to the sin bin for some misdemeanour or other. (The sordidness of the sin bin is covered in Chapter 2.) However, the good blindside flankers don't get caught. So the role generally involves someone who is a bit of a lock and a bit of a number 8, as well as a powerful ball-carrier who would love to have the speed of an openside flanker.

Getting Your Backs in a Row

The general adage in rugby is the forwards win the ball, and the backs win the game. This often causes friction among the two, as the forwards see the backs as the "glory boys" who do none of the dirty work yet attract all the praise. But really it's a bit like a cheese and tomato sandwich – if you want a decent meal, you can't have one without the other.

The players in jerseys numbers 9 to 15 are often referred to collectively as the *backline or backs*.

Passing and pestering for profit: Scrum-halfs

The *scrum-half*, or number 9, is the border collie of the team. He is a shepherd, an organiser, someone who yaps away around everyone's feet, driving them mad. He's the real link man between the forwards and the backs.

The scrum-half's main aim is to be the team distributor. Because he is invariably one step away from everything that's happening, he is the person who usually distributes the ball from the scrums, lineouts, rucks and mauls, and whenever there is any form of breakdown in play. (We discuss the scrum-half's passing skills in Chapter 6.)

The scrum-half must be agile, courageous and the best passer in the team. He basically acts like a pest and doesn't mind upsetting anyone and everyone – even his own team-mates! In fact, the best scrum-halfs just cannot shut up: They are the communicator between the forwards and the backs, as well as the "eyes" of the pack, constantly urging the scrum on to greater heights, or keeping the referee honest with yet another query about a penalty decision.

The scrum-half usually works in tandem with the fly-half (see the next section), with the pair deciding what is the best attacking and defensive option. (Chapter 9 examines game tactics.) When you see the scrum-half and fly-half making all these weird hand signals, or cupping their hands around the mouth so that they won't be heard by the opposition, it means they are getting serious, and something interesting is about to occur.

Better by more than half: Dawson and Howley

British rugby has been blessed with outstanding number 9s. In the past decade, it can boast two scrum-halfs the envy of the rugby-playing world. Matt Dawson has played a pivotal role in England's rise as a world rugby power, and while he may not be the most orthodox scrum-half, his running close to rucks, mauls and scrums, makes him one of the most dangerous.

Rob Howley is a more traditional scrum-half than Dawson, but just as prominent and effective, because of his resourcefulness and the searing speed with which he turns defence into attack. Although he retired from international rugby with Wales in 2002, Howley proved on the Lions tours of 1997 and 2001 that he is world-class.

The scrum-half is the easiest to pick out in a team as he is usually the smallest player on the field. He has to go into areas of the field that no-one else would. Mean-looking forwards, irritated by his constant babbling, love nothing better than running at, and running over, that painful, pesky number 9. This is where the scrum-half really shows whether he is up to it or not. The great ones, like Matt Dawson (Northampton & England) and Rob Howley (Wasps & Wales), take it in their stride (as we explain in the sidebar about them). The scrum-halfs who aren't up to scratch usually let the forwards run all over them, which means their days on the field are numbered.

Feeling footloose and fancy-free: The fly-half

The *fly-half*, or number 10, is the chief play-maker of the team, the man who makes all the big decisions that so often determine whether a team wins or loses.

While this position has a number of names, "fly-half" is the one most widely used in the British Isles. They are known Down Under as a five-eighth. This is because he stands between the scrum-half and the centres, which are sometimes called three quarters. Half, five-eighth, fly-half, three-quarters – get it? Rugby is such a mathematical pursuit!

The number 10 position is usually taken by the artiste or self-proclaimed intellect of the team. The fly-half is known as the pivot – and understandably so. So much pivots on what the fly-half does because he often dictates the flow and meaning of the game. He determines whether his team adopts a running game or relies on midfield kicking to upset the opposition, whether to mix it up or to use forward power to grind out a victory. (Chapter 9 further discusses the fly-half's role in devising winning tactics.)

The fly-half must be a talented kicker and passer. He can determine the speed and flow of the match because he has the ability to slow play down, especially if he opts for a kicking game rather than a running game. He may consider the best option is to return the focus of play back towards the forwards by running the ball towards his pack. As he is in the most central position on the pitch, and always stands close to his forward pack, it is understandable that the fly-half becomes a vital tactician.

A fly-half of any note must have a very cool demeanour and an ability to think clearly under pressure. He also needs to possess good all-round skills, because every one of those skills are usually put to the test. Fly-half is a demanding position, but it is also one of the most rewarding.

Focusing on centres

While both go under the name *centre*, the players wearing numbers 12 (inside centre) and 13 (outside centre) involve slightly different roles. The aim remains the same: trying to elude their opponents so that they can set up tries.

Attacking from the inside out

Number 12 is the *inside centre*, the man who stands closest in attack to the fly-half (number 10) and who often acts as a back-up fly-half, being the second midfield organiser of the attack. In simple terms, the inside centre is the man who keeps the attack in some sort of formation by providing the ideal link between the fly-half and the outside backs.

The prime aim of the inside centre is to be the link man. Like the fly-half, he often has to decide whether to straighten the attack by running straight with the ball, or push the attack wider by passing to either his outside centre or fullback (mostly a back-up position, discussed later in this chapter). He often plays a "battering ram" role in taking the ball up to the opposition defensive line, allowing himself to be tackled. Hopefully he can recycle the ball at the tackle area so his team can regain possession and attack again – the quicker the better! (We talk about tackling in Chapter 6.)

A good inside centre must be dependable, able to straighten the attack when required and fearless in all facets of play. Few players touch the ball more often than the inside centre, so he needs to have exceptional ball-handling skills and great judgement, knowing when exactly to pass, when to have a run himself, or when to try and mix it up a bit with a *chip kick* (kicking skills are explained in Chapter 6). Most importantly, he cannot drop the ball, especially as he is invariably playing in a confined area with opponents hovering all around him. He has to be the coolest of customers.

Attacking from the outside in

Number 13 is the *outside centre*, who is generally the faster of the two centres and, along with the wingers, is among the team's more important attacking players. (Be patient – wingers are discussed in the next section.) The prime aim of the outside centre is to set up team-mates playing outside him, in particular the fullback and winger. This usually involves luring the opposition defence into pursuing him and, through that, creating enough room to throw what must be a perfectly timed pass, putting a team-mate through the opposition's defensive line. But he must also have the attacking instinct to know when to attack the line himself, and to have faith in his own speed to get him through. The outside centre is the player who tries to ruin any formation in the opposition defence by producing that unpredictable, attacking spark.

The outside centre usually has more space to work with than the inside centre; he must also be an expert kicker. Many tries have been achieved after a number 13 has broken his way through the opposition defence, and then put his winger or fullback over the tryline with a precise kick into the corner of the field, well behind the opposition defence. (Shown in Figure 4-1, the tryline is the line over which the attacking team must ground the ball in order to score a try.)

Just as important, the outside centre must also be one of the best defenders, especially as a fast-running fullback is usually charging at him with ball in hand, and by the time he hits him, running at full speed. This is no position for the faint-hearted.

To be effective, centres need to work in pairs. For example, there have been few better centre pairings than the 1997 Lions combination of Scott Gibbs and Jerry Guscott, which combined flair with midfield authority. Gibbs, at number 12, was immensely powerful and utterly dependable, especially when a team was under pressure, as he knew the importance of retaining possession and staying within reach of the Lions forwards. Guscott was the adventurer, knowing when to stick right on Gibbs's shoulder, or be more outlandish and go for the wide open spaces.

Running wild with the wingers

Each side has two *wingers*: Number 11 is usually the left wing, and number 14 the right wing. Left and right are determined by which way a team is running, with 11 on the left-hand side of the attack and 14 on the right-hand side.

Wingers are regarded as the "show ponies" of the team, whose primary function is to finish off attacking moves and score tons of tries. In any team, they should be the most prolific try scorers, especially as their team-mates devote so much of their energies into putting them in a perfect position to get over the opposition tryline.

The demands of playing on the left and right wing are basically the same. However, who plays on which wing is usually determined by which foot a player kicks the ball with, or if he has a better left- or right-footed *side-step* (side-stepping is where you dart off in a different direction to that anticipated by the opposition; we discuss it further in Chapter 6).

Because the winger spends most of his time close to the sideline, it is no use having a strong left-footed kicker on the left wing, where he is unable to gain any distance with his *clearing kick* for the line; the same logic works in reverse for the other side of the field. (We discuss the best technique for a clearing kick in Chapter 6.)

Understandably, wingers have to be the great speedsters in the team, possessing extraordinary acceleration and the ability to beat their opposite man and then out-sprint him for the tryline. Wingers need to be fast in attack and able to work well in a limited amount of space; they also need to be fast and fearless in defence, especially when the attack is focused on the outer reaches of the field.

Mr Versatile: Neil Back

Most players stick to one position. That usually has a lot to do with size, physique, ability and certain skills. But there are those who have made radical diversions during their career and become stars in positions totally foreign to where they started out. So for those who do not believe in specialisation and would like to try out different positions, there are definite avenues. But you still have to choose wisely.

One of the most successful England players of recent times who made a dramatic change to his rugby career is openside flanker Neil Back. At schools level Back was a promising scrum-half, and also a talented football player, who only switched to openside when he was 18.

Back wanted higher honours and had always admired Jean-Pierre Rives, the great French openside (who was blond-haired and under 6 foot, like Back), so he switched position. For most players this would seem like lunacy, considering that the responsibilities are totally different. But in Back's s favour, he was supremely fit and, despite his height, had the physique and strength to make the radical leap. Initially, he had to overcome the prejudice that, at 5 foot 10 inches, he was too small to play international rugby. He has played brilliantly for Leicester and England, and has proved in the process that size does not matter.

The pressure on the winger to score has intensified since the introduction of bonus points in tournaments like the Zurich Premiership, where they are on offer for teams scoring four tries or more, and the Heineken Cup, where superior try totals count when teams are tied on points. And who do teams call upon to score these elusive tries? The wingers.

Roaming with the fullback

The *fullback* wears the number 15 jersey and has more freedom to roam than any other player on the pitch. The fullback's prime responsibility is to be Mr Back-Up. When the opposition has the ball, he has to know where and when to join in his team's defensive line, to ensure that the right number of players are in the right spot to stop the opposition from scoring.

This could mean joining the defensive line between the centres, or among the forwards, to fill any gaps that may occur. Or it could mean placing himself in a strategic position behind the defensive line so he is in the right spot to catch a clearing kick from the opposition, or even a chip kick, which is aimed at turning around and disorientating his side.

Forwards and the midfield attackers have relatively defined areas of ground to work in and cover. However, the fullback, as the team's "gatekeeper", has a lot of territory to patrol.

A fullback's normal position on the pitch is standing several metres behind his attacking line. This means he usually has half the pitch to cover, and even more when his own side is close to the opposition's tryline. So it is important that he knows how to cover that area. No other player on the pitch is on his own so often without the support of a team-mate. It's a demanding position, which explains why a good fullback is so vital to a team's prospects of winning.

A good fullback is a bit like a snooker player – he has to have the intuition to anticipate what's going to happen a few moves ahead and get himself into the right place to deal with it. The best fullbacks also use their skills to correctly "read their opponents" and anticipate what the opposition plan to do before they even know they're going to do it.

While it is probably the most stressful position on the field, it can also be among the most enjoyable because you actually get to see the sunlight – you don't spend half the game at the bottom of a ruck or maul.

Surprising the enemy

It is in attack where a fullback can really make his mark on the field. Due to his relative freedom of movement, the fullback should be used as the surprise attack weapon – he can appear anywhere on the field. A running fullback radically improves the attacking prowess of any backline, particularly if he is able to read the play and has the timing to know exactly when to "hit the line" and create the extra man.

The aim of most rugby attacks is to create an overlap where the attacking team has more players than the defensive line in front of them. The fullback can create that overlap if he chooses to appear in the backline either near the centres or wingers at an opportune moment.

Defusing bombs

The fullback needs the mental strength and courage of a bomb disposal expert because during a game few other players are put under such mental and physical pressure. To break up their attacking patterns, teams often kick high balls, which are known variously as "bombs", "up-and-unders", or Garryowens, to test the fullback. It takes great intestinal fortitude for the number 15 to continually risk his neck in catching these high kicks. A bomb is a kick from the opposition which is aimed high in the air, usually 20–30 metres above the heads of the players. As the high ball, or bomb, usually swirls in the air, it is often tricky to catch, and is the fullback's nightmare.

The fullback is usually the first opposing player a team tests. If he's not up to the task of fielding bombs, he's a disaster area, as the bombs just keep on dropping. If you can imagine trying to catch a ball with someone the size of a small mobile home bearing down on you, you get the general idea.

Changing codes: Jason Robinson

Even though rugby league and rugby union have for many decades been at arms-length in Britain, the rise of professionalism in the union ranks has prompted a lot of code-switching. League players are trying their luck in the union game, primarily because of the big salaries on offer and the temptation of playing an international game that involves more than three or four nations.

Despite the similarities between the two codes who play with an odd-shaped ball, many players have discovered that the transition is not as easy as it first looks. The biggest exception to the rule has been Jason Robinson, the former Wigan Warriors and Great Britain star, who was one of rugby league's most devastatingly effective wingers.

On joining the ranks of English rugby union in 2000 – joining Sale Sharks amid a blaze of publicity – Robinson worked his proverbials off in an attempt to learn the new code, practising his kicking and ball retention skills in particular. It paid off when Robinson not only managed to break into the England side in his first season, but was also selected for the Lions tour of Australia in 2001. Robinson made a devastating impact, scoring a brilliant opening try to the test series. His ability to change direction at lightening speed in tight spaces is a talent that transfers directly to union, and the way he has applied himself to understanding the distinct structural and tactical differences between the codes has paid big dividends already.

Chapter 5

Laying Down the Laws

· ·

In This Chapter

▶ Getting acquainted with the five most important laws

▶ Knowing how to tell your offside from your onside

▶ Recognising what the ref's up to

▶ Appreciating what a touch judge does

▶ Running the game: becoming a referee or a touch judge

· ·

*W*hen followers of rugby used to discuss the difference between football and rugby union, a popular saying was often quoted: "Football is a game for gentlemen played by hooligans, while rugby is a game for hooligans played by gentlemen."

It's a quaint load of old tosh, and nothing illustrates this better than the way that the rules governing the game are interpreted by rugby union players. They pick the rules up, bend them, bounce them, shake them and generally manipulate them every which way they can in order to squeeze out every ounce of advantage. You can always tell when a player has tried to push things to the limit – the referee points an accusing finger at the offending player who gazes back at him with all the innocence of a choirboy.

Rules are rules and they are meant to be obeyed, not only because without them anarchy would reign, but also because flagrant disregard of them could lead to serious injury.

In this chapter, we discuss the law book and focus on those laws that warrant particularly close attention. We also discuss the role of referees and touch judges. And – if you are the type of person who likes to rule – we even tell you how to become a referee...just make sure you've got the skin of an elephant, the eyes of a hawk and the disposition of a saint.

Introducing the Laws

To the rugby novice, the laws that govern the game appear complicated. At first glance, the law book is rather intimidating: It's closely written and goes into detail on every small issue. In addition, when rugby purists talk about the law book there's often so much jargon that others might be forgiven for thinking it's written in ancient Greek.

Nonetheless, the law book is a lot simpler than the rugby zealots make out, particularly as the main laws that govern the game, those that directly affect the flow of a match, can be narrowed down to just five – "The Big Five". They are *offside*, *forward pass*, *knock on*, what goes on at the *tackle*, and what is deemed *foul play*. When you know these laws backwards, you are well on your way to becoming a rugby expert.

Whenever you are discussing what is and isn't allowed on the rugby field, talk about the "laws" and not the "rules". Rugby purists, who can be very pedantic at times, love the word "laws" and frown on "rules", believing the former term sounds more dignified. You discover as you journey through this book that rugbyites are heavily into the aura of the game.

Finding out about the laws

If you want a copy of the full law book, it can be obtained through the *Rugby Football Union (RFU)* or its Welsh, Scots or Irish counterparts, and from various rugby bodies such as clubs. (We give details of these organisations in Appendix C.)

Nonplussed players

If you have studied the law book and grasped the basics, you are already on a higher level than the majority of players, who usually haven't any idea what the whistle blower is babbling on about, or why he's throwing his arms in all different directions.

This is not the referee's fault. Many modern players love the money they earn playing rugby, but don't do the research. That is why so many representative players spend most of the game looking totally befuddled. It is not because they have suffered too many hits to the head over the years; it's because they genuinely don't know the finer points of the laws.

To its eternal credit, though, the RFU has attempted to simplify the laws in the law book and has published a booklet in which the cardinal laws are summarised to make them more easily accessible to everyone who wants to be involved with the game. The RFU booklet cuts to the chase and explains the laws in plain English. Entitled *Instant Rugby (A Brief Summary of Rugby Union and Its Laws)* it is readily available through the RFU (the Rugby Store on the internet on) or rugby clubs. You can also obtain the complete law book from the same sources. Make sure you get the latest edition by checking the year on the cover.

Instant Rugby is a 10 page booklet produced by the RFU with the multi-functional aim of giving a concise, easily understood account of the main laws. It is used to induct new referees, who sometimes have no rugby union background, into the game, and can do the same for spectators and players. There are nine main headings, and each page is illustrated. They are: The Try & Touchdown, Knock-On or Throw Forward, The Scrum, The Tackle, Ruck & Maul, The Line-Out, Offside, Advantage, and Player Safety. In 2003 some 4,000 prospective referees went through the induction course in England – so whistle blowing is alive and well!

Building up your knowledge

You don't have to spend days poring over the laws, far from it. However, an hour or two going through the main points of the law – whether your reference is the full law book or the simplified version – is time well spent.

You begin to have a better understanding of what the referee is doing on the pitch if you've done a bit of study. In fact, you are more likely to know what's going on than some players, who, sad to say, don't have a clue what the referee is going on about.

Watching the ref

A good way to familiarise yourself with the laws in action is to focus on the referee during a game. Watch his every move and try and guess why he makes the decisions he does. Through close observation like this, you get to know the various signals and recognise the types of play that lead to important decisions. (We go into detail about the signals the referee makes later in this chapter.)

Pestering the ref

You can quickly shed your law book L-plates by approaching the referees themselves – they are usually struggling to find someone to talk to and most of them are obsessed with the law book and love talking about it. Also, referees are probably the most co-operative and friendly group to deal with in the rugby world, and are always eager to help someone improve their knowledge of the laws of the game.

Just approach referees in a friendly manner that reassures them that you aren't going to start arguing the merits of a decision they just made. You soon find yourself immersed in the intrigue of what actually happened at the bottom of the rucks and mauls, and beginning to understand the finer points of some laws that were hitherto absolutely bewildering.

Keeping in with the coach

Your rugby coach is often a good source of information about the laws. You find that coaches are instant experts on referees, even though their views may be more derogatory than flattering. For all this, however, most coaches have a good knowledge of the law book – it's an essential requirement if they want their team to succeed. (See Chapter 11 for more information on coaches.)

Your coach soon tells you at training sessions if you do something that a referee is likely to come down on like a ton of bricks. If you do it in a match, your coach's behaviour towards you is going to be on the frosty side, to say the least. Finding yourself banished to the reserve bench is a good indication that your knowledge of the laws is somewhat flimsy, and that you need to spend a bit of quiet time with the law book.

Observing the Offside Law

Without doubt, the most important rugby law revolves around what is offside and what is onside in general play. Like football, rugby union is a sporting code that revolves around the offside law. The main difference is that in football, offside is really only a concern near the goal, whereas in rugby, offside is in operation across the whole field of play.

Unfortunately, spectators and players alike often get totally bewildered by the offside law, but it really is quite simple, as we explain.

Going offside and coming onside

A player is *offside* in general play if he is in front of a team-mate who is carrying the ball, or in front of a team-mate who last played the ball. If you are behind a ball-carrying team-mate, you are *onside*. Offside means that a player is temporarily out of the game and should stand where he is or otherwise get back onside. Figure 5-1 shows a team moving towards the opposition's try-line, with two of its players in the offside position.

To become onside and thus able to take part in the game again, a player must get back behind his team-mates. A player can return to the onside in one of four ways:

✔ The offside player runs behind the team-mate who last kicked, touched or carried the ball.

✔ A team-mate carrying the ball runs in front of the offside player.

✔ A team-mate who has kicked the ball forward runs in front of the offside player.

✔ Team-mates can bring a player back onside by running past him towards the opponent's tryline.

A player can also be put onside by the opposition:

✔ When an opponent carrying the ball runs five metres.

✔ When an opponent kicks or passes the ball.

✔ When an opponent voluntarily touches the ball, but does not catch it.

A good way to remember this law is to imagine that you are the player with the ball. Everyone who is in your team and who is standing behind you is onside, and any team-mate who is standing in front of you for whatever reason is offside. Now you have mastered the first mysterious law of rugby.

Getting penalised for going offside

At some stage of the game, all players find themselves offside. However, it's important to remember that a player is not penalised for being in an offside position unless he

✔ interferes with play

✔ moves forward towards the ball or

✔ fails to comply with the 10 metre law (We talk about this law in the next section).

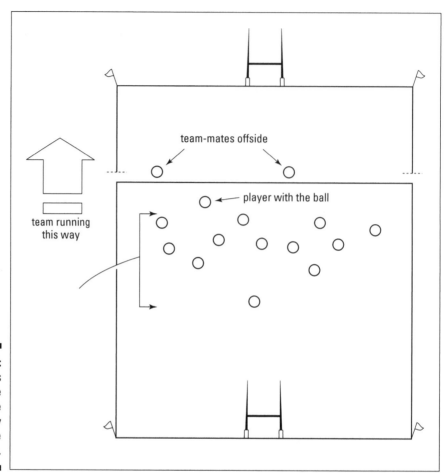

Figure 5-1:
Players
who are
offside are
temporarily
out of the
game.

If the referee catches you offside – and you are offending – he awards the opposition a penalty kick and the chance of adding three points to their score with a penalty goal. (See Chapter 2 for details of the scoring system.)

Players must also remember that if they are in front of the offside line, they can be ruled offside at a scrum, ruck, maul or lineout. (Full details of scrums, rucks and mauls can be found in Chapter 7, and Chapter 8 is all about lineouts.)

When a player knocks the ball on, a team-mate can be penalised if he prevents an opponent from running forward, picking up the loose ball and playing it. (We discuss the knock on a little further on in this chapter.)

Offside players must be careful that they are not caught *loitering,* or *lazy running*. These quaint rugby terms refer to someone who is standing in an offside position and preventing the opposing team from playing the ball as they wish. If you find yourself in this situation, move on fast or attract the ire of the referee!

The offside law may sound rather tricky, but one simple solution applies if you are concerned about attracting a penalty for being offside – get behind your team-mates.

Crossing the 10 metre line

A player is penalised if he fails to comply with the *10 metre law*. This law applies when the team-mate of a player standing in an offside position has kicked the ball ahead. The player in the offside position is unable to move towards the opposition or go within 10 metres of the opponent waiting to play the ball.

The offside player is considered to be taking part in the game if he is in front of an imaginary line across the field which is ten metres from the opponent waiting to play the ball, or from where the ball lands. The offside player must immediately move behind the imaginary 10 metre line. If he doesn't, the referee penalises him for being offside and intentionally obstructing an opponent by awarding the opposition a penalty kick, and therefore a chance at gaining three more points.

Figure 5-2 shows a player who is outside the 10 metre line and who must move back behind it if he is not to be penalised.

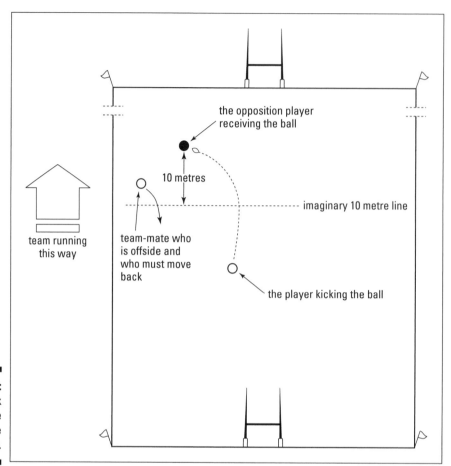

the opposition player receiving the ball

10 metres

team running this way

team-mate who is offside and who must move back

imaginary 10 metre line

the player kicking the ball

Figure 5-2:
Move back or break the 10 metre law.

Passing Forward

A player is not allowed to pass the ball forward to a team-mate towards the opposition's tryline – the pass must always be backwards, or behind the off-side line.

If a forward pass occurs, and the team-mate picks the ball up, the referee stops play and sets a scrum, with the non-offending team getting the scrum feed. (A scrum feed is described in Chapter 7.)

If the ball goes forward, and the opposition gains possession, play continues, with the opposition getting *advantage*, in that they can continue on with the ball. (We describe getting advantage in the section on the referee's signals later in this chapter.)

If the opposition is unable to do anything positive with the ball, the referee stops play and calls a scrum, with the non-offending team again getting the scrum feed.

Knocking On

If a player drops the ball "forward" – that is, towards the opposing team's try-line – or loses possession of the ball and it goes forward, a scrum is set, with the non-offending team getting the scrum feed. (The dead ball line is illustrated in Chapter 2.)

When the player knocks the ball forward in this manner, it is called a *knock on* (see Figure 5-3). If the opposition picks up the knock on, the referee gives the opposition advantage, allowing them the chance to do something positive with the ball.

If the opposition is unable to gain ground with the ball, the referee stops play and calls a scrum, with the non-offending team getting the scrum feed.

Figure 5-3: A knock out blow as the ball is knocked on.

Tackling the Tackle Area

Rugby administrators have been fiddling around with the tackle area laws for years in a bid to quicken up the game. Concerned that matches were being slowed down by unsightly pile-ups of bodies fighting for the ball, the law makers have tried to simplify everything.

Now the tackle law reads like this: A tackle occurs when a ball-carrier, in a standing position, is held by one or more opponents, and is brought to the ground, and/or the ball touches the ground. That player is known as the tackled player. Any opponents of the tackled player who go to ground are known as tacklers.

The tackled player

When a player is tackled, he must place the ball, pass it, or let go of it immediately when his body hits the ground so that play can continue. He is not allowed to hit the ground and keep tight hold of the ball. Repeat: He must either pass the ball immediately or release it immediately by putting it on the ground in any direction.

The tackled player must attempt to move away from the area, and then can return to the tackle area from the onside position. If the tackled player tries to grab the ball while still on the ground, he is penalised and the referee awards the opposition a penalty kick.

The tackler

When a player tackles an opponent and they both go to the ground, the tackler must immediately release the tackled player. He must immediately get up or move away from the tackled player and away from the ball. Exactly how far away the tackler must go has not been defined, but he must be up on his feet before he can play the ball.

Usually, the tackler re-approaches the tackle area from an onside position, from behind several of his team-mates. If he makes the mistake of grabbing the ball while he's still on the ground, he attracts a penalty and the opposition is awarded a penalty kick.

After a tackle, all other players must be on their feet when they play the ball. Players are on their feet if no other parts of their body are supported by the ground or players on the ground.

Tackling turn-offs

In addition to the restrictions we've just described, the following also apply:

- ✔ A player cannot stop a tackled player from passing the ball.

- ✔ A player cannot stop a tackled player from releasing the ball, or from getting up and moving away from it.

- ✔ A player is not allowed to pull the ball from a tackled player before the tackled player has released it.

What happens if it all becomes a mess, and the ball doesn't come out? If the ball becomes unplayable at a tackle, the referee orders a scrum, with the throw-in given to the team that was moving forward prior to the stoppage. If no team was moving forward, the scrum feed goes to the attacking team.

Playing Foul

A player cannot get away with anything that is against the letter and spirit of the laws of the game. Playing foul includes obstruction, unfair play and misconduct.

- ✔ **Obstruction:** When a player and an opponent are running for the ball, neither player can charge or push his opponent. Other players cannot run in front of the player carrying the ball or block the tackler.

- ✔ **Unfair play:** A player cannot waste time, throw the ball *into touch*, which means over the sideline, over the dead ball line, or repeatedly infringe.

- ✔ **Misconduct:** A player cannot punch, strike, stamp, trample, kick or trip an opponent. A shoulder-only tackle is also deemed dangerous: A player must not tackle an opponent above the shoulders, tackle an opponent who has jumped into the air to catch a high ball, or *late charge* someone who has kicked the ball. A late charge means to tackle or hit someone late, or well after the ball has left the area.

The referee can issue a yellow or red card to a player who is guilty of illegal or foul play. If the referee waves a yellow card in front of the offending player, it means that he has been temporarily suspended and must sit in the sin bin for ten minutes. (See Chapter 2 for a detailed explanation of the sin bin.)

If the referee waves a red card, the player is in big trouble: It not only means that he has been sent off and cannot take any further part in the match, but it also means that he has to appear before a *judiciary committee hearing*. A judiciary committee usually comprises three officials who determine during a hearing attended by the offending player whether or not he should be suspended for the offence. If the hearing finds against him, the player may be suspended for further matches, depending on the severity of his actions.

The Referee Rules

Whether you are a player or a spectator, the referee is the man to watch. The *referee* is the official who has the ultimate power over what occurs in a rugby match. What he says, goes. The referee's position is probably the most demanding of all, requiring a broad depth of knowledge, a high level of fitness and a very thick skin.

Your rugby-playing experience is far better if you try and keep the referee happy; antagonising the man with the whistle is not a good idea. Most rugby players treat the referee with respect with youngsters often referring to him as "Sir". This doesn't happen in many sports these days.

To avoid being targeted by the referee act as if you don't want to break the law, always be courteous and attempt to understand his decisions. Never, ever, push or manhandle the referee, irrespective of how much you disagree with a decision, or you will get a minimum six month ban.

How to be the ref's pet

Apart from having the right-size boots, perfectly ironed shorts and a clean jersey, it's important that every player's kitbag contains a well-thumbed copy of the law book.

If you know the laws, you can determine whether you can use them to your advantage, and be a step ahead of the other 29 players on the pitch. You may also be the only one to have an intelligent conversation with the referee during the match.

Apart from being able to chat with the referee, it's really easy to stay on the right side of him.

All you have to do is act like a saint, always stand behind your team-mates so you are never caught offside, never get involved in fights or altercations, never say a word out of turn, never make a false step at the breakdown, always release the ball when you are tackled, never play the ball when you're flat on the ground, never drop the ball and never commit a foul tackle.

As we said, easy.

Recognising the Referee's Signals

Match organisers often try to make the spectator's lot easier by explaining on the scoreboard, or via the public address system, what each refereeing decision means. This has helped immensely in explaining what is happening on the pitch.

Another important innovation has been the introduction of small radio receivers which spectators can buy at major rugby grounds, enabling the listener to hear what the referee is saying to the players on the field.

You are hooked up to the referee's microphone, eavesdropping on every conversation he has with the players and his touch judges. (We discuss the role of touch judges later in this chapter.) Listening in like this is endlessly entertaining and also informative, as the referee tells the players why he has made a certain decision.

The referees' signalling system is much clearer than it used to be. Many signals a referee makes are immediately understandable, reflecting what has just occurred on the field. Referees give signals to indicate to the players and to the spectators what penalties have been awarded, all scoring plays, and whether a team has been given a free kick or advantage in play. Some signals are not so easily understood, though, and may take a little time to learn. But don't worry; the signalling system all suddenly becomes very clear.

The referee also signals when time is added. While the time left in the game is often shown on the scoreboard, remember the referee is the final arbiter of time – what he says, goes.

The signals you are most likely to see the referee make during a rugby match are shown in Table 5-1.

Table 5-1	The Referee's Signalling System
Signal	*What It Means*
 	Advantage: This means that rather than stop play to award a penalty, the referee has decided to give the non-offending team the advantage of continuing on with the ball, or continue their attacking move. To indicate that a team has advantage, the referee stretches out his arm at waist-height, pointing it towards the non-offending team.

(continued)

Table 5-1 (continued)

Signal	What It Means
	Award of scrum feed: The referee faces the sideline and, with his arm horizontal and at shoulder height, points towards the team that gets the scrum feed, that is, the team to put the ball into the scrum.
	Forward pass: The referee makes an exaggerated hand gesture as if he has just made an imaginary pass which has gone well forward.
	Knock on: The referee puts his hand near his head and makes a tapping motion with his fingers, as if he has pushed a ball forward.
	Penalty kick: The referee faces the sideline and with his arm straight and angled upwards, points towards the non-offending team. The non-offending team can then take a penalty kick.
	Slow release: If in the referee's opinion a player has not released the ball immediately at the tackle, he makes a signal as if he is cradling a baby. He brings both hands to his chest, as if he is holding an imaginary ball.
	Try: The referee stands on the tryline and, facing the team that scored, raises his arm vertically and blows his whistle.

Taking Note of the Men in Charge

Running the game is a tough job which often attracts more criticism than praise. Should you want to become involved in this side of the game, though, several avenues are open to you. If you aspire to become a referee or a *touch judge*, this section is for you.

Referees: Men in the middle

Referees must be part-time psychologists, because they are in charge of an unruly classroom where they must know when to exert authority, when to give the pupils a bit of leeway, when to advise and when to bring out the big stick.

Players prefer referees who speak on their level and are not on an authoritarian kick. No-one likes a dictator. Try to understand what the players are doing, be sympathetic to their demands and whenever possible try to let the game flow. Players prefer referees who stay out of the way and try to allow them to play their game. But don't get bluffed – players frequently try to bend the laws and you can't let them get away with too much.

Referees fervently believe they have the best job in the world. They are the most passionate of breeds and protect their own. The referee's job is also now a lucrative position; because, with the rise of professional rugby, has come the need for full-time referees. For the Six Nations, Heineken Cup and other main competitions in the northern hemisphere, the English, Welsh, Irish, Scots, French and Italian unions employ a group of referees who travel the globe officiating games. (See Chapter 13 for information on the Six Nations, and Chapter 14 for details of the Heineken Cup).

Travel is often long distance, because northern hemisphere referees officiate at southern hemisphere matches, and vice versa. The money is reasonable, and if you don't mind spending time in lavish hotel rooms, all expenses paid, in some of the more entertaining cities of the world, then it could be the position for you.

Touch judges: On the sidelines

Becoming a specialist touch judge is difficult, because the position is usually filled by a referee. Normal procedure is for two referees who have officiated in lower level matches prior to the main game to become touch judges for the big match. A touch judge plays a very important role, as he determines a number of crucial points, such as where a lineout has to be formed and which team throws the ball in to the lineout (We cover lineouts in Chapter 8).

A touch judge also has to determine exactly where the ball crossed the sideline, which team was the last to touch it and which team is allowed to throw the ball back in. He also determines whether kicks for goal have been successful.

A touch judge also acts as the referee's right-hand man or as his second pair of eyes. He advises the referee whenever foul play has occurred and when incidents have occurred off the ball that the referee might not have seen, all the while making certain that players are in an onside position. At international and elite club level, a touch judge is in radio contact with the referee and can alert him via a microphone that is inserted into the top of his flag. In matches at the lower levels, a touch judge has to alert the referee by raising his flag above his head.

Once you've watched a few games, you begin to realise that the touch judges are almost as important as the referee, and have to be as fit and alert as the man in the middle.

Video referees: In front of the screen

At major matches, from Heineken Cup up, a referee is also required for a third important job, that of video referee. He spends the match in a quiet room up in the grandstand perched in front of a television set. In case you're thinking this sounds like a cosy little job, the video referee has to be an actual referee, and not a television soap addict, because it requires someone with an intimate knowledge of the laws.

The video referee's role is to help the referee in determining whether a player has actually scored a try, and, from 2003, he also helps the referee clarify who has been involved in instances of foul play.

- **Scoring a try:** If the referee is uncertain whether a player has properly grounded the ball over the tryline, or if he has been knocked over the sideline, he makes a hand signal, as if he's outlining a large box, to indicate a television screen. This means he's asked for the video referee to watch a replay of the incident and determine whether or not someone actually scored a try. At the same time, the referee contacts the video referee via a radio microphone hook-up and explains what he wants the video referee to look for. Usually the video referee watches the incident several times before informing the referee through the radio microphone hook-up whether a try was scored or not.

- **Identifying foul play:** For the 2003 southern hemisphere Super 12 tournament, the video referee could be called upon if the match referee is uncertain who was involved in an incident of foul play. The referee again gets in contact with the video referee and asks him to look at the incident to clarify who was involved. The video referee can only look at the incident specified by the referee.

We discuss television coverage of rugby union games in Chapter 16.

Becoming a Referee or a Touch Judge

Referees and touch judges are often former players who have either been forced to retire because of injury or believe that their vocation was in the middle, blowing the whistle.

Rugby authorities throughout the world are always looking for referees and touch judges, as the numbers are generally small. Anyone who wishes to become a referee or touch judge is encouraged. Major organisations have officials who are focused on ensuring that aspiring referees and touch judges are properly trained, properly recruited and properly nurtured through the grades.

The easiest way to become a referee or touch judge is to contact your main local rugby body, such as the Rugby Football Union in England or the national unions of Scotland, Ireland or Wales, which can put you in touch with their referees manager. (See Appendix C for contact details.)

To become a fully fledged referee, you undergo numerous teaching and coaching courses where the basics are explained by well-established, high-profile referees. As part of your training you are also taught everything that is required to be a top-notch touch judge. Although being a touch judge is not a specialised position, it can be as rewarding as refereeing. You still play a very active part in the game.

The first step, though, is to watch a lot of matches, observing how the referees and touch judges go about their business and trying to get an intimate feel of the game. Just as important is to get yourself a law book and read it over and over again, because before you are allowed to have a whistle in your hand, the refereeing authorities want to be sure that you know the laws backwards, inside-out and upside-down.

If you have any queries, do not hesitate about approaching a referee. Referees are very helpful and co-operative and gladly provide help to anyone who wants to become one of them. Punt high and whistle on.

Chapter 6

Honing Your Skills

*T*he best way to play winning rugby is to score more tries than your opponents. To score tries, you must win precious possession, and to win possession means you need to dominate the lineouts, the scrums, the ruck and mauls and just about everywhere that the ball is contested.

To be able to dominate a game, you need to have a good grounding in the basic skills. In this chapter, we guide you through some of the silky skills you need to go from rugby zero to rugby hero. We show you how to run, pass, tackle and kick like a champion. Before long, you'll be earning man-of-the-match honours.

Running Rampant

Running is just a matter of putting one foot in front of the other as quickly as possible – well, almost. Certainly, as with most sports, in rugby the quicker you run, the better your game. The same basics apply when you are practising to run in a 100m, 200m or 400m race: Namely, you need good leg drive, effective balance and a strong, confident stride. Unfortunately, running with a rugby ball in your hands requires slightly different skills and thought processes to just simply sprinting down a straight track.

To adopt the best running position for rugby, a player leans forward to provide balance and effective weight distribution. The rugby running style enables the player to adapt to whatever is going on around him: He has to be able to react to different situations, which could see him tackling one moment, side-stepping the next. After you can run full tilt in this position you're ready to try it with a rugby ball.

Running at full tilt with the ball may take a little practice before you feel entirely comfortable. A rugby player usually runs holding the ball in both hands in front of him. However, the player with the ball generally gets a lot of attention, most of it unwelcome. While he's trying to hang on to the ball, his opponents are trying to get it off him.

To prevent the ball being ripped off you during a match, practice running while carrying the ball under one arm. This skill requires the ball to be tucked or cradled within the arm, where it is protected from the grasp of the opposition's defending players. Carry the ball in the arm furthest away from the defending player and you can use the other arm to either hand-off your opponent or push away from him when he attempts the tackle.

Receiving a pass on the run

Knowing how to receive a *pass* from a team-mate while running at full pace is an important skill. A fast-running player becomes a target for his team-mate and gets ready to receive the ball by extending his arms and offering his hands as a marker, spreading his fingers.

When a team-mate passes the ball to you, don't take your eyes off the flight of the ball until you catch it. One of the most common mistakes when a player is receiving a pass is that he blinks or momentarily loses sight of the ball at the last moment. Taking your eyes off the ball can cause you to fumble and even drop the ball.

Nifty side-stepping

The *side-step* is one of the easiest and most effective ways of getting past an opponent. A side-step occurs when a ball-carrier appears to be heading in one direction, then at the last moment suddenly pushes off from his left or right foot and heads off in a different direction.

For example, you are running with the ball and a defender gets in your way. You slow down a bit and tuck the ball under one arm for safety (see Figure 6-1a). If you want to side-step to your right, drop your body weight onto your bent left leg, planting the foot firmly on the ground, drop your shoulder to your left, and then drive in hard with your left leg and push away in a sideways direction to your right (see Figure 6-1b).

To add to the deception, before you push off towards the right, feint with your upper body and make your opponent think you are about to go left. Once you have side-stepped around your opponent, continue your run (see Figure 6-1c).

While the side-step may sound a bit like a move from a line-dancing routine, it's a great manoeuvre on the rugby field because, if it comes off, the defender in front of you looks pretty foolish, grabbing thin air as you cruise past.

Curving into the swerve

The manoeuvre where the ball-carrier runs directly at the defender but, just before getting to him, curves away is called the *swerve*. The ball-carrier usually makes only a slight swerve of the body, and if done at high pace, it can be very effective in getting past a defender.

Figure 6-1:
Stepping
out with the
sidestep.

To make a swerve to your right, bob to the left with a slight turn of the shoulders as your right leg moves forward. Then take a long stride across the running line with your left leg and move the body away to the right as your right leg comes through.

Fending off the opposition

Sometimes you can't get past an opponent using either a side-step or a swerve. However, you can use the momentum of a defender to your advantage in order to get past him. The most effective way is a *hand-off* (or a *fend-off*).

In this manoeuvre, the ball-carrier runs directly at the defender, with the ball carried in one hand, before sliding to one side (see Figure 6-2a).

As the defender attempts to tackle the ball-carrier, the ball-carrier thrusts his free hand, palm-first (the hand which is not carrying the ball) directly at the closest part of the defender's body, usually his head or shoulders (see Figure 6-2b). The ball-carrier pushes his opponent away and down with his palm (see Figure 6-2c). This action gives the ball-carrier leverage and pushes him off the defender, so he can pick up speed and accelerate away before his opponent has time to recover (see Figure 6-2d).

Figure 6-2:
Fending off an opponent.

Going into a hit and spin

The *hit-and-spin* manoeuvre is one where the ball-carrier commits himself to being tackled and then extricates himself. He runs towards the tackler and drops his shoulder into the tackler's upper body before spinning or rolling out of the tackle. He accomplishes this by quickly twisting, swivelling his hips, and turning his back on the tackler.

The ball-carrier spins his way out of the tackle and can either pass the ball to a nearby team-mate or continue running.

Doing the goose step

The *goose step* is a tricky, fairly advanced move, looking not unlike the Can-Can. The ball-carrier takes three or four quick steps, lifting the legs with the knees locked straight (as shown in Figure 6-3). If done quickly, it has the desired effect of leaving the defence totally bamboozled as to which way the ball-carrier is about to run.

Australian Test winger David Campese was the master of this step – look for footage of his high-stepping style.

Figure 6-3:
Goose-
stepping
your way
around the
opposition.

Notable running styles

The greatest example of running rampant in recent history was New Zealand's rugby colossus, Jonah Lomu, knocking over everyone in sight to score four tries against England in the 1995 World Cup semi-final in Cape Town. Lomu (6 foot 5 inches and 18 stone) simply ran through, over and around everyone and everything.

Players, both past and present, use guile and brilliant changes of pace and direction to make them extremely dangerous when they have the ball in their hands. Great wingers like Wales's Gerald Davies and Australia's David Campese were so unpredictable that at times no-one, not even them, knew exactly what they were about to do. They did not restrict themselves to one particular running style, but would try anything if they thought it would upset a defence.

Kicking Cleverly

If you are just starting to coach youngsters – or "youngsters of all ages" – you can do your team no greater service than making sure every player has good *kicking (punting)* skills (we discuss kicking in the next sections).

You can guarantee that sometime, somewhere in a game, every player is going to be called upon to boot the ball. And you can become an instant hero if you know what you are doing and if your skilful footwork puts pressure on the opposition and your team scores.

An adept kicker is an asset on any rugby team and, like every other basic skill, knowing how to kick effectively requires a bit of practice.

Screw-kick

This all-purpose kick is usually the first one you learn. The most effective type of *kick-from-hand* is called a *screw-kick* (shown in Figure 6-4). The screw-kick has been in use for decades because it is extremely effective – when kicked properly it goes the longest distance and is accurate.

TIP

The screw-kick is relatively easy to learn. When you want to kick the ball deep into opposition territory with a *clearing kick*, this is the kick you want.

1. Hold the ball in both hands well out in front of your body, with the ball at an angle to enable it to spiral off your foot when kicked.

2. Drop the ball at an angle of about 30 degrees towards the centre of your body (see Figure 6-4a).

3. Anchor the non-kicking foot to the ground while flinging the kicking foot back (see Figure 6-4b).

4. Bring your kicking foot swinging straight through so that it strikes the ball with power. Point the toe of your rugby boot out as you make the kick.

After the ball is dropped onto the foot, the boot moves slightly across the ball, somewhat like a corner kick in soccer. Watch the ball all the way onto your boot, and then follow through.

If the kick is done properly, the ball spirals off your boot. A spiralling movement makes the ball go further than the usual punt kick, which usually floats in the air with no great distance. In the case of a right-footed kick, the ball spins from left to right, and of course spins the other way for a left-footed kick.

Never kick the ball too hard. Through trial and error you quickly discover just how much force you need to accurately send the ball the full distance.

Punt

A _punt_, shown in Figure 6-5, is similar to the screw-kick though it is far easier to kick. The punt uses the same kicking technique except that the ball is held in the hands in such a way as to ensure that the point and not the side of the ball is hit by the boot. One of the pointed ends of the ball faces down and towards the kicking boot.

A punt is a good kick for accuracy and for high kicks when you are trying to upset the opposition. The kick is accurate because the ball is hit on only a small point and it usually goes straight ahead rather than curling in the breeze.

Drop kick

A player trying to kick a drop goal makes a _drop kick_. The kicker moves forward with the ball in his hands and just as he's about to make his last long stride, he drops the ball vertically to a spot about 25–30cm in front of and about 15cm to the right of his left foot (if he's right-footed). (See Chapter 2 for more information on the drop kick.)

What the player wants to do is make contact with the ball with his right foot at virtually the same time as the ball hits the ground. Timing the kick, and being able to control the dropping of the ball, takes a long time to perfect. Spend a few hours practising this routine before you even think of trying it in a match, otherwise the fans in row Z could get a rugby ball on the nose.

Figure 6-4:
Using a
screw-kick
for distance
and
accuracy.

Figure 6-5:
Confusing
the
opposition
with a punt.

Chip kick

The ball kicker aims a short kick just over the heads of the opposition in the hope that it can be re-gathered on the other side of the defensive line; this short kick is called a *chip kick*.

Attacking teams often use the kicking style of a punt to make a chip kick. The ball can be accurately kicked just over the opposition defence, often bouncing up nicely for one of the attacking players, usually the winger who has been able to get through the defensive line quickly, to re-gather it without too much trouble.

Grubber kick

A short, low kick, known as a *grubber kick,* can be very effective where the ball is only kicked a short distance, usually along the ground. The ball-carrier drops the ball as he swings his kicking foot back (see Figure 6-6a). He then gets top spin on the ball by kicking the back half of the ball, the side closest to him, causing the ball to quickly roll forward end over end (see Figure 6-6b).

Use the grubber kick when trying to upset the opposition defence, or to make quick kicks towards the sideline. This is a good tactical kick, because when kicked properly, the ball shoots along the ground, bouncing erratically. Because the opposition players can't judge how the ball is going to bounce, the tactic causes indecision in the ranks of the opposition.

Figure 6-6:
Rolling out a grubber kick.

Goal kicking

Because penalty goals often settle the outcome of a big match (see Chapter 2 for more information on penalty goals), having a good goal kicker in your team is a real advantage. *Goal kicking* is a specialist skill, so usually only one or two players in a team handle the responsibility.

Nevertheless, all rugby players should practice goal kicking whenever they have the opportunity, because an accurate goal kicker is worth his weight in gold and is usually the first person picked in any team.

Kicking goals starts with the way you place the ball on the ground, how you approach the ball and how you follow through. The two main techniques for goal kicking are as follows:

- ✔ **Straight-line goal kick:** For a straight-line goal kick, the ball is struck with the toe of the boot, with the kicking leg swinging straight along the line of the kick.

- ✔ **Round-the-corner goal kick:** For a round-the-corner kick, the ball is struck with the top of the foot, near the big toe, with the kicking leg swinging in an arc across and through the line of the kick.

For either technique, you need an adequate run-up of about four or five strides before you kick the ball. Your non-kicking leg acts as a stable anchor when you swing your kicking leg through.

Whether you use a straight-line or round-the-corner goal kick is determined by how comfortable you feel with the techniques. Once you have done a bit of practice with both methods you know which you prefer – it varies from person to person.

Concentrate on the ball until the moment of impact. Always remember to follow through properly when kicking for goal: The follow-through provides the balance and coordination that's needed to put the ball through the goal-posts.

Straight-line goal kick

When you are positioning the ball for a straight-line goal kick, stand the ball on the ground angled towards you.

1. **Run in slowly in a straight line, with your eyes focused on the ball, as shown in Figure 6-7.**

   If you kick with your right foot, your last stride should be long, with your left foot about 20cm behind and 15cm to the left of the ball.

2. **With your left foot firmly anchored, swing your right foot through with ankle flexed and your arms extended to help keep your balance.**

   Flex your ankles to enable you to strike the ball powerfully with the toe of your boot.

3. **Kick the ball.**

   Kick the ball just below its centre.

Figure 6-7:
Kicking for goal along a straight line.

Round-the-corner goal kick

The usual way to position the ball for a round-the-corner kick is to stand it upright on one of its pointed ends. Alternatively, you can stand the ball slightly angled towards the goalposts you are aiming for.

Walk back from the ball about four paces and then take two paces to the left, if you kick with your right foot. (If you kick with your left foot, take two paces to the right.) The round-the-corner goal kick, shown in Figure 6-8, requires the following approach.

1. **Run towards the ball in a slight arc, in a slow, relaxed manner, with your eyes focused on the part of the ball you intend to kick.**

   Running towards the ball in a slight arc gives the required curl to the run as you approach the ball from the left, if you kick with your right foot.

The curl to your run-up helps get a slight right-to-left curl to the ball in the air, helping its trajectory and helping it keep its line. The curl also improves the distance of the kick.

2. **Push your hips forward with the final stride, and extend your arms to help you balance.**

   The last stride with your left foot must be long, with your left foot ending up about 20cm behind and 15cm to the left of the ball.

3. **Swing through with your right foot and kick the ball.**

   Your right foot should hit the ball well below its centre, with the ball connecting across the top of the foot, near the big toe and instep. Your foot should be extended as you swing your leg through, pointed in the direction of the target.

Figure 6-8:
Kicking
round the
corner.

Getting into goal-kicking form

Both goal-kicking techniques, straight line and round-the-corner, require a lot of practice to get right. So get a ball, go down to the local park and experiment until you are comfortable with a goal kick that suits you and the level of rugby you want to play.

The kick that won the game

There is no shortage of games which revolve around last-minute kicks. A famous example occurred in 2000 when Australia met New Zealand in Wellington. Wallaby captain John Eales was only given a few seconds to compose himself before taking a kick that would determine where the Bledisloe Cup would end up.

Five minutes into extra time, New Zealand were leading 23–21 when All Black replacement prop Craig Dowd was penalised for an infringement at the breakdown. Eales assumed that the team's regular goal kicker Stirling Mortlock would take the shot, until he was informed that

Mortlock had left the field a few minutes earlier with severe cramp. So it was up to the skipper.

Eales, a lock, had the onerous responsibility of kicking a penalty goal about 25m out from the goalposts and 15m in from the sideline, in a swirling breeze, to determine who would win the Bledisloe Cup. A poor attempt, and the cup stayed in New Zealand.

Rising to the occasion, Eales casually tapped the ball straight through the goalposts, prompting scenes of ecstasy among the Wallabies as they celebrated the tightest of victories over their great rivals.

Watching expert goal kickers in action is always rewarding. For example, watch England's Jonny Wilkinson, Wales's Neil Jenkins or New Zealand's Andrew Mehrtens. Each of these players has a smooth, precise approach and an effective, relaxed kicking style, which in some ways resembles a perfect golf swing. As a result, they are among the most accurate and reliable goal kickers in international rugby.

Passing with Panache

Passing a rugby ball is one of the most elementary of rugby skills; the technique for making a good pass is shown in Figure 6-9.

The player running with the ball holds it in both hands, with a hand on either side of the ball, fingers spread wide to ensure control and balance. When he is ready to pass the ball, the player swings it across his body in the opposite direction to the one in which he is going to pass it. If the player wants to pass the ball to his right, he first swings the ball to the left side of his body. The player then swings his arms and shoulders back towards the team-mate he wants to pass to and flings the ball across. The ball leaves the player's hand quickly and with a snap.

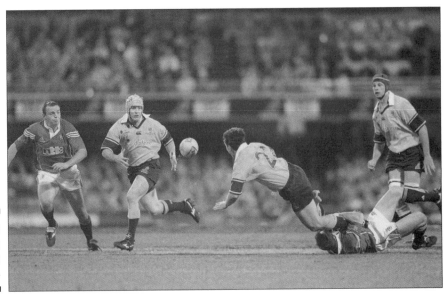

Figure 6-9:
Passing
with flying
colours.

To make your pass more effective, propel the ball towards your team-mate by slightly bending your arms and flicking the ball with the two small fingers of each hand, turning the wrists slightly.

Making a good pass means you involve your whole body and are well co-ordinated. Other factors that are critical to a good pass are the following:

- **Accuracy:** Accuracy is vital. Throw the ball to your team-mate, but not straight at him; if you throw it slightly in front of him, he can run on and collect the ball at pace. And throw the ball towards your team-mate at a height that is somewhere between his waist and his chest so he can easily see it and easily catch it – throwing the ball to your team-mate's shoes or over his head is not very wise.

- **Velocity:** Speed is important. Throw the ball with some velocity to ensure that it maintains its height and does not drop before reaching the player who is going to receive it.

- **Tactical awareness:** Only throw the ball to a team-mate when that team-mate is better placed to continue the attack. Passing the ball to a team-mate who is surrounded by defenders just waiting to hit him when he receives the ball is not only pointless, it's also dangerous. Such a danger-ous pass is called a *hospital pass*, because it usually sees the receiver, being pummelled by defenders! And you'll be the one bringing the grapes to the bedside if your team-mate ends up in casualty.

Bringing tactics into play

Once you know how to pass, and can execute a fast, straight and well-timed pass, use the pass to frustrate the opposition. One of the most effective tactics is for the player with the ball to succeed in drawing his man. In other words, while the player with the ball is covered closely by a defender, a team-mate to whom he can pass is in the clear and does not have an opponent hovering around him.

If the player with the ball throws it straightaway, the defender might have enough time to change direction and chase down the player who receives the pass. To avoid this, the ball-carrier lures the defender by running at him, as if to try to get around him; this compels the defender to tackle him. But just before the ball-carrier gets to the defender, who is on the verge of tackling him, the ball-carrier passes the ball to his team-mate, who is completely in the clear and not troubled by any defenders in front of him.

The ball-carrier can also delay the pass slightly, a tactic which often has the desired effect of bamboozling the opposition. Or the ball-carrier may allow a team-mate to run onto the pass at full speed – this means the ball-carrier shields the ball before popping it up to a team-mate sprinting in at top speed. This tactic can confuse the opposition, because they momentarily lose sight of the ball and are caught out of position. It's a bit like the old three-card trick – now you see it, now you don't.

Spiral pass

To achieve a successful *spiral pass* means the player puts a bit of spin on the ball. The hand farthest away from the direction in which the ball is about to be thrown moves up over the ball as the ball is thrown, which effectively makes the ball spin.

If the ball is being thrown to the left, the right hand comes up over the ball, and gives it side and top spin, as shown in Figure 6-10.

The advantage of a spiral pass is that it is aerodynamically superior to a ball which does not have any spin and the pass is often straighter and flatter.

Cut-out pass

A tactic that aims to cut out one or more attacking players is called a *cut-out pass (or miss-pass)* and is shown in Figure 6-11. The ball-carrier deliberately throws the ball so that it goes past a team-mate in the attacking line, and goes instead towards players further out in the advancing line. The phrase *two-man cut-out* means that the ball-carrier has thrown the ball past the first two players next to him in the attacking line, sending it instead to the third man in the line.

For example, the fly-half may throw the ball past the inside centre and outside centre, and straight to the winger (see Chapter 4 for an explanation of where each player stands on the field). This is usually a predetermined move, aimed at totally upsetting the opposition.

The player or players who are not going to be on the receiving end of the ball do their best to deceive the opposition by giving a good imitation of someone expecting to get the ball. The pantomime includes having their hands ready for a pass and running in their usual positions in the backline. At this point, the ball-carrier needs to make a fast spiral pass, because speed is paramount to ensure that the cut-out is effective. The ball has to be thrown quickly, effectively and accurately so that the outer backs have the maximum amount of time to do something positive with the ball.

Lob pass

A high, looping throw of the ball, aimed to go over the heads of the opposition and into the waiting arms of a team-mate who is in the clear is called a *lob pass*. You use this type of pass when you are on the attack and find yourself crowded by the opposition's defending players. The only way out of your situation is to throw the ball over the top.

Building up your passing skills

Rugby coaches have tried all sorts of methods to ensure that their players know how and when to properly execute a pass. In the rugby heartland of south-west France, an area renowned for great passers, teams often train with balls filled with sand in order to help players learn to weight a pass.

The 1980 New Zealand team passed bricks to each other in training, to prepare for a game against Australia. This prompted the newspaper headline: "Look out Australia: Here come the All Bricks". Two days later, Australia recorded a rare victory over the All Bricks, 26–10.

The All Blacks got their revenge when, in 1996, Sean Fitzpatrick's outstanding side beat Australia 43–6, scoring six tries in the mud and rain of Athletic Park, Wellington, barely dropping a single ball in one of the greatest wet weather displays ever seen.

Figure 6-10:
Spinning
out with a
spiral pass.

Figure 6-11:
Making a
two-man
cut-out
pass.

Dive pass

A fast pass made by a player who dives forward at the same time as he flicks the ball from underneath his body with a scooping motion is called a *dive pass*. This pass is usually thrown by the scrum-half when he finds himself under pressure from the opposition defence and needs to get the ball away quickly.

Scrum-half pass

The *scrum-half pass* is where the scrum-half throws a flat spiral pass which is fast and accurate, and which often gives the opposition little warning because of its speed. Why? Because the element of surprise is a crucial part of the scrum-half's armoury.

Although the scrum-half occasionally uses the dive pass, he mostly relies on a deceptive pass when he wants to clear the ball away from the breakdown or from the back of the scrum. The scrum-half pass is a totally different type of pass to any other. Often, the scrum-half doesn't even look at the receiver, he just knows they are going to be there. Rugby telepathy, if you like.

Through practice, the scrum-half knows exactly where to pass to his closest team-mates. The skill is acquired after hours of training, where the scrum-half throws the ball to his fly-half, centres and wingers without looking. In this area particularly, practice makes perfect. (We discuss the scrum-half's skills further in Chapter 4.)

When the ball is available at the back of a scrum, ruck or maul, the scrum-half swings his arms through in an over-extended arc, using the power of his whole body to fling the ball. If he is about to pass the ball to the right, he places his left foot near the ball with his right foot pointing in the direction he is about to pass. When executed properly, the ball goes straight to the target, quickly and with a nice trajectory, making it easy to catch.

Flick pass

A *flick pass* is a short, effective pass, thrown quickly by using only a flick of the wrists to send the ball on its way. This pass is used when attacking players want to pass the ball very quickly along the backline in a bid to outpace the opposition's defence.

Tackling Tough

For a rugby beginner, the prospect of having to tackle someone is often daunting. Throwing yourself at someone who may be bigger, stronger and faster than you are isn't everyone's idea of a great way to spend the weekend.

Don't worry. When you join a rugby club, great emphasis is placed on teaching players how to tackle properly. Large *tackle bags* are used to help players perfect their technique without getting hurt, and to ensure players get everything right well before they actually have to try it out on a fellow human being. Tackle bags are large bags, usually packed with foam, that are enthusiastically bashed, smashed and crashed into by players trying to improve their tackling skills.

With a proper understanding of the basics and confidence in yourself, tackling can become one of the more enjoyable parts of the game. Bear the following in mind:

- ✔ **The fear factor:** You can overcome the injury fear factor. While it is natural to think that trying to stop a crazed lunatic who is running straight at you is going to inflict damage on your person, the reality is that you won't get hurt if you tackle correctly.

- ✔ **The focus factor:** To be a good tackler, you must possess the ability to block everything else out of your mind as you prepare to make the tackle. Tackling is a precise battle of mind over matter.

The real secret of tackling tough is to convince yourself that you can do it. When you have overcome that hurdle, you discover that it really doesn't matter what shape or size you are – you can effectively tackle any opponent and not get hurt.

Although acquiring a good tackling technique takes time, remember that tackling is not all that difficult. Once you've acquired the skill, you can improve it at training sessions – even the best players regularly return to the tackle bags to keep their tackling techniques up to scratch.

When tackling tough, don't be cautious or half-hearted about it. Those who do not tackle with 100 per cent commitment are the first to get hurt, whereas those who trust their instincts become great tacklers and a vital team asset.

As with passes, there are different types of tackle, which require different techniques.

Making a front-on tackle

To make a front-on *driving tackle* correctly and effectively, follow these steps:

1. **Assess the situation as your opponent approaches.**

   Work out the best way to tackle your opponent, where you should direct the tackle and how to achieve it – and convince yourself that you are going to be successful.

2. **Lean forward and use one of your shoulders to aim at the spot where you want to hit your opponent.**

   As you prepare to tackle, push forward with your shoulder to aim at the spot where you want to hit the other player, as shown in Figure 6-12a. You are allowed to tackle anywhere between the player's knees and chest.

3. **Use your legs to drive into your opponent.**

   It is important that you launch your tackle from both feet as you drive powerfully with your shoulders. You need to make such an impact on the body of the ball-carrier that he loses the ball.

4. **Keep your head aimed to the side of your opponent's body.**

   Your head position is important. Your chin should be tucked in on your chest, which has the effect of hunching your shoulders, while your back should be straight.

5. **Drive into your opponent, grabbing him tightly around the waist.**

   Drive hard into the ball-carrier to push him backwards and upwards. Wrap your arms tightly around him to begin with, then slide your arms down, behind and around his thighs (see Figure 6-12b). If done properly, the tackle knocks the ball-carrier off-balance and you fall on top of him.

6. **Try to get the ball from your opponent.**

   Keeping a strong hold on your opponent so that he cannot push you away, try and get some part of your body or your hands on the ball, because that can often have the effect of your opponent losing his grip on the ball.

Side-on tackle

When a ball-carrier is trying to run in between defending players, he is some-times stopped by a *side-on* tackle, a variation of the driving tackle. If you are the tackler trying to stop the ball-carrier, aim your shoulder at the ball-carrier's waist, near the hip.

After hitting the ball-carrier with your shoulder, put your arms around his thighs and keep a tight hold. Keeping a strong grip on your opponent's thighs has the effect of stopping him, and the momentum sees him hit the ground.

Tackle from behind

Another variation of the driving tackle is the tackle from behind. When chasing the ball-carrier from behind, the tackler aims or dives at the ball-carrier's lower back, as shown in Figure 6-13. The tackler's arms encircle his opponent's waist or hips with a firm grip, then slide down his legs, which effectively traps his legs and trips him over.

Figure 6-12:
Going for a front-on driving tackle.

Figure 6-13:
Diving in to tackle from behind.

Smother tackle

When a ball-carrier is running straight at the tackler, the tackler aims high, at the ball-carrier's chest, and attempts a *smother tackle*. The tackler throws himself at his opponent, and gives him a tight bear hug while leaning back, in the hope that either his weight or their combined weights topple him over. The objective is to at least stop the ball-carrier from passing the ball to anyone else.

Stationary tackle

The *stationary tackle* is a variation on the smother tackle. The ball-carrier is running right at the tackler, who is usually stationary. The tackler prepares himself for the front-on impact and, when it comes, holds on tightly, using the ball-carrier's momentum to topple his opponent forwards and over the tackler.

Use the stationary tackle if you are a smaller player confronted by a large forward. If you hold on doggedly and vigorously, you can upset your opponent's balance and topple him.

Ankle tap

Even if you are not in the right position to tackle a ball-carrying opponent, you are still allowed to hit his ankles with your hand in an attempt to trip him. An *ankle tap* takes perfect timing, and an effective tap, but it does work.

A defending rugby player uses the ankle tap when an attacking player has sped past the other defenders and looks like breaking through completely. In a last-bid attempt to stop the attack, the remaining defender throws himself full length in an attempt to tap the attacker's ankles. The ankle tap is basically a clever and legal form of a trip.

Chapter 7

Breaking Down the Breakdown

*I*t may surprise you to learn that not every game is an 80-minute feast of fast-moving rugby, featuring terrific tries, thumping tackles and desperate defending. Sometimes it can become quite frustrating, punctuated with more stops and starts than a learner driver's first lesson.

And it may surprise you even more to discover that when we talk about a breakdown on a rugby field it has nothing to do with a stranded motorist or psychoanalysis. It's far more straightforward than that. In rugby terms, a breakdown in play occurs when the well thought-out tactics of a rugby team don't quite go according to plan and they have to resort to Plan B.

This chapter is dedicated to explaining that area of forward play that is often called "the dark arts", because a lot of what happens is not always seen by the spectator, and thankfully so. We separate the breakdown into its three major components – rucks, mauls and scrums – and go into the glorious technicalities of each. We also tell you how to tell the difference between a ruck and a maul.

Roughing It in the Rucks

A *ruck* takes place after a tackle has been made or when the ball is loose on the ground. A ruck is formed when at least one player from each side is standing above the ball and they are in physical contact with each other.

The player who has been tackled with the ball is allowed to place it on the ground, or push it somewhere near his own team-mates. He must do this almost immediately. The referee gives him a few seconds, then he must release the ball; if the player hangs onto the ball too long, perhaps to allow his team-mates time to catch up or to prevent a defender picking the ball up, the referee blows his whistle and awards a penalty to the other side.

The first forwards to arrive at a ruck usually bind together, as shown in Figure 7-1. The players grab each other around the shoulders or waist, as if they are a scrum on the run, before stepping over the ball. They then attempt to drive the opposition back and away from the loose ball. It's a bit like a game of push and shove in the school playground, only with bigger kids.

Figure 7-1:
Forming a
ruck.

When the ruck is formed, the prime aim is to remove the ball. Players are not allowed to touch the ball with their hands, only with their feet which they use to rake the ball back to a waiting team-mate. Alternatively, the attacking group of players can drive forward, stepping over the ball so that it comes out on their side and into the hands of the waiting scrum-half, who decides how the team attacks next.

Players do not make deliberate contact with an opponent's body. Kicking, trampling, or hacking away at an opponent who may have fallen to the ground and who appears to be blocking access to the ball is not tolerated, and can result in the referee sending the offender off. Heeling an obstructing player backwards from a ruck with the ball is permitted.

The kings of rucking

The New Zealand All Blacks have a mantra: Their players are told to "Bend, Bind, Drive". This mantra is worth remembering, because for more than 60 years, the All Blacks have been the kings of rucking. Sixty years ago, Vic Cavanagh, a coach from Dunedin, turned his Otago provincial team into an immense rugby power, thanks mainly to their ability to form the most effective of loose scrums, driving over the loose ball in unison to regain possession.

With their concentration on "Bend, Bind and Drive", Otago's game eventually became one of the main weapons in the arsenal of the All Blacks. For decades they have been virtually unstoppable in ensuring that whenever play has broken down, usually coinciding with a player being tackled, they have immediately regained possession of the ball by rucking it their way. The rest of the world watched in amazement before realising that they, too, had better adopt this effective form of attack, or they would be left far, far behind.

The ball is won from the ruck when the attacking players successfully bind together, drive forward over the ball and present it to the scrum-half at the back of the ruck, who then distributes it. Good rucking means giving the ball quickly to the scrum-half, which in turn ensures fast, quality backline play. This gives a team the chance to take advantage of the opposition defence. If the opposition hasn't had time to align itself properly before the next attacking wave, it's likely to have holes in its defence.

Attacking with the "pick-and-go"

One slight variation to a ruck that can be used as a successful attacking strategy is the *pick-and-go*. In a pick-and-go move, an attacking player falls to the ground, strategically placing the ball some distance from his prostrate body. Hot on his heels are several of his team-mates, who quickly drive their opponents away from the ball, but leave the ball behind.

Another attacking forward, who now has a clear run to the ball, picks it up and charges several metres before being tackled, setting up yet another ruck or another "pick-and-go". This tactic, if done properly, can be carried out five or six times and allows a team to gain a lot of ground.

And why is it called a pick-and-go? Well, you *pick* up the ball, and off you *go* — as fast as your legs can carry you.

Directing the ruck

Perhaps the most important player at the ruck is the scrum-half, who directs proceedings by telling his forwards exactly where to go. Also, the scrum-half is often the only person who can actually see where the ball is, how many opposing players are committed to the ruck and where the defence is standing. He can then decide if more of his forwards are required at the ruck, whether the ball should be released or driven, and exactly where his teammates need to concentrate their efforts in a defensive ruck to ensure they get the ball back. (The role of the scrum-half is described in detail in Chapter 4.)

The scrum-half is basically the on-site director of a ruck, telling his forwards where to go, what to do and whether they are being successful in getting the ball back to him. Imagine Stephen Spielberg on a rugby pitch and you get the general picture.

Rucking rules

A ruck can be a highly effective, and sometimes devastating, attacking tool. But it is also an area where countless infringements occur. The scope for foul play in a ruck is enormous and referees strictly enforce the rules. The whistle is blown if players who join a ruck

- ✔ Do not come from an onside position
- ✔ Come into the ruck at an unfair angle
- ✔ Use their legs to pick the ball up
- ✔ Use their hands mischievously to get the ball back to their side

Players are not allowed to kick the ball back into a ruck, because once the ball is out of a ruck, it must leave that area. And as the ball is coming out of a ruck, no player is allowed to fall on or over it.

Kick the ball, not the man

You often hear the term "over-vigorous rucking". This means someone has been caught unnecessarily attacking an opponent with his feet and includes a situation where a player stomps all over an opponent who has fallen and is lying near the ball. However, a player is not allowed to lie all over the ball and, within reason, an opponent can attempt to get him out of the way with a well-aimed back-heel of the boot.

A player must strictly ruck for the ball and not ruck the man. If his boot is aimed at the ball and it collides with a body lying near the ball, he usually gets away with it. But if a player strikes an opponent with his boot and he is a long way from the ball, he could find himself in a lot of trouble. This law is inter-preted differently by referees throughout the world; some countries are more lenient than others in what they allow players to do at the ruck.

Stay on your feet

Perhaps the most important law is that players joining or forming a ruck must have their heads and shoulders no lower than their hips. Players in a ruck must be on their feet and they must endeavour to stay on their feet. A player cannot deliberately

- Fall or kneel in a ruck
- Collapse a ruck
- Jump on top of a ruck

Rucks can be dangerous and sometimes collapse, especially when players use the wrong technique or do the wrong thing. For a ruck to be successful, players have to be well-drilled, well co-ordinated and disciplined – and know the laws.

Monstering in the Mauls

A *maul* is formed when a player who is carrying the ball and who is still on his feet is held by one or more of his opponents. In addition, at least one team-mate must be attached to the player holding the ball. These rather con-voluted relationships are illustrated in Figure 7-2.

Figure 7-2:
Hanging on
in a maul.

Mauls are usually created when a player carries the ball into a tackle and then turns to face his supporting team-mates in an effort to protect the ball and stop it being wrestled away by an opponent. His team-mates grab him between the waist and shoulders to protect him from the opposition and retain possession of the ball.

To the spectator, it looks like three or four people have got tangled up with one other in a washing machine going through the spin cycle. It may look like a confusion of bodies, but most of the time it is focussed on one prime target – the ball.

The two main types of mauls are *driving mauls* and *rolling mauls* which evolve after the maul has been formed.

Attacking in a driving maul

When the attacking team tries to drive through the opposition, the tactic is called a *driving maul* – no surprises there. The ball is usually smuggled to a player in the second or third line of the maul to protect it from the opposition. The players in the front line of the maul stay relatively upright, with their team-mates behind them, adopting a lower body position so they can get better leg drive and better leverage to push the maul forward. In effect, the maul becomes a driving scrum charging straight ahead, but the big difference is that the ball is being held by one of the players and is not on the ground.

Spinning into a rolling maul

A *rolling maul* occurs when the attacking team transfers the ball into the hands of a player on the side of the maul where the opposition appears weakest or has the least number of players. His team-mates roll around to that side, pushing the player with the ball forward in a fairly good imitation of a cyclone. The maul resembles a spinning top, with one player rolling onto another, enabling the maul to move forward as the ball is transferred from one player to the next.

When executed properly, a rolling maul is a devastating attacking strategy because it is so difficult to defend against, especially when the team in possession changes its direction, going from one side of the field to the other. Most of the time the opposition has its work cut out just trying to stop the rolling maul from advancing, and has no real chance of getting the ball back.

For this reason, lots of tries can be scored from rolling mauls. Whoever is currently holding the ball watches for the moment when the opposition defence in front of him is in disarray. He then peels off and crosses over the tryline (see Chapter 2 for an illustration of the field markings).

Directing the maul

As with rucks, the scrum-half again acts as the co-ordinator at mauls. He doesn't get directly involved in the maul, but stands behind, right next to the action. The scrum-half looks for opportunities, decides where the opposition defence is weakest and tells his forwards where to go. He advises his teammates where they should join the maul, and who needs support to ensure that the maul keeps rolling on towards the opposition tryline.

Once a maul is formed, it must continue to move. If it stops, the team that has the ball must either use it immediately or try to get the maul moving within a few seconds. If they do neither, the referee awards the ball to the defending team with a scrum being set.

Mauling laws

To the spectator, mauls can look totally confusing, like an out of control amusement ride. On the pitch, though, a well-executed maul can ensure that one team totally controls the game. It requires an enormous amount of dedication and discipline, and a proper understanding of the laws.

An important rule is that players can only join a maul from an onside position. The mauling manual includes other basic rules:

- ✔ **Players who are in a maul must endeavour to stay on their feet:** Referees regard it to be dangerous play if anyone tries to collapse a maul or jumps on top of it.

- ✔ **Players are not allowed to drag an opponent out of a maul:** While the ball-carrier in a maul can go to ground, he must make the ball available immediately.

- ✔ **Players must respond when it is no longer a maul but a ruck:** If the ball drops to the ground, it is no longer a maul, but a ruck, and players must recognise this and react accordingly. It is forbidden to use hands in a ruck, only feet.

From time to time, check that your law book is up-to-date – the year of issue is stated on the cover. For many years, the laws governing rucks and mauls have been constantly reworded and amended. If you have an up-to-date law book by your bed, while you may not find enlightenment, it's a top cure for insomnia. (Chapter 5 goes into detail on the laws.)

Knowing a Ruck from a Maul

Every rugby spectator, and we mean *every* rugby spectator, has at some stage become befuddled and bemused working out which activity is a ruck and which is a maul. So don't worry – you are not alone.

The difference between a ruck and a maul is that in a ruck, the ball is on the ground, while in a maul, the ball is generally in the hands of a player. To put it simply: Off the ground, it's a maul; on the ground, it's a ruck.

Rucks and mauls serve the same purpose, in that the forwards are trying to retain possession of the ball which is fairly important if a team wants to dominate its opponent and achieve its prime aim – to win the game. That's why forwards get very, very passionate talking about scrums, rucks and mauls. From the way some forwards talk, these manoeuvres justify their very existence. Some forwards actually enjoy being at the bottom of a pile of bodies. Scary, but true.

Sorting Out the Scrums

A *scrum* is pretty easy to identify, and comprises the eight forwards on each team doing their best impression of a human spider. However, what is going on inside a scrum is not so clear – whatever it is, it is usually being done under a pile of bodies and to the uninitiated may appear a total shambles.

A scrum formation is rather like a battering ram: The front row of three players is reinforced with five more players strategically placed behind them in positions that best stabilise the formation and push the opposition backwards. (See Chapter 4 for further details of player positions.)

Scrums are often described as the engine room of rugby union, delivering a team's prime power source. If a team is dominant in the scrum, it usually means they are well on their way to winning the match, because what happens in this area of the game affects so many other aspects of the match.

Scrummaging for position

A scrum (which actually is an abbreviation of the word "scrummage") is a way of restarting the game. As explained in the law book, the purpose of the scrum is to restart play quickly, safely and fairly, after a minor infringement or a stoppage.

"Scrummaging" is an intense, precise science, so the best way to explain it is to go through the scrum positions, describing how each player in a scrum formation arranges himself.

The Front Row

There are three front rowers. The formation of a scrum starts with the hooker, who wears number 2 on his back. The hooker is the central figure, and when a scrum is called he raises his arms, enabling the two props (numbers 1 and 3) to bind under them. The hooker then grips the props, binding onto their rugby jerseys. The props place their arms around the hooker, so that the three are closely bound together.

Once all linked up, as shown in Figure 7-3, these three players lean backwards so that they are properly prepared to withstand the pressure when the second row and back row bind in behind them. The three front-rowers also spread their legs and bend their knees, looking directly at the opposition's front row in readiness for the battle ahead.

Figure 7-3: Binding together: the front row gets ready for a scrum.

The Second Row

When the front row is ready, the two lock forwards, also known as the second row, place an arm around each other, gripping onto their jerseys at waist level. The players wearing the number 4 and 5 jerseys bend over forwards and place one shoulder against the hooker's thigh and the other against either the tight-head or loose-head prop, depending on which side of the scrum the second-rower is standing. The head of a lock finishes up between the prop and the hooker's shorts, enabling him to peek through the gap and look at the opposition's front row.

The lock then binds with his spare hand, the one that isn't holding on to his second row colleague, on to the waistband of the prop in front, so that he can grip and hold on. A lock's lot is all very intimate and touchy-feely, considering where he's got his head stuck: You need to be fairly easy-going to play in this position.

The Back Row

The back row consists of two flankers and the Number 8, who have their own important roles to play in the scrum.

The Flankers

To complete the scrum formation, the two flankers (in jersey numbers 6 and 7) bind onto the second-rowers. For example, if the scrum is set on the left-hand side of the field, the openside flanker puts his left shoulder against the backside of the prop on the right hand side of the scrum, and the blindside flanker does the same with his right shoulder to the prop on the left-hand side of the scrum.

The Number 8

The last piece in the scrum jigsaw is the player in the number 8 jersey, who puts himself at the back of the scrum, leaning forward to place both shoulders against the backsides of the two second-rowers. In order to keep his grip on this twisting mass of humanity, he places his arms around their hips and puts his head between them.

Ready to rumble

By this stage, the eight forwards should be bound together into one powerful unit. The players in the front row crouch relatively low, with their shoulders slightly above hip level.

The opposition forwards get into scrum formation in exactly the same way. The two groups now face each other in an attitude not unlike that of an enraged bull lowering its horns.

When the two sets of players are about a metre or two from each other, the referee calls upon them to crouch, hold, and engage. The moment of impact is usually accompanied by the sound of loud grunting, and the heads of the front-rowers interlock with those of their opposite numbers (see Figure 7-4). The heads of the loose-head props are the only ones that can be sighted on the outside.

All 16 players in the scrum flex their legs forwards and keep their backs straight. It is now up to the scrum-half to put the ball into the scrum in the tunnel formed between the two front rows. The scrum-half knows when to feed the ball into the scrum because he is given a signal by his team's hooker who has the responsibility of striking the ball back behind him towards his second-row and the number 8.

Figure 7-4:
Locking
horns in a
scrum.

The usual signal that the hooker is ready for the *scrum put-in* is for the hooker to tap with the hand around his loose-head prop's shoulders. When the scrum-half sees the signal, he knows the hooker is in position and ready to strike ("hook") the ball back.

Two things need to be borne in mind here:

- ✔ The scrum-half puts the ball into the scrum by standing square onto the tunnel between the front rows. He must put the ball in straight (see the next bullet point for the reason why he must do this).

- ✔ The scrum-half cannot throw it directly towards his hooker's feet or the referee penalises him for what is termed a *crooked feed*, and the opposition are awarded a free kick.

Getting a shove on

When the ball is thrown in, the players in the attacking scrum push in unison; this is known as the *shove or shunt*. The players in the defending scrum want to frustrate their opponents and also try to win the shove – their aim is to wear down the opposition forwards, win the ball, and force the opposition to retreat. But the attacking scrum has most of the advantages and usually retains possession unless it is wheeled.

Should the attacking hooker fail to win the scrum feed, he is likely to be on the receiving end of immediate and intensive counselling. His failure is known as a *tighthead,* or *strike against the head*, meaning that the team which didn't put the ball into the scrum won the scrum. The term is derived from the fact that the team which won the scrum had the disadvantage of their tighthead prop being the closest to where the ball was thrown in. As the tighthead prop cannot see the ball going into the scrum, to win such a scrum is a great feat.

A tighthead is treated as a big, black mark against the losing hooker, especially if it happens several times in a match. It earns him a truly miserable week when he is laughed at, ridiculed and then dropped by the team selectors. For the opposing hooker who has won the tighthead, all his Christmases have come at once.

After the ball has been hooked back by the hooker, the second row forwards attempt to channel it to the back of the scrum, where it can be picked up by either the number 8 or the scrum-half. The ball can go through one of several different channels on its way through the scrum – the most common route is for the ball to go between the two locks and towards the number 8, who finds the ball near his right-hand side. This is the best way for the ball to go through the scrum, because it is protected from the opposition scrum-half who is usually hovering around, hoping that someone makes a mistake and the ball squirts loose.

Whatever happens in the scrummaging, no-one is allowed to touch the ball until it has been cleared from the scrum.

Pack animals

When rugby fans get talking about greats of the game, the names of legendary English, Scottish, Welsh, French, Irish, South African, Australian, and New Zealand forwards are inevitably mentioned.

However, the forward battle at international level has never been a saintly business. It is too competitive for that, and it is little surprise that forwards account for the vast majority of the 50-plus players sent off in top tier rugby since 1925.

One of the most notorious incidents was the "Battle of Ballymore" when England played Australia in Brisbane in the second test of their 1975 tour. Australia began the match with an unprecedented outburst of violent play, which appeared to be pre-planned. Fists and feet were used at the first ruck, and at the first lineout each Wallaby forward appeared to aim a punch at the Englishman opposite. The Australian referee, Bob Burnett, took no action. After retaliating by punching an opponent, and getting away with it, Mike Burton became the first English player to be dismissed at international level, when was sent off for a late tackle on Wallaby winger Doug

Osborne. The match, and the Australian violence which provoked Burton's anger, was justifiably condemned as a disgrace.

Another infamous set-to came in the 1992 Five Nations match between France and England in Paris at the Parc des Princes when France selected Vincent Moscato and Philippe Gimbert, two front row forwards who had been dubbed the "Beasts of Begles", after a series of unsavoury incidents playing for their Bordeaux-based club. A war of words occurred before the game had started, with England hooker Brian Moore goading the French, leading to a highly charged atmosphere. When England started to get ahead on the scoreboard, French discipline disintegrated in the last ten minutes of the match, with prop Gregoire Lascube sent off for stamping on England lock Martin Bayfield's head. Moscato – one of the "Beasts of Begles" – was sent off at a scrum for trying to head-butt England prop Jeff Probyn. England kept their cool to record a 31–13 victory, while Moscato, who never played for France again, took up boxing – with some success!

Laying down the laws of scrum

With so much activity taking place in a scrum, it's not surprising that scrums are governed by numerous laws. Fortunately, the most important scrummaging laws are relatively simple.

- ✔ A scrum must have eight players from each side; if a forward has already been sent off, seven players are allowed.

- ✔ Each front-rower must be a specialist in his position; a fill-in from the reserve bench is not allowed because of safety concerns.

- ✔ All eight players must stay bound to the scrum until the ball has left the scrum.

- A front row cannot form at a distance from its opponents and charge at it.

- Until the ball leaves the scrum-half's hands, the scrum must be stationary, and the players cannot put on the shove until the ball is inside the scrum.

- If a scrum collapses, the referee must blow his whistle immediately to ensure that players stop pushing.

- If a player in a scrum is lifted in the air, or is forced upwards out of the scrum, the referee must blow the whistle immediately so that players stop pushing.

- As soon as the front rows have come together, the scrum-half must throw the ball in without delay.

- The scrum-half must throw the ball straight down the middle of the tunnel between the two front rows.

- Once the ball touches the ground in the tunnel, any front-rower may use either foot to win possession of the ball.

- Front rowers are not allowed to twist or lower their bodies, pull opponents, or do anything untoward which may lead to the scrum collapsing. A player must not fall or kneel in a scrum, because this is regarded as dangerous play.

- Players are not allowed to handle the ball in a scrum, or pick it up with their legs. Players can only use their foot or lower leg to win the ball in the scrum. When the ball has left the scrum, a player is not allowed to bring it back into the scrum.

- If a scrum is turned, or has wheeled through more than 90 degrees, the referee must stop play and demand another scrum. The possession goes to the team that had not thrown the ball into the previous scrum.

Banter and "sledging"

Many intimate moments occur on a rugby field, especially when forwards come face-to-face, cheek-to-cheek and mouth-to-mouth at the bottom of a ruck or maul, and these moments afford ample opportunity for a bit of banter.

When friendly banter turns nasty, it's known as "sledging". While sledging has gained most of its notoriety on the cricket pitch, it's also commonplace on the rugby field. If, while watching a game, you start wondering why a player suddenly starts throwing punches, or gets all hot and bothered, it may not be because he has been the victim of a tackle or has lost a good opportunity to attack. More likely, he has been abused by an opponent, which has had the desired effect of unnerving and distracting him.

Sledging can be cheeky, vicious, witty or clever, but it only works if it has the desired effect of demoralising the victim. Sometimes sledging rebounds, though, and it's the sledgers who get demoralised – don't sledge unless you can back it up.

Chapter 8

Leaping Lineouts

- -

In This Chapter

▶ Making sense of a lineout

▶ Bringing players into line

▶ Doing it according to the rules

▶ Working out tactics to fool the opposition

▶ Picking up the tallest players

▶ Using code to win the lineout

- -

*T*he lineout is one of the most interesting and constantly changing aspects of the game. Unique to rugby union, it helps distinguish the game from every other sporting code. Spectators regard a lineout as one of the highlights of the game because of the athleticism and skill involved.

You can't miss a lineout. A lineout always takes place on a sideline and is, therefore, about the closest the spectators ever get to the action. A row of players from each team faces the crowd in similar fashion to the Saturday morning check-out queues at your local supermarket, but minus the trolleys and the bored expressions. A quick game of "statues" before the ball gets thrown in and they soar skywards, creating more aerial activity than the inbound flight path at Heathrow or Gatwick.

This chapter is dedicated to the tall men of the team, the players who take off like a rocket to compete in the unique rugby union phenomenon that is the lineout. We give you a full description of a lineout and when and where it occurs on the rugby pitch. We also describe what each player should be doing when a lineout takes place, and the tactics that players use to take advantage of any opportunities that come their way.

Lining up for a Lineout

In a lineout, designated players, almost always forwards, from each side line up facing the sideline in two straight rows. The ball is thrown in between the two lines of men (the *throw-in*) and the jumpers spring upwards, to try to catch or otherwise deflect the ball in the direction that gives their team the best opportunity to attack.

The basic aim of a lineout is to restart the game after the ball has crossed the sideline and gone out of play. The law book explains that the purpose of the lineout is to restart play, quickly, safely and fairly, after the ball has gone into touch, with a throw-in between two lines of players. (You may want to take another look at Chapter 2 to refresh your memory about the line markings on the field of play; Chapter 5 is all about the contents of the all-important law book.)

Calling a lineout

Lineouts are called in the following situations:

- When the ball goes over the sideline
- When the ball is kicked out over a sideline
- When a player has run over the sideline while carrying the ball
- When a player has been tackled while in possession of the ball and the force of the tackle has carried him over the sideline

The last scenario is the hardest for referees and touch judges to rule upon as the player with the ball twists and turns like a conger eel to avoid being taken *into touch*.

The ball goes into touch when it goes over the sideline – and out of play. Players don't like the ball going into touch because it means that they lose possession. The two touch judges, the officials on the sidelines helping the referee, determine when and where a lineout is played.

Locating a lineout

Quite often, the team-mates of the player in possession of the ball arrive on the scene and try and prevent him being carried over the sideline. Sometimes, it's quite hard to figure out which player is holding the ball before the whole bunch crash into the nearest advertising hoarding.

Once the wreckage is removed, the player who touched the ball last is regarded as having taken it out of play. The following rules dictate where on the sideline the ball is thrown in and which team throws it:

- ✔ If a team kicks the ball out, with the player who kicked it standing in his own 22 (between his own tryline and the 22 metre line), or in-goal area (behind his own tryline), the lineout is formed where the ball went out. The opposition gets the throw-in.

- ✔ If the kicker is not in his own 22 and the ball went over the sideline without touching the rugby field at all, the lineout is taken back to where the kicker was when he took the kick. In other words, he loses ground, and friends. Tired and emotional forwards hate having to run back 50 metres when a player has kicked the ball out *on the full*, as it is known. The opposition gets the throw-in.

In the case of a penalty kick, where a player opts against kicking for goal and instead kicks for the sideline and creates a lineout, it doesn't matter where the kicker is standing on the field. The lineout takes place where the ball went over the sideline. This time, the team which kicks the ball out gets the advantage of the throw-in – because it is a penalty kick.

A lineout is formed at the exact spot where the ball goes over the sideline, as determined by the touch judge.

Forming a lineout

The referee stops the game when the ball goes over the sideline and demands that it is restarted through the formation of a lineout. With one arm raised in the air to indicate where the lineout is to be formed, the touch judge uses his other arm to signal which team is going to throw the ball in.

The number of players to take part in the lineout is determined by the team's forward leader who decides the best tactical way to win the lineout. His decision varies from lineout to lineout. At least two players must participate, and the side throwing in often puts eight players into the line-out, although there is no defined maximum number – but they are almost invariably forwards due to their size. Occasionally you see a back participating in a lineout, but it's very rare. The opposing team can choose to have fewer players in the lineout, but they cannot have more.

Before the lineout forms, the attacking team decides which of their jumpers should try to catch the ball and what moves should be attempted after winning the ball. Another important role belongs to the scrum-half who stands a little way behind the lineout and whose role it is to gather the ball after it has been won by his forwards.

Once it has been decided how many players from each side contest the line-out, those players make their way to the spot on the sideline where the touch judge has his arm raised.

The players face the sideline in two straight rows, with a gap of about a metre between the rows; the players in each line stand about an arm's length apart from each other (see Figure 8-1).

A few basic rules here:

- ✔ The front of the lineout cannot be less than 5 metres from the sideline.
- ✔ The back of the lineout must not be more than 15 metres from the sideline.
- ✔ The lineout players must stand between these two points.

Figure 8-1 illustrates a typical lineout formation.

Figure 8-1:
Preparing
for action at
a lineout.

Throwing in the ball

The lineout throw is usually made by the team's hooker (the player in the number 2 jersey), but anyone in the team can restart play if necessary. The player who throws the ball in must throw it in at the precise height and speed so that the lineout player he is aiming at can catch the ball at the right moment, robbing the opposition of any chance of getting their hands on the ball.

How does the thrower know when to throw the ball or how hard to throw it? Well, for the answers to that one, we have to crack the code.

Communication between thrower and his lineout players is done through signals or code words which the *lineout boss*, usually the forward leader, yells out to the thrower so everyone on their side knows exactly what type of throw is required. (We talk more about codes later in this chapter.)

The throw could be short, long, high, flat, lobbed, or bullet-like, depending on the signal or code words used. The throw, which can be propelled any way the thrower pleases, as long as it goes between the two lines of forwards, must also go at least five metres into the field of play.

Reaching for the ball

When the ball is thrown in, the players in the lineout try and win it by jumping, catching, deflecting or tapping the ball back towards their scrum-half, who stands a couple of metres behind the lineout ready to catch the ball when it comes his way.

When jumping for the ball, *lineout jumpers* can use both hands to either catch, grab or redirect the ball.

To help a player jump higher in the lineout, his team-mates give him every assistance – to the extent that the players standing directly in front of him and behind him support his jump by gripping onto his waistband to help him up towards the heavens.

The opposition's jumpers try to work out where the ball is likely to go when it's thrown in and try to lift their jumpers at the right spot to win the ball. Sometimes it works – sometimes it doesn't.

This manoeuvre takes a lot of skill and practice. In order to give the jumping player maximum support to catch the ball, players use whatever comes to hand – whether it be skin, tape, shorts or a mixture of both. (We talk more about tactics and roles later in this chapter.)

Observing lineout laws

Even though the lineout looks a relatively simple affair, with two rows of players jumping for the ball, it is one of those areas where referees have zillions of reasons to penalise a team. Well, at least 20 anyway.

Certain laws govern how the ball is to be thrown in at a lineout. Not only must the ball must be thrown at least 5 metres but, most important of all, the throw-in must also be straight and between the two rows of forwards.

Players cannot support a jumping team-mate from below the waist (although at elite club and international level players are consistently lifted by the strapping on their legs), neither can the lineout jumper do the following:

- ✔ Use an opponent as a support when jumping
- ✔ Hold, push, charge, obstruct or grab an opponent not holding the ball at the lineout, except when a ruck or maul has formed
- ✔ Charge an opponent, except to tackle the opponent after the lineout, or to play the ball

Some referees allow a throw that is slightly in the direction of the thrower's team-mates even though it is against the letter of the law, but none should allow a throw that clearly favours them. If the throw-in at the lineout is deemed incorrect, the opposing team has the choice of throwing the ball in, or having a scrum set. (See Chapter 7 for details of scrums.)

The casual spectator or rugby newcomer does not need to know every detail of the lineout laws; many of them are self-explanatory. After watching a number of games, you soon understand all the nuances of a lineout and can quickly work out what's going on.

A lineout can be as much fun for the spectator as it is for the player, although spectating is a far less energetic occupation.

Lineout legends

Every country has its line-out heroes, and Six Nations and Lions rugby has been blessed with some of the modern greats. Pride of place goes to England and Lions captain Martin Johnson. After 10 years at the top, Johnson, 6ft 6ins and 18st 7lbs, was still hitting the peaks as England claimed their first victory on Australian soil 24–15 in Melbourne on their summer tour of 2003. A week after beating New Zealand in Wellington, Johnson gave a towering performance as the "go-to man" at the front of the line-out as England produced a 100% return on their own throw.

Revenge was sweet for Johnson because it was his line-out loss to Justin Harrison in the decisive third test of the 2001 Lions tour that denied the tourists the chance of a series-clinching try in the closing stages. Johnson's England partner Ben Kay is another athletic jumper, who prides himself on trying to crack the opposition's code.

England have not been short of great line-out men. In the early 1990s they could boast the formidable pairing of Paul Ackford and Wade Dooley, and, although other northern hemisphere sides have not been as blessed, Ireland have had fine leapers in Neil Francis, and his modern equivalent, Malcolm O'Kelly, Wales in Bob Norster, and Scotland in Doddie Weir.

Taking Tactics Down the Line

Before the invention of the faster, fitter brand of rugby we are seeing these days, all that was required at the lineout was for someone to grab the ball and run as fast as their little hairy legs would carry them. Now it has become more elaborate, almost scientific, with designated jumpers, special jumps, decoy moves and more subterfuge than a James Bond movie.

The basic aim remains the same: Win the lineout and set up a good platform to launch an attack, either through a forward running at the defence and setting up a maul, or by passing the ball out to the backs. As the winner of the lineout is protected by a number of team-mates, he has the scope for a variety of actions, including passing to one of his backs, running himself, or working in tandem with his forward team-mates to set up a driving maul. The options are limitless.

Those in the lineout who do not jump for the ball must concentrate on protecting their jumping team-mate, to ensure that the opposition doesn't pilfer the ball from him.

While rugby players are clever when it comes to evading the laws, defending players at the lineout have to be very careful that they don't overstep the line. Teams try to vary their lineout calls, and who they throw to in the line-out, so that the opposition never feels totally confident about which jumper to target.

The element of surprise often wins important lineouts. Some of the tactics you are likely to see include:

- ✔ **A front peel:** This is a quick throw to the front of the lineout where the ball is passed quickly from the catcher to a player "peeling" round from the back of the line-out with the aim of bursting down the tramlines.

- ✔ **The catcher throws it back to the thrower:** Sometimes the player who catches the ball throws it straight back to the hooker who threw it, who then charges down the sideline in the hope of catching everyone in the opposition napping.

- ✔ **The ball is thrown to the scrum-half or a forward:** Sometimes the ball is thrown to the scrum-half, who has charged through at speed, or to a forward who has peeled round from the back of the lineout. This tactic doesn't always work, but sometimes it does, and it's produced its fair share of tries over the years.

- ✔ **The jumper deflects the ball to a fellow forward:** The jumping player taps the ball down to a fellow forward, who then peels round behind the lineout before making a charge at the defensive line. This player is then supported by his other forwards to ensure that if he gets through an unprepared defensive line, he has numbers to pass to, or if he is stopped and tackled, enough forwards are in place for his team to win the ensuing ruck or maul. The attacking team hopes that this move sucks in plenty of defenders, and that with the quick recycling of the ball at the tackle, a gap emerges somewhere further out in the defensive line that the flying backs can exploit.

Keystone Kops

Not all modern lineout developments have been good. Some coaches and players have become too fond of trying to flummox opposing coaches and teams by devising complex and elaborate lineout tactics. Often they outsmart themselves.

Whacky lineout manoeuvres have players running this way and that, some making dummy runs and others being used as decoys. In the end it looks like a totally out-of-control Keystone Kops routine where everything goes wrong and the opposition wins the lineout ball.

And when it goes horribly wrong, the hometown supporters find it far from amusing.

Lineout star

If you want to be a lineout jumping star, it helps if you are tall, are not too self-conscious about other people touching you around the waist, and do not suffer from vertigo.

If you want to be a lineout lifting star, get big muscles and use them.

If you want to be a lineout throwing star, take up darts; accuracy is imperative.

If you want to be a star at upsetting opposition lineouts, get used to putting your hands where they are not invited.

If you want to be a lineout star overall, it is advisable that you know how to protect yourself, because a lot of pushing and shoving goes on.

A lineout is not the place for the timid or faint-hearted.

The bottom line is: If in doubt or in trouble, keep it simple. Throw the ball to the front of the lineout, where your best jumper should be situated, and get it out of the area as soon as possible. It is better to be simple rather than be a show-off.

Starring Roles in a Lineout

Representative teams throughout the world spend hour upon hour on the training pitch, perfecting their lineout tactics. These tactics centre around the jumper, the players who support the jumper, and the player who throws the ball into the lineout.

Jumping for the ball

Before players were allowed to lift one another in a lineout, each player had a designated position. (The law was introduced in the late 1990s.) Looking at a lineout head-on from the sideline, the jumpers – usually the three tallest players in the team – were placed second, fourth and sixth in the row. This enabled the thrower to vary his throws and so bamboozle the opposition. He could

✔ Throw short to the number two jumper

✔ Throw a bit longer to the number four jumper (who was usually the best lineout player in the team)

✔ Throw deep to the back of the lineout to the number six jumper.

Mixing up the throws also enabled the team to vary the spot where they could attack from the lineout, especially if the ball went deep to the number six. This player could take the ball and charge into the attack in the hope of delivering a nasty wake-up call to some sleepy defenders.

Taking possession of the ball deep into the lineout can help your backs because they are placed further away from the opposing forwards, who don't have as much time to get into position following the lineout.

Nowadays the lineout jumpers are not so carefully aligned, as lifting enables the jumpers to move here, there and everywhere. Yet many teams still stick to the number two, four and six formula.

A lineout jumper's objective is to deliver good, clean ball to the scrum-half, which means the jumper deflects the ball back directly to the scrum-half, not over his head or to his side. Getting the ball directly to the scrum-half enables the scrum-half to quickly pass the ball to his inner backs in plenty of time, before the opposition pounces on him.

The scrum-half's backline players also win valuable seconds. When the ball is tapped back directly to the scrum-half, his backline players also have that vital bit of extra time to get their attack organised. If the ball does not go straight to the scrum-half and bounces here, there and everywhere, well away from him, he wastes valuable time trying to retrieve it. Usually by that stage, the opposition players have reached the scrum-half, hassled him, knocked the ball away from him and thoroughly ruined his chances of getting the ball away quickly from the lineout.

Lifting the jumper

The responsibilities of the two lifters are as important as those of the lineout jumper. One lifter is positioned in front of the jumper and one behind him, and they must work in tandem and be perfectly coordinated to ensure that the jumper reaches the top of his leap at exactly the same moment as the ball passes over his head. Figure 8-2 shows a jumper being assisted as he reaches for the ball.

Lifters need to be well-proportioned and strong to be able to confidently lift one of the biggest players on the field. It may sound simple, but achieving the necessary skill takes an enormous amount of practice.

Figure 8-2:
Getting a lift
as the ball is
thrown in.

Winning the throw-in

You can usually find lineout throwers in the local park tossing a ball at the crossbar of the rugby posts until darkness beats them. Why? Because the crossbar is around about the right height for a proper lineout jump, and because it is a small target, difficult to hit.

The skill of the thrower, usually the hooker, is a major ingredient in the success of a team's lineout. The thrower must be accurate and possess the ability to throw the ball different distances. He must know how to counter any type of weather condition, in particular swirling breezes, and know what type of throw each jumper prefers – some players like nice looping throws, others prefer dart-like throws.

Achieving the technique

Practice throwing techniques as often as you can: Three important ingredients are a steady eye, power...and guile. You can throw several different ways. The overarm cricket bowling action is one alternative, but most throwers use a spiral throw, where the ball is thrown from over the top of the head. Imagine you are playing darts with the ball.

Cracking the code

The hooker, the player who usually throws the ball into the lineout, has to work closely with his forwards. Before each lineout, the attacking team decides which one of their jumpers should catch the ball and what move should be attempted after winning the ball. To ensure that everyone knows what is going on, the pack leader, or a designated line-out boss, is given the important task of making the lineout calls. The lineout caller then tells the other players and the scrum-half what is about to happen, through the use of the code system, so that the opposition doesn't know what they are up to.

At training, the lineout players, who are nearly always the eight forwards, work on a list of codes for various jumps. It may involve numbers or code names, but it must be known by everyone to avoid confusion.

In the simplest terms, a team may use the codeword "Frog", which means the ball is going to be thrown to one of the jumpers at the front of the line. If the codeword is "Dog", however, it may mean that the ball is thrown to those at the back of the line.

Codes are also used between the thrower and the lineout jumper so that the thrower knows exactly what type of throw the lineout jumper wants at that moment. It could be a flat, dart throw, or one that is high and looping. It could be a fast throw, or delayed slightly to upset the opposition. All this is worked out at the training sessions.

Notoriety in the lineout

The most notorious lineout occurred in the final moments of the 1978 Wales versus New Zealand international match at Cardiff Arms Park. With the final bell about to sound and the All Blacks trailing by two points, a lineout was formed close to the Welsh tryline.

As the ball was thrown in by New Zealand, their second-rower Andy Haden catapulted out of the lineout, falling to the ground. The referee penalised Wales, enabling New Zealand to kick a penalty goal to win the game.

Haden was immediately accused of cheating and milking a penalty, by making out that he had been fouled by a Welsh forward through his outlandish act of diving to the turf. However, the referee later explained that he had penalised a Welsh forward for impeding another All Black. This information failed to quell the anger of the Welsh fans, who still blame Haden for their unfairly losing a Test. To this day in Wales, the All Black player is called "Hollywood Haden", due to his theatrical skills.

Chapter 9

Talking Tactics

*T*his chapter has nothing to do with the art of public speaking. You have reached the part of the book where you can use all the information we've given you on rugby skills and turn it to your best advantage. Tactics and strategy are the key words now.

In this chapter, we give you tips on how to outsmart the opposition on the rugby pitch, using calculated and well-planned tactics. You can draw from a variety of methods and strategies – from how to attack with single-minded precision, to how to defend your end of the pitch as if it were the Bank of England. And, as this chapter is about the tactics that various players use, you might want to refresh your memory about player positions and roles by having another look at Chapter 4.

Beating the Opposition

Standing on the pitch just looking at those great hulks in the opposition ranks can in itself be very intimidating. You wonder to yourself: "How am I going to get past all those immovable objects?" While at first your prospects may not look promising, you discover ways and means...

- ✔ **Rely on your own self-confidence:** Convince yourself that you have the ability to beat any opponent. That self-confidence depends upon your willingness and enthusiasm to do the hard work on the training pitch to ensure that you have a solid grasp of the basics of the game before becoming a bit more adventurous.

- ✔ **Avoid making mistakes that hand the ball to the opposition:** When you can kick, pass, catch and hold a rugby ball, and when you've figured out how to side-step, swerve and hit top speed virtually from a standing start, you have discovered the best tactics to confound the opposition.

- ✔ **Devise a good plan, both in attack and defence:** Before a match, winning teams work out the best, most instinctive moves to overcome their opposition. Plans usually involve the whole team. A good attacking plan can be simple or complex, but revolves around a precise, easy-to-learn way of getting the ball past the opposition defence. A good defensive pattern relies on each member of the team knowing exactly where his team-mates are, so the whole team can move in unison to ensure no attackers get through.

- ✔ **Work on your strategy:** Many clever moves are worked out on the blackboard by the coach, often with the input of players. After you sit down and start working out tactics and plans with your team-mates and the coaching staff, you slowly walk through those tactics and plans until you have them all committed to memory. Players then know exactly where they have to be every second of the duration of a particular move – and they practice that move at real speed until it becomes part of the team's regular bag of tricks. Good rugby teams usually have at least a dozen different attacking moves, practiced for hours on the training pitch until players know them by heart, before trying any out in a game.

- ✔ **Have a solid forward base:** The best way to guarantee that a team has every chance to beat an opponent is to have a solid forward structure, which means that the forwards must attempt to dominate in all areas of their play. These players must win their own ball in the scrum and at lineouts, must pressure the opposition's set-piece ball, must win their fair share of the ball at the tackle area, and must get the ball out to a backline that is fast, efficient and, most importantly, doesn't drop the ball under pressure. (Chapter 8 is all about lineouts.)

Despite all this pre-planning, winning still revolves around the basics, ensuring that every part of the team's game reflects a commitment to precision and good timing before trying to become too creative. When you watch high-profile teams scoring tries, a lot of what they do may look simple. In fact, most of the best-scoring moves evolved only after a great deal of groundwork and a coach who can add a little bit of wizardry.

Making the Best Move

A successful team is a patient team, waiting for the right moment to strike and take advantage of the opposition, which may have suddenly lost focus or unexpectedly offered an opening in its defence.

The aim of any team is to try and overcome their opponents through pressure. That aim is usually achieved when all players in the team have acquired the basic rugby skills and can keep the ball for as long as possible, until a crack appears in the opposition's defensive line. (You can read all about basic skills in Chapter 6.)

Bringing on the forwards

The forwards in a team must do everything in their power to dominate their opponents. The basis of any good team is a powerful and dynamic forward pack. A team is certain to have consistent possession of the ball if it is on top in the scrums, lineouts, rucks and mauls (Chapter 7 goes into the details of rucks, mauls and scrums).

Keeping the ball in those areas is ensured if the forwards are prepared to use back row moves from the scrum, attack from the lineout, and drive from the rucks and mauls. If the forwards dominate in these areas, the work of the backline is so much easier; good consistent possession gives those out in the open field more opportunities, time and space to weave their magic.

If the forwards are poor, however, a good backline is totally wasted on them.

Coordinating strategy

In addition to having basic skills, a successful team makes a point of assessing the opposition's strengths and weaknesses in advance, and devises a strategy that it believes can beat the opposing team.

A successful team strategy involves a good mix of powerful forward play and exhilarating backline play. The attack should never be predictable because the opposition can soon work out how to stop a team that keeps trying to push through the same channel. Good attacks involve varied handling and running movements, tactical kicking by the halfback and fly-half, and the willingness of everyone in the team to have the confidence to try something different and trust their own ability.

Backlines adopt different styles in order to get over the *advantage line,* or *gain-line.* The *advantage line* is an imaginary line across the field that indicates where the attacking play first starts, so that you can see whether the backs have actually gained ground or not. Some backlines adopt a very steep attacking line so that each player is running onto the pass from deep and is at near top speed when receiving the pass, while others follow an alignment popularised by Bob Dwyer, the 1991 World Cup winning Wallaby coach. The essential feature of Dwyer's tactic is that the backs line up across the field much flatter than usual, and they must run straight. By lining up flatter – almost in a straight line across the field – the backs have far less distance to travel before they get over the advantage line. For a team to get over the advantage line, it must be able to get the ball over that imaginary line. In other words, the team moves forward and gains territory. By using a flatter formation across the field, and where their noses are almost in the faces of the opposition players, the backs immediately put the opposition defence under pressure, but it also means that their passing has to be quick and very accurate.

New Zealand provincial coach Vic Cavanagh was an outstanding tactician. During his time with the Otago team, Cavanagh stressed the importance of ensuring that the ball stayed in front of the forward pack, who dominated proceedings with good strong rucking skills, before delivering good quality possession to the backline. The backline would then attack primarily through keeping the ball in their hands, rather than kicking it.

Watching and analysing your opponents during a game is important. Note any obvious chinks in their armour and take advantage of them. For example, you may notice that the opposition fullback is nervous when the ball is kicked high into the air. You may sense that an opponent seems hesitant to tackle when you run towards the left-hand side of his body. A defender struggles to pass the ball from right to left, or is clumsy when the ball is kicked straight at him, or when he has to bend down.

These observations all indicate potential weaknesses that are ripe for exploitation. By being observant, you are able to take advantage of them the moment an opportunity presents itself.

Nowadays, top-level rugby coaches rely heavily on the video camera in a bid to find weaknesses in the opposition's game and identify areas where they can focus the attack. Before the game, all the top coaches analyse their opponents' play through watching videos of matches and using the slow-motion button to find potential weaknesses.

During most games, however, no television cameras or statisticians are around, so the coach and his players have to rely on their own gut instincts, knowledge and experience. With or without high technology, the aim of the game is the same – get an edge on the opposition.

Unorthodox tactics

The Lions have often come across southern hemisphere opponents who would stop at nothing to put one over them. On the victorious 1989 tour of Australia, their penultimate game of the tour was against New South Wales Country. The Country coach, Daryl Haberecht, realising his side would be seriously outgunned, developed a novel, if painful, tactic. When Country finally managed to get a scrum near the Lions' tryline, Haberecht had his winger take the ball at full pelt and attempt to run over the top of the scrum, using the backs and shoulders of his own forwards as a ramp to get to the tryline. He didn't

quite make it, the Lions duly won 72–13, and Haberecht's ruse was immediately outlawed.

Another Haberecht ploy which was quickly outlawed was getting his players to turn their backs to the opposition at a tap penalty, and then have them running in all directions, pretending they had the ball tucked under their jerseys. This "up the jumper" ploy bamboozled the defence as to who exactly had the ball – and not surprisingly, his team scored. Again, this move was immediately outlawed.

Weathering the game

Any number of outside factors can affect how you approach a game: factors such as the ground and weather conditions, the length of the grass, the state of the pitch, how strong the wind is blowing and in which direction, and whether it is boiling hot or bucketing down. These all have an effect on how the game is played and, if you're a player, it's a case of adapting.

If the pitch gets wetter than a shark's bathing suit, avoid madly throwing the ball around, because the risk of dropping a slippery ball increases. If the day is windy, you may find some advantage in trying to upset the opposition by kicking high balls at them, because such kicks can swirl, dip and drop in the breeze.

Take all these factors into account when working out the best way to dominate and win a match. You've heard the cliché that making the right move revolves around playing to your team's strengths and attacking the opposition's weaknesses. But also remember that you must be adaptable, forever willing to change your tactics on the spot. Like the ability to read the weather from the clouds in the sky, that adaptability comes from practice and experience.

Cheeky chappies

The players who thrill and entertain crowds are invariably those who have the gift for doing the unexpected. James Simpson-Daniel, the gifted young Gloucester and England back, crowned his England debut against the Barbarians in 2002 by leaving his marker, the massive All Black Jonah Lomu, in his wake with a superb piece of sleight of hand. Simpson-Daniel "fixed" both Lomu and Percy Montgomery, by throwing a pass to himself which he half-shielded from their view. When they hesitated, he rounded them, sprinting clear to score.

Austin Healey, the England and Leicester utility back, is another crafty customer. In one match for Leicester he took what looked at first like a routine tap penalty, with his back to the opposition, but then kicked the ball straight over his head. With his chasers primed, and the defence caught flat, Leicester scored.

Geordan Murphy, the Ireland and Leicester full-back, is also an accomplished trickster. Murphy's party pieces include kneeing the ball over the head of defenders rather than chipping it.

Jo Maso, the French centre of the late 1960s, could have taught even the players mentioned above a thing or two. One of Maso's favourite ploys was to befuddle defenders by moving the ball behind his back while he was running; this often confused them into thinking he had made a reverse pass, only for Maso to recover the ball with his other hand – and head towards the tryline!

Among the greatest entertainers was David Campese, the Aussie winger who is also the world record try-scorer (64 in 101 internationals from 1982 to 1996). Nothing illustrated this better than the looped over-the-shoulder scoring pass he threw to Tim Horan during Australia's 16–6 semi-final defeat of New Zealand in the 1991 World Cup semi-final.

Defending Devilishly

To the casual observer, a rugby match can often look like a disorganised game of catch-me-if-you can, where someone carrying a funny-shaped ball is chased by everyone else. The reality is that a lot more science is involved, especially among those who are trying to stop the person who has the ball.

To gain a real advantage over the opposing team, your defensive skills need to be both fearless and precise. Remember, you are always endeavouring to stop your opponents – and they should know you mean business.

Coordinating the defence

The key to any team's success revolves around their ability to defend their own goal line, and that relies on a determined plan and pattern. (To refresh your memory about line markings on the pitch, turn to Chapter 2.)

The defensive plan relies upon every player in the team knowing exactly how and where to tackle, making sure that every tackle is effective, and understanding what every other player in the team's defensive line is doing. Each defending player also needs to know exactly which person in the opposition attack they are marking, because that person is not always their exact opposite. For example, often the defending winger is not marking the opposition winger, but the full back or the outside centre. Backs often mark forwards and vice versa.

An effective defensive team plan relies upon players working together as a unit, communicating and backing each other up at every available opportunity. The purpose of this is to put pressure on the opposition and ruin their attacking moves so that the defending team regains possession. Pressure means the defenders always fiercely contest the ball – even when the ball appears lost, they needs to keep up the pressure in the hope of halting the opposition's advance.

Above all else, the art of defending devilishly is knowing exactly what you're doing and, at all times, telling your team-mates what you're up to and where and when you need help. And the best way to do that is simple – use your mouth. Talk to them, even yell at them if you have to. Do whatever is required to let your team-mates know exactly what is going on.

Blocking the advance: Defensive systems

When the ball is away from the rucks and mauls, defensive systems can be brought in. Two main forms exist:

- ✔ **The man-on-man defence:** The defending players tackle their opposite numbers, the aim being to isolate the ball-carrier from his team-mates.

- ✔ **The drift defence:** Each player in the defensive line drifts onto the player outside.

Man-on-man defence

In the *man-on-man defence* system, a defending player goes to tackle his opposite number. The defender gets in between the ball-carrier and his closest supporting team-mates, and tackles the ball-carrier before he is able to get rid of the ball.

If the opposition brings an extra man into the backline, the defenders all move as one to cover the additional attacking player. As a result of this movement, the last outside player in the attacking move is unmarked. To counter that threat, the defence is directed towards the sideline, and the responsibility of covering the last player usually goes to the fullback.

Figure 9-1 shows a scrum in action, with the defending players ready to mark players of the attacking team (as shown by the arrows). For example, the defending fly-half (number 10) marks the attacking team's number 10. In order to cover the last player in the attack formation, the defending fullback moves towards the sideline and the attacking team's left-winger.

Drift defence

The *drift defence* often occurs after a lineout or a scrum. To an observer, it looks as if the defending players are drifting across the field like a chorus line, a very purposeful chorus line.

In Figure 9-2, a scrum is in action, with the defending players getting ready to mount a drift defence. What usually happens is that the openside flanker has the responsibility of taking the opposite fly-half, the fly-half pursues the opposite inside centre, the inside centre pursues the opposition's outside centre, the outside centre the opposite fullback and so forth. In other words, the defence has to drift across the field to make the tackle. Tricky, but a tactic that usually works.

If executed properly, a drift defence gives the defensive line a way of countering and tackling any player who is brought in by the opposition attack. It also has the effect of forcing the opposition's attack across the pitch towards the sideline, an area with often no room to move. In fact, a drift defence can often see an attack pushed over the sideline.

The effect of drift defence is that when an opposition player enters the attacking line in place of the man that the defender was originally planning to tackle, then that defender tackles the new person.

So, if an attacker enters the line between the inside centre and outside centre, that player should be tackled by the defending inside centre, with those outside him in the defensive line consequently lining up against their exact opposite number and working on a man-on-man defence.

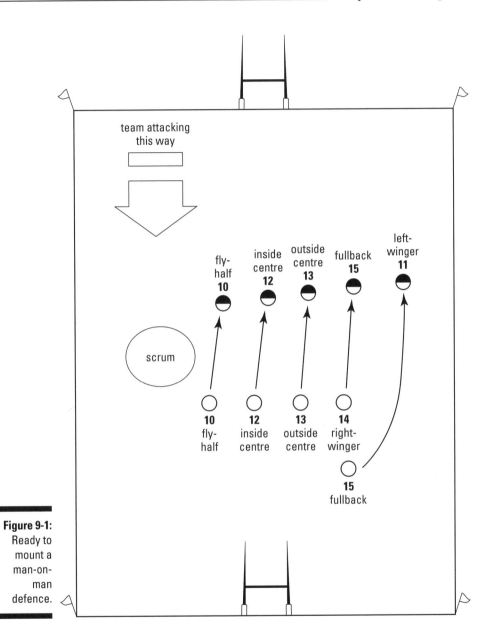

team attacking
this way

fly-
half
10

inside
centre
12

outside
centre
13

fullback
15

left-
winger
11

scrum

10
fly-
half

12
inside
centre

13
outside
centre

14
right-
winger

15
fullback

Figure 9-1:
Ready to
mount a
man-on-
man
defence.

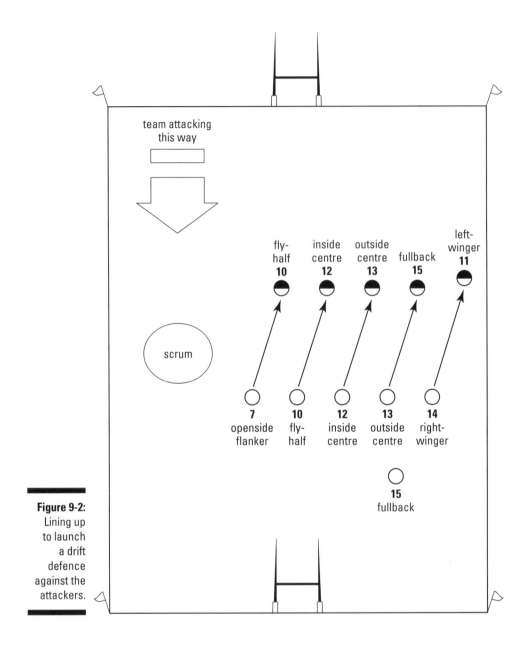

Figure 9-2:
Lining up
to launch
a drift
defence
against the
attackers.

Attacking Artistically

The attack plan of a successful team, like its defence strategy, relies on prede-termined patterns and plans. When a team goes into a game, it should have practised a variety of attacking moves during training, and each player knows exactly what he has to do. Figure 9-3 shows an attack in action..

While attack plans don't have to be elaborate, great attacking moves are always innovative and are such that the opposition finds it near impossible to know exactly what's going to happen next.

Figure 9-3:
A team
going on
the attack.

A good attacking move revolves around two players:

- **The playmaker:** This player gets the plan going with a precise pass or an action that creates the time and space needed to start the attack.

- **The instigator:** The playmaker is followed by the instigator, who can break through the opposition's defensive line, followed by the supporting players who assist in the attack and whose responsibility it is to finish it off, hopefully with a try.

In a backline attack, the playmaker is often the scrum-half or fly-half. The instigator is either one of the centres or the fly-half (if he is not the playmaker). And the supporting players are usually the wingers and the fullback. However, a great attack usually sees these roles becoming totally interchangeable, with any one of the 15 players having the ability to play any part in a constructive and successful attacking move.

Launching an effective attack

A good attacking move relies on what is known as *quality possession*, where the ball is delivered cleanly to the backline, usually by the halfback, giving the backs enough time to work out what exactly they are going to do before starting their attack.

Quality possession can be enhanced by a *cut-out pass (or miss-pass)* or by a *scissors pass*, as follows:

- ✔ **A cut-out pass:** In this move, the ball is thrown past one or more players to someone further out in the attacking line in the hope of catching the defence on the hop. (I describe this move in detail in Chapter 6.)
- ✔ **A scissors pass:** In this option, the ball-carrier moves in front of one of his team-mates and then twists back to pass it to the team-mate, again in the hope of distracting the opposition. The ball-carrier may run around in a kind of loop. After passing the ball to a team-mate behind him, he runs around that team-mate who then passes the ball back to him. This manoeuvre has the effect of bringing an extra man into the attack.

The attacking team may also try to attack on the *blindside*, which is the short side of the field, where the defence may be lacking in numbers.

Attacking players may also change the angle of attack in an effort to outwit the opposition. An attacking player radically changes the direction in which he is running, usually cutting in behind a team-mate.

A *decoy run* is another useful attacking tool. A decoy run occurs when several players pretend they are about to receive the ball in a bid to distract the opposition and thus create open space further out in the attacking line.

Breaking through

Getting through a defensive line requires a lot of preliminary work. A team's coach needs to work in tandem with his players to figure out the attacking moves that work best for them and, most importantly, have that element of surprise.

Many good attacking moves rely on careful alignment, choosing the right angles, the introduction of speed and the ability to penetrate at key spots on the field. Major international teams work on a particular move for weeks or months before they try it in an international match.

Good teams practise a new move over and over again, first in slow motion, and then gradually at speed until everyone knows exactly where to be and what to do to ensure that one of their players successfully grounds the ball over the goal line.

As with defending devilishly, attacking artistically relies on good communication more than anything else. The communications usually rely on the playmaker calling out in code what the move is going to be, and the rest of the attack getting into the right position to complete the move.

You can usually pick when a set move is about to happen because the playmaker starts talking and gesticulating to the players in his backline.

The great escape

One of the greatest escapes in international rugby history came in the 1991 World Cup quarter-final between Ireland and Australia in Dublin. The Wallabies led 15–12 with four minutes remaining when Irish flanker Gordon Hamilton intercepted the ball and ran half the length of the pitch to score. At 18–15 ahead Ireland were set to spring the biggest of upsets, but the Wallabies – or one Wallaby in particular – managed to remain ice cool. Salvation came in the form of fly-half Michael Lynagh.

Lynagh's plan was to do what they had done many times during training. Lynagh told his forwards to get the ball to the Wallaby backs, and let them do the rest. And if anyone was in any doubt as to who to pass to, they should just hold onto the ball and run towards the goal line.

The first priority for Australia was to kick to the other end of the field, knowing that Ireland would immediately kick the ball over the sideline in response, giving Australia the lineout throw. The plan remained intact when the Wallabies won the lineout through John Eales.

Australia then set up the midfield platform from which to attack: The ball was passed from scrum-half Peter Slattery to Lynagh, on to centre Tim Horan and then winger David Campese, who ran back towards his covering forwards. The attack was stopped by the Irish defence, but Australia got the put-in at the scrum. The scrum was in the ideal position for Australia – about 8 metres out from the Irish try-line and to the left of the posts. This gave Australia room to try a loop move, which had worked in the first half, enabling the Wallabies to break through the Irish defence.

The move revolved around a *cut-out pass*, where the person with the ball misses the player beside him and throws it instead to the next person in the attacking line. So, after Slattery had passed to Lynagh, Horan passed to fullback Marty Roebuck, rather than to outside centre Jason Little. Little then looped around Roebuck, a tactic which had the effect of destabilising the Irish defence.

While Little prepared to pass to Campese, Lynagh was scurrying across the field to get outside Campese. When Campese was tackled the ball bounced backwards towards Lynagh, who finished what he started by catching the half-volley and scoring in the corner.

Australia won the game 19–18 and went on to win the World Cup.

Playing the Ten-Man Game

You may hear rugby aficionados talk about the *ten-man game.* The term is used to describe a team that has decided to focus most of its play around the eight forwards, the half-back and fly-half. The backline is usually neglected and hardly sees the ball, confined as it is to the forward base. This form of play was popular during the 1970s and 1980s.

The ten-man game is not commonly played now. The speed of the modern game and the importance of teams having fast, expressive backs make the ten-man game a thing of the past – much to the relief of the spectator. The ten-man game was often slow and boring to watch.

Nonetheless, the teams that still want to play the ten-man game do so for important reasons. Teams with powerful packs and dominant lineouts find it a comfortable way to dominate possession and territory while wearing down the opposition. The forwards usually keep the ball, especially if they can gain territory by using driving mauls and quick rucking. If that doesn't work, the half-back passes the ball to the fly-half, who then either kicks the ball towards the sideline for a lineout, or puts it in front of the forwards.

The fly-half kicks for the sideline, knowing that the team has enough good lineout jumpers to win the ball, even if the opposition has the throw-in at the lineout. Inevitably, the team finds itself perched close to the opposition try-line, and through brute force is able to charge through at close range and score the tries required for victory.

The tactics are not pretty, as the ball is hardly sighted in open play, and watching a big bullock of a forward bustle his way over the line from a few metres out isn't exactly a moment of aesthetic beauty. Nevertheless, playing the ten-man game often ensured victory.

The ten-man game relies upon an outstanding and totally dominant forward pack, an efficient scrum-half who can get the ball to the fly-half, who must be able to kick the ball accurately, efficiently and with a minimum of fuss. As for the rest of the backline, they are reduced to chasers, rather than runners and handlers. Those who still love and preach the ten-man game are very much in the minority – the modern game of rugby has overtaken them. Most teams believe that more advantage can be gained by attacking from all areas of the field, although they might resort to the ten-man model to protect a hard-won lead. Thankfully, most of the people who populate the world of rugby union now realise that a balanced 15-man game is the best route to success.

Chapter 10

Talented Training

· ·

In This Chapter

▶ Getting ready to run on

▶ Stretching your way to fitness

▶ Making low-cost training pay off

▶ Winning with your wits

▶ Knowing the best foods for fitness

· ·

So you've got the right equipment, you know how to run in a straight line and you know how to pass the ball to the player next to you. You also know that if someone wearing a jersey that's a different colour from yours is running straight at you, you are supposed to stop him in his tracks. You are already well on the way to calling yourself a rugby player. But can you call yourself a fit rugby player?

Very few of the world's greatest sportsmen and women would claim to have conquered their own particular sport without having shed a swimming pool full of tears and a considerable amount of sweat – and, in some cases, drops of blood. Unless God has smiled on you and said: "Here's a bucket-load of talent, now get on with it," you are unlikely to excel in your chosen sport without doing the "hard yards".

The hard yards? Well, if you want to be the next Steve Redgrave, it means you get up at 4 a.m. every day to row five miles before going to work. Or if you're a budding Tiger Woods, you hit 500 golf balls for a couple of hours every day. Or, if you want to be the next Jonny Wilkinson you spend hour upon hour on the training pitch, practising your kicking, catching and running skills. In short, you have to work hard at sport if you want to be better than the next guy.

To be good on the rugby pitch, you have to be fit, and fitness is acquired in the hours off the pitch. Nothing can take the place of hard work. However, make sure that you are doing the kind of hard work that gets you the results you want.

In this chapter, we describe some of the more essential exercises you need to do to improve your performance as a rugby player. Eating the right kinds of food is also imperative, as is mental preparation. What you feed your mind is as important as what you feed your stomach, and both have a crucial bearing on how far you go in this game. Mind and matter – mind over matter.

Getting Match Fit

Before deciding which exercises to do, think carefully about the physical demands that are made on you in a match. You need to maintain a level of fitness that ensures you have plenty of the following:

- **Stamina:** As a match is played over 80 minutes and you are expected to maintain a constant work-rate, you need to have plenty of stamina. The only break you get in a match is a short one after 40 minutes.

- **Strength and power:** Because you constantly encounter opposing forces who want to run over the top of you, you need to be tough yourself. And at numerous points in a match, probably at the tackle or when there is a breakdown in play, you are required to push against a mass of bodies.

- **Flexibility:** When you have the ball in your own hands, you need a supple and flexible body so that you can move quickly at different angles and at varying levels of speed.

Even in the final minutes of the game, you should be breathing easily. Sprawled face-down in the turf, suffering from exhaustion or cramps, is not where you want to be.

Focus on exercises that are not over-strenuous and target those parts of your body that you want to strengthen. As with any form of physical exertion, don't overdo it – we don't want legions of *Rugby Union For Dummies* readers turning up at the doctor's tomorrow with strains, sprains and broken bones. Fitness is not acquired in a day. Only do as much as you feel comfortable with, and take your time.

Warming up with a good stretch

Rule number one about getting the body tight, taut and terrific is that every practice or fitness session starts with a well-organised and carefully planned warm-up. As well as stretching exercises, your warm-up could include lighter aerobic exercises such as short periods of jogging, cycling or skipping.

A good warm-up and stretching routine minimises the risk of injury and also prepares your body for the harder work to come. Improving your flexibility prevents ligaments, joints and muscles from going "piiiiing" on the big day.

Devote at least 10–15 minutes to stretching before you commence the more strenuous training. All the stretches we describe help your body become flexible and ready for action.

 Only do these exercises if you are absolutely sure you can manage them. If you are in any doubt whatsoever about whether the exercises we describe are right for you – perhaps because you have an old injury or some other kind of weakness – check with your coach or your doctor.

Neck stretches

This exercise is designed to stretch the muscles around your neck and shoulders. Repeat the stretch four or five times, alternating arms.

1. With your right arm at your side and using your left arm, pull your head towards the point of your left shoulder.

2. Hold this position for about 15 seconds, then release.

3. Repeat steps 1 and 2 in the opposite direction with your other arm.

Shoulder and upper body stretches

These stretches focus on the main muscles in your upper body. Repeat the exercise five to ten times, alternating arms.

1. Lift your right arm above and behind your head so it is touching the back of your neck.

2. With the left hand touching the right elbow, push the elbow back slightly.

3. Hold this position for about ten seconds, then release.

4. Repeat this stretch with your other arm.

Abdomen and lower back stretches

These exercises, shown in Figure 10-1, help to strengthen the abdomen and extend and stretch the back. Repeat the following steps five times.

1. Lie on your back and slowly pull your knees to your chest.

2. Hold this position for ten seconds, then release.

3. Roll over onto your stomach.

4. Keeping your knees and hips on the ground, push up your upper body.

5. Hold this position for ten seconds, then release.

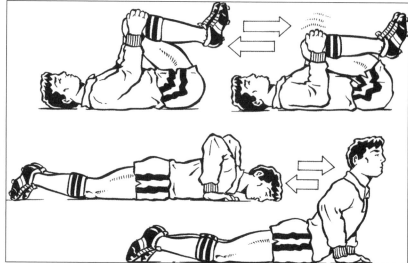

Figure 10-1:
Stretching the abdomen and lower back.

Thigh stretches

This stretch helps keep your thighs flexible. Repeat this exercise five times for each leg.

1. Stand upright, keeping your back straight.

2. Bending at the knee, extend your right leg up behind you.

3. With your right hand, grab your right leg near your ankles.

4. Slowly pull your right leg back, stretching the front of the thigh.

5. Hold this position for ten seconds, then release.

6. Repeat this stretch with your left leg.

Hamstring stretch

For this exercise, you need the assistance of a piece of furniture like a desk, table or sideboard (if you're exercising at home) or a boundary fence (if you're at the rugby field), to prop your leg on. Make sure that your prop is a comfortable height for you.

This exercise stretches the muscles at the backs of your thighs. Repeat the stretch five times for each leg.

1. Place your right leg fully extended on the top of the piece of furniture or fence, so that your leg is horizontal with the ground.

2. Bend forward (see Figure 10-2) and grab hold of your leg with your right hand; take it slowly and don't overexert yourself.

3. Hold this position for 20 seconds then release.

4. Repeat this stretch with your left leg.

Figure 10-2:
Stretching
the
hamstrings,
carefully.

Lower leg stretches

This exercises and flexes your calf muscles. Repeat the stretches five times for each leg.

1. Adopt a stance as if you were about to start a race, with your left foot about 60 centimetres in front of the other and both feet pointing forwards.

2. Bend your left knee and, keeping your body upright, shift your body weight forwards onto your left leg.

3. Straighten the right leg, keeping the heel on the ground.

4. Hold for ten seconds, then release.

5. Change legs and repeat steps 1–5.

Liquorice Allsorts stretches

You can also limber up with an assortment of other stretches. Never under estimate the value of the following:

- ✔ **Touching your toes:** Stand upright with your feet slightly apart with arms above your head. Bend down, with knees slightly flexed, and touch your toes with your fingertips. Do this exercise 10–20 times.

- ✔ **Bending sideways:** Stand upright with your feet apart and put your hands on your waist. Bend your body sideways, hold for ten seconds, and then go the other way. Don't twist – just bend your body 20–30 centimetres first to one side and then to the other.

- ✔ **Kicking high:** Stand upright and bring your right leg through as if trying to kick a football. Swing your leg back and forth several times. Repeat with your left leg.

Developing a fitness programme

To prepare yourself properly for rugby, you need a fitness programme that improves speed, muscular strength, agility and endurance – in particular, cardiovascular endurance. To improve your cardiovascular endurance, that is, to increase the fitness of your heart and lung system, you need a series of exercises that improves the body's ability to take in oxygen and circulate it throughout the body, particularly to those muscles that maintain stamina. If you have plenty of stamina, you won't flag or tire excessively while playing or training.

Improving your stamina

One of the best ways to improve stamina is to run, varying the distances from a few hundred metres to five or even six kilometres. A good combination is to do some sprinting (which we discuss in the next section) and then some distance work. Try running around your training pitches for about 15 minutes at a slow but steady rate.

If you are not used to running, increase the distances slowly. For example, begin with 500 metres and keep to that distance until you can run effortlessly and at the same time hold a conversation with the team-mate who is running with you. Then you may want to increase the distance by a third and so on, in increments.

Don't do too much too early, otherwise you may cause muscle damage. Run well within your own limits and slow down or stop if you suddenly find yourself struggling. Your distance and speed improve over time, not overnight!

Running at full tilt: sprint training

You can mix up your longer runs with shorter ones. Try running at a brisker rate from one end of the pitch to the other, have a 30-second break, run back the other way and take another break. Do this three or four times. You may struggle early on, but within days you discover that the number of sprints you can make before collapsing in a heap rise remarkably.

Sprint training is an important element in building up speed. During a game, a player often has to accelerate from a standing start and hit top speed within a couple of seconds. Good players rely on sprint work to improve their speed, and a training schedule commonly includes a series of sprints.

An effective sequence is to do ten 30-metre sprints with a 10-second rest between each sprint, then five 50-metre sprints with a 20-second rest between each, ending up with two 100-metre sprints with a rest of at least one minute between each.

Sprint training is demanding fitness work and should only be done if a player has warmed up properly before starting. If you haven't done your warm-up, you could easily suffer serious muscle injuries.

Working on your agility

To improve your agility, construct an obstacle course, involving markers placed at intervals of 4–5 metres. With a rugby ball in your hands, weave through the markers and practise bounding off first your left foot and then your right foot, as if trying to get past a defender with the side-step. You can also practise how to swerve (Chapter 6 explains these moves). Begin slowly, then pick up the pace.

You are welcome to try this in your own backyard. You not only improve your agility, you also keep the neighbours entertained. Watch out for the small dogs yapping at your heels, though.

Another good drill is to run at speed through the same obstacle course, throwing the ball up and re-gathering it. Let the ball bounce occasionally, so you are accustomed to picking the ball up from the ground while on the run.

Building up your strength

With rugby now a professional game, players have become more dependent on lifting weights to improve body strength and physique. While weight-lifting is recommended for the advanced or mature player, it is not essential for new-comers or youngsters, who can build up their strength by going down a different, perhaps safer path.

Good old fashioned push-ups and sit-ups are perfect for toning the body and increasing upper body strength. If you begin slowly and gradually build up the number of push-ups and sit-ups, your strength is sure to improve.

A heavy weight-lifting program can cause permanent damage to bones and muscles if the body is not yet ready to accept heavy weights. If you want to lift weights, seek out either the club's trainer or a gymnasium instructor and get their advice on an appropriate, safe and effective weight-lifting program.

Varying your routines

An important aspect about training is to vary the ways in which you do it and attempt new drills. If you get bored while practising, you eventually won't bother, which won't do much to improve your skills.

Get adventurous: Invent your own drills that involve a rugby ball. The more you have a ball in your hands, the better you become. Before long, the ball feels like a natural extension of your hands.

Tooling up on the Cheap

Most training tools are usually free! To get fit for rugby, you don't have to install a gymnasium in your garage or build sand hills in your backyard to run up and down. Your local playing field does quite nicely for your sprint and stamina training.

Most good rugby clubs have either their own gymnasium or access to a local facility where you can work out on equipment that strengthens the muscles you need for rugby. So now you don't have to stay up late watching midnight-to-dawn television in the hope of getting a "gut-buster" machine at a bargain price.

Training tools that are cheap, if not free, include

- ✔ **Small cones:** A worthwhile and cheap investment would be to buy several small cones which are available from most sporting shops. Sometimes called "witches hats", they are those small, plastic orange-coloured cones used by road workers to indicate the areas of the road they are working on. Use these cones for running drills – running in and out of them is a good way to improve your swerving and side-stepping capabilities.

✔ **Goalposts:** Most playing fields have goalposts of one description or another. Use them for goal kicking practice and to work on improving your ability to kick a field goal. Sometime, somewhere in a game, you could find yourself in the right position to kick a match-winning drop goal. If you can't do it, the moment is lost; if you can, you become an instant hero.

✔ **Tackle bags:** Rugby clubs usually help you practise your tackling skills by providing tackle bags (sometimes called *tackle dummies*). These are the large bags, usually packed with foam, that players use to improve their tackling skills.

Your team-mates become live training tools when you want to work on improving other skills. To improve your tackling techniques, walk through them first using a team-mate as the target. To improve your passing techniques don't hesitate to grab a team-mate, either before or after training, and run up and down the field with him throwing different passes to each other. Both of you improve your passing and catching skills.

Psyching up for a Star Performance

While it's terrific to look good, have the body beautiful and be overflowing with energy, the mind also has to be healthy. Getting mentally prepared doesn't mean spending days on a psychologist's couch, moaning about your parents and how they messed up your life. Nor does it mean staying up late and contacting the psychic hotline to find out what the stars say about your team's chances in the match tomorrow.

Player superstitions

Many top players have little quirks or routines that they like to adhere to with an almost religious zeal before big matches. One of the most quirky is Rob Howley, the Wasps and former Wales and Lions scrum-half. Howley, who goes by the nickname "Stan" (because he bears some resemblance to Stan Laurel, the thin character in the old black-and-white Laurel and Hardy comedies), once gave an insight into his world of superstitions. There's a place for everything, and everything in its place before a match with Howley. He always puts his left boot on before his right, he makes sure he's the last man in the changing-room to have a rub down by the physio, he never walks under ladders, and he also never fails to salute magpies when he sees them.

Countless players go through the lucky boots, shorts, socks, jockstrap, or underpants syndrome in rugby changing rooms throughout the world every weekend. Others insist on running out onto the field last. It's a weird and wacky world out there!

Pride of place

Players react in different ways to the pre-match speeches from coaches and captains designed to give them unshakeable resolve. Eric Evans, an inspirational England captain of the 1950s, used to encourage his men to great things by delivering the Agincourt speech from Shakespeare's *Henry V*. Some players are suitably inspired by such oratory, others come close to breaking down – with laughter. Jerry Guscott found himself in the latter category when the 1997 Lions were addressed by manager Fran Cotton, just before the series-clinching second test in Durban.

As Guscott explains in *The Lions Diary* (Penguin), his entertaining account of the tour, Cotton had clearly given his speech plenty of thought. "After exhorting us not to let this chance of rugby immortality slip through our fingers, there was a dramatic pause as he let it sink in", Guscott recalled. "He then referred us to the famous words of Napoleon that 'we all knew'. Then there was another dramatic pause – but this time an unscheduled one – as Cotton had to remind himself of those famous words by looking at the piece of paper he had written them on." When Napoleon's words were eventually uttered, Guscott did not hear them because he was choking back tears of mirth. A couple of hours later it was Guscott's drop-goal which won the series for the Lions.

There is also no shortage of post-match humour. During the 1977 Lions tour of New Zealand, the England hooker Peter Wheeler went into the changing room to see his teammates after a hard fought win over New Zealand Universities in appalling quagmire conditions. He asked Moss Keane, the big Irish lock, how the game had been, to which Keane replied: "The first half was even, the second half even worse."

Being mentally prepared means that a player has his wits about him and can instantly sum up a situation and work out the best way to handle it. Rugby can often be like a chess game, revolving around intricate tactics and manoeuvres.

Before a game, give yourself some space to quietly think about:

- ✔ What is likely to happen in the game
- ✔ How you can best take advantage of any opportunity that presents itself
- ✔ What you want to and are expected to achieve in the game

Don't hesitate to mentally picture yourself scoring the winning try, or kicking the winning goal, or leading your team to an international triumph. It is anything but puerile – all the great players have done it during their careers, and keep doing it, as a way of improving their confidence and belief in themselves. If it works for them, it can work for you.

Good mental preparation means you are less likely to be intimidated when a big, beefy neanderthal runs straight at you. You know that so often it's the smaller rugby players, those who don't have the physique to confront the over-sized players and so compensate with skill and cunning, who pull off the greatest tactical triumphs. All you need is willpower and confidence.

Fear is important. All players, at some stage of their playing lives, experience the fear of failure or the fear of injury. It is a natural feeling, so use the adrenaline flow to your advantage. No matter the level of rugby at which you play, being nervous before a game means you are in the right frame of mind to do your best.

Eating Your Way to Victory

The era when rugby players believed that loading up their breakfast plates with steak, eggs and grilled tomatoes was the only way to win has mostly disappeared. A frugal diet that allows you only one celery stick a day is not the answer either if you want to be a successful rugby player. Common sense prevails – eating and drinking in moderation is the smart route.

The rugby dietician

Colin Meads is a legend not just in New Zealand, but throughout the rugby world. A farmer from the North Island, the teak-tough Meads, who played in the 1960s and 1970s, was brought up at a time when rugby and dieting didn't mix, and became the All Blacks team manager in the 1990s.

On one occasion before a Test match, Meads was at the back of the room when a well-known dietician talked to the team. The dietician explained that if a player was to build up properly for a Saturday international, they should not eat meat after Wednesday night. Meads was aghast.

After the talk, Meads approached the dietician and told her what his diet had been during his playing days. He told her that on the day of a big test match, he had steak and eggs for breakfast, and then three hours before kick-off, a large meal of cold meat and mashed potatoes. The potatoes would be smeared with melted butter.

He said, "I've listened to you – no butter either, you say – no meat after Wednesday night. Jesus, I used to get my mashed potatoes and put a big blob of butter in, wait until it melted, stir it all up and…." The dietician stopped Meads and said, "You don't know how good a player you could have been."

Brian Turner, *Meads* (Hodder)

Choosing a balanced diet

Nowadays, most rugby clubs have a dietician hovering somewhere in the shadows, who can recommend the optimal diet for rugby fitness. While no one single food is likely to make you a superstar, as a rugby player, you have more energy requirements than the average bloke walking down the street.

We recommend you mix up your diet, ensuring that it provides you with adequate kilojoules (energy) as well as essential nutrients. A balanced diet is one that includes proteins, carbohydrates, fats and fibre, and which provides essential nutrients, vitamins and minerals. This means concentrating on foods like meat, chicken and fish; bread, pasta and potatoes; and salads, vegetables and fruit.

A typical day for a rugby player would begin with a breakfast of cereal, toast, fruit and orange juice. Coffee and tea are fine, though beverages like this should not be drunk in large quantities. For lunch, salad sandwiches and pasta are recommended, along with yoghurt and fruit. Dinners should include meat or fish and salad or vegetables, preferably steamed vegetables.

Rugby players need an energy boost from time to time and muesli bars and fresh fruit are recommended here.

The best thing a rugby player in training can drink is not a pint of beer – it's water. We highly recommend it. Water from the tap is more-or-less free, though you may prefer the taste of a particular brand of bottled water.

While junk food is usually off-limits, an occasional hamburger, or fish and chips can't do the body that much harm – but note the word "occasional"! Stick to the healthier foodstuffs as much as you can, though, because coaches love nothing better than torturing anyone they think is getting a bit paunchy around the midriff.

We hasten to add that rugby players are permitted to fall off the health food wagon now and then. Constantly saying no to chocolate cake when it's offered can be demoralising – and in the end, send you absolutely mad. Don't feel guilty about tucking into the occasional dessert.

Taking on fuel

Most matches take place in the afternoon, so you probably don't need to vary too much from your normal mealtimes on the days you are playing. You may prefer to have lunch earlier than normal to ensure that you digest your food well before you have to digest what the opposition dishes up for you on the pitch.

Smokers and drinkers

In 1975, Irish prop Phil O'Callaghan came onto the field as a replacement in a match at Lansdowne Road. During the first scrum, a packet of cigarettes and a lighter fell out of his pocket. With a straight face O'Callaghan handed the cigarettes and lighter to the referee, saying, "Hold onto these until half-time. I'm not too keen on oranges."

Pilecki was notorious among room-mates as a chain-smoker who wasn't a great lover of training. On one training run from the team's London hotel, Pilecki soon dropped off the back. When the players eventually returned to the hotel and were milling around in the foyer, a taxi drove up. In the back was Stan, smoking a cigarette. He had apparently got lost and borrowed some money off the cabbie to buy a packet of smokes.

Rugby players are also well known for enjoying a post-match tipple or two, but it was England prop Colin Smart who made it headline news at the post-match dinner at the Grand Hotel in Paris after England had beaten France. Smart was tricked into drinking a gift bottle of after-shave by a team-mate, who, having poured out the contents of the aftershave bottle and refilled it with wine, remarked that the stuff was perfectly drinkable. Smart quaffed his with one gulp, but soon had to be taken to hospital to have his stomach pumped (he made a full and rapid recovery).

Over the last few years, with the demands made of the professional rugby player intensifying – not to mention their salaries multiplying each season – the leading performers have become very, very careful over how they treat their bodies. Smoking and regular drinking is right out of the window these days.

Professional players involved in night matches have to eat earlier than they normally would on the day of the match. However, they can cope relatively easily, enjoying a reasonable-sized meal at least two hours before the match starts. So if kick-off is at 7:30 p.m. the players eat around 5 p.m., concentrating on foods that provide plenty of energy and avoiding over-indulging.

Eating on the way to a game, or just before kick-off, should be avoided at all costs. Nothing is guaranteed to make a player more sluggish than running on a full stomach.

Choosing your supplements carefully

By and large, the following saying holds true: Good food ain't cheap, cheap food ain't good. Paying extra for good-quality fruit, vegetables, meat, chicken and fish pays dividends where your health and general well-being are concerned. So head to good supermarkets, fruit and vegetable shops, butchers and fish shops where you know that the produce on offer is fresh and reliable.

People who play sport tend to visit health food stores which stock every elixir under the sun. Some of these food supplements work and, among other things, boost the energy levels of rugby enthusiasts. Unfortunately, many don't.

While sports novices (and new coaches) probably had their mothers tell them to eat their fresh greens and fruit and avoid junk food, their mothers never anticipated all the choices they would be facing in the sports drink aisle of their local supermarket, or the dangers of some modern diet supplements.

Before you buy any vitamins, sports diet drinks or whatever, get advice from your coach, your club trainer or a sports dietician. These people know what's safe and effective for the budding rugby player and can warn you off products that are no more than a passing fad.

Avoiding Accidents: Easy as Falling off a Log

At the start of the season, most rugby clubs run various defensive drills to ensure that players know how to fall properly and how to offload the ball in a tackle. Defensive training means you are tackled endlessly, but it builds up your confidence as well as your skills – confidence that you know exactly what to do when tackled.

However, there is no avoiding the fact that injuries are a part of rugby life, as is dealing with them. Mouthguards are a must. If you have a head-wound, or ear abrasions, then headguards make sense, but a lot of padding will not protect injuries that have already occurred. If you are injured, stop playing, make sure you follow a proper rehabilitation programme, and do not return to contact sports or playing until the injury is healed and tested. If you wish to read more about protective equipment, Chapter 3 will tell you what you need to know.

Too many players make the mistake of coming back from injury too soon, often compounding the problem. Let nature, and proper rehab, take their course.

Knowing how to fall when you are tackled

An important rugby skill is knowing how to fall properly. Admittedly, you find yourself being tackled from every angle, but good players know how to turn or roll their bodies to minimise the impact when they hit the ground.

A good way to practise falling correctly is to ask a friend or team-mate to tackle you from different angles. As you fall, land on your side or in such a way that the impact feels minimal. You know you're doing it right when you can immediately jump to your feet. Just think of all those old war movies where characters are trained to make parachute jumps; they are always taught to roll over to one side when they land properly.

When you are tackled, tighten the muscles of your arm and shoulders and attempt to roll onto the ground, allowing the whole upper body to absorb the impact. The impact is cushioned when it is spread out along a large section of the body.

Injuries often occur when a small area of the body lands heavily. When you have been tackled, it is crucial that you do not use your arm to break the fall because this can often lead to fractured bones.

Playing hard helps avoid accidents

If you are the aggressor in a tackle, remember not to do anything in a half-hearted fashion. The players who hold back are usually the ones who get hurt, whereas those who run hard or tackle hard and show courage are usually the ones who are happily running around at the end of the match.

We are not going to pretend that accidents don't happen – accidents are a fact of rugby life. While some accidents simply cannot be avoided, enthusiasm and courage often get you out of a sticky situation.

Chapter 11

Coaching

*P*icture the scene. It's the end of the tournament, the winner stands there clutching the trophy with a smile as wide as the Severn Estuary, a cheque for umpteen thousands tucked under a sweaty armpit. An interviewer pushes through the crowd and shoves a microphone under his nose, asking him to explain just how he managed to beat all-comers. The inevitable response is, "I'd just like to thank my coach for getting me where I am today." Cue to rapturous applause, hugs and kisses all round.

While natural talent and a strong work ethic take you a long way, to make it to the very top in any sport you need the trained eye, dedication and cajoling of a coach. Someone who cares enough about you to coax, nag, bully and pester the very best out of you. Someone who is there to monitor your progress at that 5a.m. training run or to demand you do another 30 minutes on the tackle bag when all you want to do is have a shower and go home. While sometimes you hate them, coaches can make the difference between you being good, or being great.

In this chapter, we explain how to become a great coach, and just what abilities and talents the job requires. Should you decide that the hot seat is just a little too hot for you, you can choose from a range of other jobs that give vital support to the team. You may not get the same amount of credit as the coach does, but without coaching assistants, a team runs about as smoothly as a car with a faulty fuel line.

Grand Obsession: What Makes a Good Coach?

Coaching is not really a profession; rather, it's an obsession, attracting some of the strongest (and often the strangest) of individuals. Nevertheless, the effectiveness of the coach is what matters, because good players without a good coach make a dud team.

While the rugby players often get all the kudos, much of the credit should go to the coach. Which one is the coach? Well, he's pretty easy to pick out at a rugby game – he's the deranged bloke trotting along the sideline, gesticulating at the players on the pitch, laughing out of context and screaming incoherently. He is invariably the most emotional person at the ground. Welcome to the weirdest breed of all – the coaching fraternity.

Tackling a tough job with everything you've got

The coach is a bit like the director of a play – he has to ensure that, come performance time, all the members of his cast perform to the best of their ability (see Figure 11-1). The coach has the onerous task of successfully putting together the most bewildering of jigsaws. He has to mould 15 very different, often diverse and sometimes unco-operative individuals into one perfectly interlocking unit.

The coach has to be an adviser, mentor, psychologist, teacher, diplomat, comrade, leader in arms, man in the shadows, butcher, baker and candlestick maker. If you aspire to be a coach, you need to have

✔ **A good understanding of the game:** Coaching is best learnt from practical experience because players soon suss you out. Sometimes they know more than you do. It also helps if you are a former player, though you don't have to have reached superstar level! Some of the best rugby coaches were average players who during their playing days developed a good grasp of the game, especially the laws, and the tactics and strategies required to win matches.

✔ **A genuine love of the game:** You need to love the game and be fascinated by all its subtleties. Like your players, you want to learn, because you never find yourself right on top of rugby. Rugby is a game that is continually evolving and throwing up puzzles that confound even the most brilliant of rugby minds.

> ✔ **A democratic approach:** A coach needs to be firm without being a dicta-
> tor, and have the ability to get on with, and get the best out of, a diverse
> array of characters. Many coaches fall into the trap of taking all the
> praise after a victory, and blaming everyone but themselves for a loss.
> Good coaches don't go on about how their team won because the play-
> ers followed instructions, or lost because they didn't.

Coaching can't be learnt entirely from textbooks. Coaching is a mind game, a
skill and an art, and you need initiative, imagination and an immense amount
of get-up-and-go. You soon discover whether or not coaching is for you, especially when you encounter 20 different problems at once.

Figure 11-1:
A coach
directing his
team from
the sideline.

Bob Dwyer, who coached the Wallabies in the 1980s and 1990s, has accurately described what is required to be a successful coach. According to
Dwyer, a winning coach doesn't require the intellect of a nuclear physicist,
but experience, common sense, imagination and a very, very good memory.
As far as Dwyer is concerned, if coaching is approached in the right vein, it is
an honourable profession.

The art of communication

On tour in South Africa in 1980, Noel Murphy, the Lions coach, got his troops together before a big match and screamed: "Right lads, I want 80 per cent commitment for 100 minutes." The same coach was renowned for a radical training drill, saying : "Right, lads, spread out in a bunch."

Welsh coach John Dawes once decided to get technical. One day at training, Dawes told his players that if the blindside flanker was to break quickly from the scrum, the codeword the half-back shouted would begin with the letter "P". And if the openside flanker was to break early, the codeword would begin with the letter "S". A scrum was set. Suddenly halfback Gareth Edwards screamed: 'Psychology!'

Neither flanker moved.

If you want to become the coach of a winning team, the simplest approach is the best. Taking Bob Dwyer's criteria one by one, a successful coach has

- ✔ Experience, in order to know what to do when under pressure
- ✔ Common sense, in order to stay level-headed and calm no matter what
- ✔ Imagination, in order to come up with match-winning moves and tactics
- ✔ An excellent memory, in order to remember what the opposition's weaknesses and strengths are so that tactics and strategies to exploit and counter them can be devised

No one criterion is more important than the others – each of these personal characteristics is equally important.

Bettering your team's best

You get an enormous amount of satisfaction when your team achieves greatness, or one of the players you have nurtured is selected in a representative side, such as a national team, or a top club side, and goes on to be something special.

The hard work that coaching requires is rewarded by the warm feeling of being an integral part of a team, where numerous people rely on you and depend on you for guidance. Their success is your success.

A coach has three main areas of responsibility. A coach must

- ✔ Improve a team's skill level
- ✔ Improve the fitness, strength and power of a team
- ✔ Motivate players so that the team plays at its best

For your team to succeed, you need to develop a good, simple and effective training programme for it, a programme that improves all parts of a player's game. Once you have your training programme, stick to it.

Improving skill levels

The coach does everything possible to ensure that the skill levels of all players improve as the season progresses. To improve your team's skills, put in place a challenging and mixed training schedule that maintains the interest of all the players. For example, you can mix it around by incorporating both skill drills and weight training into the schedule.

Obviously, the levels of skill vary from individual to individual, so you need to adjust the schedule to make allowances for these variations. Your main aim, though, is to improve the overall skill level of the team as a unit.

Getting your team fighting fit

A good team is a fit team, so it is important that you incorporate fitness routines into your schedule in order to build up stamina. Chapter 10 can help you devise the best exercises for your team.

Motivating your team

Motivating players depends largely on trust. And trust comes through openness and honesty. When you have to drop a player, don't make up a feeble excuse or blame your decision on someone or something else. Always tell the truth. Players quickly find out if you are toying with the truth.

Manic motivation

Players look to coaches for all forms of inspiration as this anecdote about the big, barnstorming Irish flanker Trevor Brennan, who now plays for Toulouse, makes clear. Brennan was feeling tired during Irish training sessions, so he asked Warren Gatland, then the Ireland coach (now with Wasps), if he had any remedy. Gatland, who has a broad Kiwi accent, suggested that he should try four to five bananas at training. The following day Brennan sidled over and said, "Gats, I've tried, but I've only managed 29." Gatland's response? "No. I said four to five, NOT FORTY-FIVE!"

Over the top!

David Brockhoff, the Wallaby coach during the 1970s, has achieved cult status among rugby fans in Australia for his off-the-wall antics when it came to motivating his teams. He also coached Sydney University, one of whose chief rivals was Randwick.

On one occasion these rivals met on Anzac Day, the day of remembrance for Australian and New Zealand soldiers, especially those who died in the Gallipoli campaign (in Turkey) in the First World War.

Unbeknown to his players, Brockhoff had arranged for the hinges on the Sydney University changing room door to be loosened. A few minutes before kick-off, Brockhoff had worked himself into a lather as he gave the final team talk. "This is Anzac Day, men. We are playing Randwick, the outright enemy. This is Turkey for us. If it was good enough for the boys at Gallipoli, it's good enough for us. Today, men ...WE DO BATTLE!"

Brockhoff strode towards the door, ripped it off its hinges, and hurled it on the floor, screaming over his shoulder: "Follow me out! Over the top!" Sydney University won 18–17.

Don't forget that the members of a team talk to each other and look after each other's interests, both on and off the pitch. If you lose the trust of your players, they won't do anything for you and you might as well leave the club, because you have no future. But if you win the trust of your players, they do anything for you.

Motivation also relies on saying the right words at the right time. You don't have to memorise the speeches of Winston Churchill; being positive on the training field and in the dressing room gets your players in the right frame of mind to go out there and achieve their finest hour.

Never underestimate the importance of encouragement. As long as it is not overdone, praise can cure so many ills. Guide your players and give them direction and purpose. Whatever support you give them is returned to you on the rugby pitch. The art is to keep things simple without insulting the intelligence of your players.

A smart coach has to be prepared to mix the message up a bit to avoid the problem of players getting sick and tired of just one person ranting at them. Do not hesitate calling in experts from other fields, or other authoritative voices, because they can so often inspire.

Climbing the Coaching Ladder: Official (and Unofficial) Requirements

The rungs of the rugby coaching ladder start at Mini, Age Grade, Schools, Colts, Students and local club rugby, and progress up through regional leagues to national leagues, to provincial or premiership standard, and all the way to international. (Chapter 15 discusses the organisation of rugby union clubs and how to make contact with them, while Appendix C provides their contact details.)

What you need to do in order to be put in charge of a team depends to a large extent on how far up the totem pole you want to go in the coaching game. On the bottom rung of the game, such as juniors, being an accredited rugby coach is not vital.

If you are striving to coach at a higher level, such as a professional team, it is advisable, rather than compulsory, that you gain accreditation. The officials who select coaches for elite club, provincial or national teams are impressed if the candidates have undertaken a coaching course and have acquired one or more certificates – it demonstrates that they have done the hard work and know exactly what is required to be a good coach. (We explain the different coaching levels later in this chapter.)

Coaching courses for each level are provided by the national unions within the Six Nations. For instance, the RFU will oversee the whole process in England. Whereas if you live in Wales, contact the Welsh Rugby Union (WRU), who can explain when and where coaching courses are conducted.

Experienced, professional coaches and teachers provide course participants with a good grounding in all facets of the game to enable them to go on to become capable coaches. While the cost of undertaking a coaching course is usually minimal and unlikely to stretch the pocket, you may like to check the cost beforehand with your national union.

Deciding whether coaching is for you

You don't really know if you have the capabilities to be a coach until you try it. You know you have the right temperament for the job when you find yourself in a muddy pitch on a Saturday morning giving orders to a bunch of children, teenagers, young men or young women – and enjoying it.

Deciding whether coaching is for you requires a bit of self-assessment. Enjoying being with other people is vital. You must

- ✔ Relate well and get on with just about everyone

- ✔ Know how to communicate with the many people relying on you to provide them with the right information

- ✔ Be even-tempered and able to handle the pressures of being in charge of up to 20 children or able-bodied men

You could also ask yourself questions: Do you like rugby? Do you like offering advice and helping other people? Are you prepared to work hard? Do you revel when under pressure? If the answer to all these is "yes", then give coaching a go.

Once you have been involved in a few games, you know whether or not coaching suits you – and you suit coaching. If you can successfully get the message across to teams which play at weekends and are difficult to organise and get motivated, you may have the coaching Midas touch!

Starting on the bottom rung

The best place to start is at the bottom. Coaching is a skill which takes time to acquire so don't aspire to the top of the coaching totem pole too early in your career. Local clubs often have five or six teams, as well as Mini and Age Grade teams, and are looking for volunteers to help out. If you think you are ready to take up the challenge, then volunteer your services. Encouraging people, especially youngsters, to give a sport everything they've got has to be one of the most rewarding jobs in the world (see Figure 11-2).

The coaching of school teams is usually the domain of school teachers and in most circumstances your help is not required.

Going up a rung: Level 1

If you find you are really keen on coaching and you want to know everything that is required to be a good coach at junior level, including knowing how to properly teach school children, you can do no better than attend a Level 1 coaching course.

The Level 1 course provides details on how to teach youngsters the basics of the game, individual skills, fitness and a simplified version of the laws of the game. The course usually involves one or two days of teaching, along with home study.

Figure 11-2:
Coaching
the kids
is very
rewarding.

You finish the course with an examination in which, among other things, your knowledge of rugby laws and safety issues are tested. If you pass that exam, you can proudly hang a Level 1 coaching certificate on your wall.

Climbing higher: Level 2

If you aspire to coach rugby at a senior level, Level 2 is the next step. You must have a Level 1 certificate, plus one year's coaching experience, before you can take the course.

The Level 2 course is run over four days and involves extensive study at home. You are taught all aspects of the game, including tactical play and how to assess the opposition. The course also covers sports science, including ways to enhance player fitness, power and endurance. In addition, you gain further insights into the role of the coach.

Naturally, the examination you take at the end of the Level 2 course requires you to have more extensive and detailed knowledge than you did for the Level 1 exam. Again, the focus is on the laws and safety. When you pass the Level 2 examination, you are presented with your Level 2 certificate.

Becoming a qualified coach: Level 3

If you are really serious about coaching at a senior level, such as a provincial, professional or national team, it is helpful if you have a Level 3 certificate. Officials who select high-profile coaches are impressed when they hear someone has obtained a Level 3 – it is like gaining your Masters degree at university. The course is long and extensive and is only for those who look at coaching as a way of life.

Only those who have gained a Level 2 certificate and who have been coaching at a senior level for five years qualify to take the Level 3 course. You attend two compulsory camps and are expected to undertake monthly projects as well as a major project which must be completed before the final examination.

Someone described as a Level 3 coach possesses in-depth and specialised knowledge. They are a fully fledged coach with a solid grounding in all that is required to be a good, rounded, intelligent leader.

The top tier: Level 4

This is for elite level coaches who have considerable experience of the professional game already.

Hymns and arias

The first hurdle in England's pursuit of a Grand Slam in 1991 was beating Wales in Cardiff, something they had been unable to achieve for 28 years. In a bid to get over the Cardiff Arms Park jinx, England manager Geoff Cooke and coach Roger Uttley decided to acclimatise their players to the atmosphere that awaited them.

The England squad were training at Gloucester in the week before the match, and no sooner had they run out at Kingsholm than the Welsh national anthem, "Land of My Fathers", blared out over the loudspeaker system. When it had finished it was rewound and played over and over again. Not only that, but whenever England got on the team bus they would get another ten renditions of it over the sound system.

By the time the rousing Welsh anthem was sung before the match, England were sick of the sound of it, totally desensitised, and went on to end the Cardiff jinx, winning 25–5.

You're Not Alone: Support Staff

A coach may sometimes feel like a rock, solitary and endlessly battered by the elements. In recent times, a strong network of support staff has been built around the head coach in order to spread the stress and responsibilities more evenly and to help the team reach its full capability. Such support occurs not just at the top levels of rugby, but at the lower echelons of the game as well.

For those who don't want the full-on responsibility of being head coach, numerous other jobs are available that could be perfect for you. A support role can be as important as that of the front man in running a rugby team properly and making it a success.

At the lower levels of the game, support staff are relatively few and no-one gets paid. You usually find a head coach, assistant coach and team manager. At the higher echelons of rugby, however, teams from the likes of the Zurich Premiership and National League 1 in England, and the Celtic League in Wales, Scotland and Ireland, are professional and their support staff can involve a cast of thousands.

For Zurich Premiership and Celtic League teams, sponsorship, television revenue, ticket receipts and grants mean that the funds are available to pay support staff good wages. A professional team like Leicester in the Zurich Premiership, has a large, paid management staff. For example, in 2003 Leicester, and teams of similar standing, had a management staff that included people who gloried in (sometimes obscure) titles like chairman, chief executive, director of rugby, head coach, backs technical adviser, defence coach, conditioning coach, physiotherapist, medical coordinator, masseuse, assistant manager, communications manger, nutrition consultant and administration assistant.

Coaching: Assistant coach

Most teams from higher ranking junior club level upwards now have at least one assistant to the head coach. At most training sessions, teams eventually divide themselves into two groups: forwards and backs. As one person cannot oversee both groups, another pair of eyes and hands is needed.

The best teams usually have a three-man coaching structure, comprising of head coach, forwards coach and backs coach. The forwards coach is usually a specialist in what is required in scrums and lineouts, rucks and mauls. The backs coach is a specialist in attacking strategies and moves and understands what is required in every position from 9 to 15. The three coaches work closely together and usually act as the team selectors.

Someone who has played forward does not necessarily make a forwards coach, nor does a back automatically turn into a backs coach.

Coaching: Defence coach

In recent years, international teams, as well as those in the Zurich Premiership and Celtic League, have employed coaches who have focused on improving the defensive strategies of the team. These coaches have often been former rugby league players who, because of the tight defensive structure of their game, have been able to pass on important tips on tactics that stop opponents. The appointment of former Great Britain rugby league coach Phil Larder as England defence coach was crucial to England's 2003 Grand Slam, and a 13-match un-defeated run, including five over Tri-Nations opposition.

Managing the team

Because the coach is focused on the on-field duties of the team, a team man-ager is needed to make sure that everything runs smoothly off the field. Team managers are important at every level of the game and at junior club level in particular. At junior level, the team manager is as important as the coach.

The team manager's job is probably the most important and most demanding one within the team structure, as it requires an abundance of commonsense, a tough hide, a willingness to work, and the ability to solve problems logi-cally. While the job can be a thankless one, many rate it as being enriching.

The team manager has to attend to the needs of the coach and the players, which means becoming mother, father, nurse and everyone's best friend. The role also encompasses that of psychotherapist, as the team manager's shoul-der is the one players usually cry on when they have been dropped from the team or feel they have failed.

You can always pick the team manager in the team photograph – they're the one looking confused.

The duties of a team manager might include ensuring that:

- ✔ Training venues have been organised.
- ✔ The players know exactly where they have to be and at what time.
- ✔ Transport for the team and support staff is organised.
- ✔ The team has the right playing and training equipment, such as rugby balls, tackle bags and kicking tees.

In addition, team managers need to have all the information that's relevant to their team on match day, including kick-off times, which dressing rooms the team can use and who the match officials are. And when required, team managers also represent their players at judiciary committee hearings.

Training the team

At local club level, a team will not always have a specialist fitness trainer. At representative level, however, teams have their own fitness gurus. The trainer puts the players through their drills during training and makes certain that when they are off the field, they are involved in appropriate weight and exercise programs.

The trainer is also easy to pick out in the team photo: He's the one wearing a tight-fitting singlet to show off his muscles.

Massaging the players: The physio

A physiotherapist works closely with the team doctor and trainer to ensure that injured players receive the right course of treatment. A rugby team's physiotherapist specialises in sports science, injury management and treatment, and is an important member of the support staff. Professional teams invariably employ the services of a physiotherapist.

When a player is injured on the pitch, the physiotherapist runs on with the doctor to treat him. Between them, they quickly assess how serious the injury is and whether or not the player should leave the pitch. The physio also doubles up and works as a *strapper* on match day and at training sessions. Strappers strap up players with bandages and tape to prevent injuries occurring or reoccurring.

Calling the team doctor

In addition to working with the physiotherapist to assess injuries sustained during a match, the team doctor helps players recover from those injuries. Team doctors diagnose injuries on the field and track the progress of the injured players while they are recovering. The coach relies on the team doctor to tell him when an injured player has recovered and is available for selection.

At professional level, the team doctor's position is full-time, while at junior club level, the doctor is usually a volunteer.

In accordance with the blood bin rule (see Chapter 2 for the gory details), the team doctor usually finds himself doing quick stitch-up work on injured players during matches so that they can get back into the game just as quickly as possible.

Running after the team

On match day, some clubs use a team runner who goes onto the pitch with messages from the coach to certain players while carrying water bottles out to the players during the game. He also hands the kicking tee to players and then retrieves it.

At professional level, a team runner is a paid employee. At junior and club level, the team runner is usually a volunteer, sometimes a parent of one of the players, who happily lends a hand at half-time by taking out to the team their bottles of water and slices of orange.

Great coaching teams

England's back-to-back away victories over New Zealand (15–13) and Australia (25–14) in the build-up to the 2003 World Cup were no accident. They were the result of England borrowing from the southern hemisphere practice of building coaching teams rather than relying on one individual to be the fount of all knowledge.

The practice of bringing in experts was started by New Zealand in the inaugural World Cup in 1987, when they were comfortably the fittest team in the tournament after bringing in conditioning coach Jim Blair. In the 1990s Australia took things further when their World Cup winning coaches, Bob Dwyer (1991) and Rod Macqueen (1999), assembled teams of coaching specialists, making their sides the best prepared in the world.

After enduring an awkward start as England head coach when he was given the job in 1997,

Clive Woodward, who was a relatively inexperienced at elite level, soon started gathering experts around him. The team of specialists that Woodward has assembled since England were bundled out of the 1999 World Cup by South Africa is second-to-none. The attention to detail is meticulous, with Woodward and coach Andy Robinson even outdoing the Aussies in terms of preparation. England have separate experts for defence, scrum, line-out, kicking and fitness. They also have a team of tactical video analysts. They have enlisted the help of leading dieticians and nutrition consultants, and even took their own chef to Australia. They employ a doctor and physios. The latest addition to the team is a visual awareness trainer. If detailed preparation is the key ingredient to success, then Woodward's England will not be found wanting.

Part III
Welcome to Planet Rugby

In this part . . .

This part explores not only the rugby competitions that are played in the British Isles and Europe, but those played at international level. We start the tour of planet rugby with an explanation of everything you need to know about the World Cup, including its history and format, as well as descriptions of some of the most memorable World Cup moments.

Next, we take you on a comprehensive guided tour of international rugby and hard-fought annual tournaments like the Six Nations, dropping in at some of the world's most famous grounds. Away from the international arena, we talk about the great club and provincial tournaments, including the Heineken Cup, the Zurich Premiership, and the Celtic League.

To round off our rugby union voyage , we provide you with everything you need to know about the different levels of the local competitions, including Mini, Age Grade, Colts and Women's rugby, and encourage you to get involved with your local rugby club, whether as a player or as a social member.

Chapter 12

The World Cup

- -

In This Chapter

▶ Finding out how teams get into the World Cup

▶ Studying form: Teams and players

▶ Seeing what the prize is

▶ Getting ready for non-stop rugby

- -

Football has one. Cricket has one. Hockey and bowls both have one. So it was inevitable that rugby union eventually proposed that once every four years all the countries that play this wonderful game get together and play for a World Cup. Although the venue for the tournament changes every four years, the atmosphere and the spectacle never change.

To a fan of rugby, the World Cup is the pinnacle of the game. Playing for a World Cup gives rugby union a chance to showcase the game to the entire planet, with the best teams and the best players in action over a six-week feast of action. The winning team can justifiably boast that it is the best in the world.

In this chapter, we describe this magnificent event, how it is organised, what the trophy is, who takes part and what happens during the tournament. We also give insights into some of the more unusual things that have happened during World Cup tournaments.

Playing up to the Final

Since the first World Cup in 1987, some adjustments have been made to its organisation regarding the number of teams participating and the number of *pools* they are divided into during the tournament. A scheme has been developed that endeavours to ensure that the best two teams finish up in the World Cup final.

A *pool* is a group of teams, usually four or five teams, who play each other once to determine which ones go through to the important finals series.

Qualifying for the 2003 tournament

The qualifying rounds for the 2003 World Cup began in September 2000 – more than three years ahead of the actual tournament – when Luxembourg defeated Norway 41–9. Overall, 92 nations entered teams into the 2003 World Cup, and over 200 matches were played during the qualifying stages.

The result is 20 teams split into four pools of five teams. The teams in each pool have been determined by a ratings system devised by World Cup officials. The eight quarter-finalists from the last World Cup immediately qualify. The automatic qualifiers for the 2003 World Cup are Australia (the defending champions) and the seven other 1999 quarter-finalists: France, South Africa, New Zealand, Wales, England, Scotland and Argentina.

The next ten countries qualify directly via a series of matches played in five regions: Africa, Asia, the Americas, Europe and Oceania, the geographical area encompassing the Pacific islands. So that accounts for 18 of the final 20 teams (eight previous quarter-finalists and ten teams qualifying directly through regional matches).

The teams to occupy the final two spots in the World Cup are determined by another series of games involving one team from each of the five regions that failed to qualify initially. This means that some teams which failed to make it the first time around get a second chance.

Winning the pool games

At the pool stage of the World Cup tournament, teams play each other in a round-robin format (every team plays each other once), with the top two teams from each pool going through to the quarter-finals.

The current scheme means that some teams get a slightly easier passage through the pool section than others, but there's usually very little in it. A team's passage is dependent on the calibre of the other teams in each pool. Only seven or eight really outstanding international teams compete in the World Cup, and teams from the lesser-known countries always suffer a thrashing or two during the tournament. However, these countries use the World Cup as a learning experience – and sometimes give their "better" opponents a bit of a surprise.

World Cup origins

Holding a World Cup tournament for rugby union has been hailed as the saviour of the modern game, giving it greater exposure and a proper global identity. However, when it was first introduced, the World Cup idea was ridiculed in some quarters.

It was only through the persistence of some forward-thinking Australian and New Zealand officials that the World Cup began in 1987. Neil Durden-Smith, an English sports promoter, first proposed a World Cup in 1982, some 24 years after the International Rugby Board (IRB) passed a resolution forbidding member nations getting together for such an event. Even though Durden-Smith's idea failed, a few southern hemisphere officials, in particular the Australian Rugby Union's Sir Nicholas Shehadie, had the incentive to keep working away.

Australia and New Zealand believed there were enough viable nations to make a World Cup work. In 1984, an Australian–New Zealand delegation presented a proposal to the International Rugby Board. The IRB were initially hesitant about the proposal, but gradually came to appreciate its benefits and called for a feasibility study, which was accepted one year later.

While some hoped to hold the first World Cup tournament in 1986, the organisers did not have enough time to get ready. Instead, 1987 was decided on. Although this gave organisers, who were an assortment of International Rugby Board officials, less than two years to prepare, there was little point in clashing with the 1988 Olympic Games in Seoul. Although the organisation of the first World Cup may have been somewhat rushed – and not helped by the fact that several leading organisers were based on the other side of the world – it did work.

Whichever pool a team finds itself in, it still faces the daunting task of becoming World Cup champions. To take the crown, a team has to win at least six games, some of them played against teams of an extremely high calibre. Over a period of six weeks, the World Cup tournament remains the best way to work out who has the most formidable talent in world rugby.

For the first time in a World Cup tournament, a bonus point system is to be used in 2003 whereby teams get extra points if they score four tries or more, or lose by seven points or less. The introduction of bonus points is to encourage every team to play an attacking game and not give up when they think they have been beaten.

Breaking Through: The Teams

The World Cup tournament has been held four times, and won four times by teams from the southern hemisphere – Australia twice, New Zealand and

South Africa. However, three of those four finals have been contested by the most prominent northern hemisphere teams, France (twice) and England, so it is far from being a one-way street. For example, in 1991, Will Carling's England got through to the final and dominated possession and territory against Australia for much of the 80 minutes but could not break an excellent defence.

France also knows how to get it together when it has to. The French team made the final of the tournament in 1987 against New Zealand and in 1999 against Australia. In the 1999 World Cup, France inflicted one of the most resoundingly unexpected victories in rugby history when they downed strong favourites New Zealand in the semi-finals (see chapter 20).

Although the tournament has witnessed what can only be called massive thrashings, it still gives the lesser-known rugby countries a chance to proudly show their wares on the international stage and prove that they are not that far off the pace. This aspect of the tournament has led international administrators to start providing funds to improve the development of the game worldwide.

However, even the struggling nations have succeeded without major financial backing. In 1991, the Western Samoan team made an enormous impact. Several impressive performances helped them make the quarter-finals, which they did again in 1995, earning them the reputation for having more good rugby players per capita of population than any country in the world. Fiji made the 1987 quarter-finals, as did Canada in 1991, reminding the rugby-playing world that the World Cup does not just revolve around the major five or six countries.

Winning Ways: Significant Players

The list of most impressive tournament players is a *Who's Who* of international rugby. In the inaugural tournament, one of New Zealand's greatest players, Michael Jones, a back-rower, was exceptional in a prominent All Black line-up, while winger John Kirwan was outstanding in attack. The first World Cup was timed to perfection because it coincided with a fine New Zealand side.

In 1991, the whole world discovered what extraordinary talent Australian winger David Campese possessed. Campese's wizardry had amazed the rugby world for some time, although it sometimes failed him and he experienced some low moments. Over the six weeks of the 1991 tournament Campese was far-and-away the best player. He almost defeated New Zealand single-handedly in the semi-final in Dublin. In that game, Campese scored what was possibly the most exhilarating solo try of the tournament. He inspired a team try which was possibly even better, proving he was the best attacking player in the world.

The memory of Campese angling across field and bamboozling his New Zealand opponents to score in the sixth minute is guaranteed to forever stay vivid in the memories of those at Lansdowne Road that afternoon. Campese's game enabled Australia to take a match-winning 13-point lead at half-time.

The 1995 World Cup in South Africa was quite different with England sending Australia tumbling out in the quarter-finals courtesy of a last-minute drop-goal by England fly-half Rob Andrew. But England's glory was short-lived as they were then smashed aside by the tournament phenomenon, All Black winger Jonah Lomu, who put four tries past them.

The 1995 tournament was South Africa's triumph. The team, expertly coached by Kitch Christie and captained by Francois Pienaar, won the World Cup trophy for South Africa at its first attempt. All triumphant World Cup teams must have an outstanding fly-half and that was certainly the case in 1995. South Africa's Joel Stransky helped them defeat an ailing New Zealand in the final, which went into extra time. (see Chapter 20).

One of rugby's veterans, Tim Horan, was the outstanding player at the 1999 World Cup, a tournament which failed to live up to the legacy of its predecessors. The Australian inside centre's courage and consistency were vital factors in allowing him to enjoy a second World Cup winners' medal when the Wallabies beat France in the final.

By invitation only: The first World Cup

For the first World Cup, the World Cup organisers opted against having qualifying rounds, instead inviting what were perceived to be the 16 strongest nations at the time. The nations perceived to be the strongest were determined by a World Cup committee who, on the basis of the national teams' recent performances, decided which ones should be part of the inaugural extravaganza.

Apart from the usual rugby powers – New Zealand, Australia, France, England, Wales, Scotland, Ireland and Argentina – teams from around the globe participated. Italy and Romania came from Europe, Fiji and Tonga were the Pacific representatives, Japan from Asia, and Zimbabwe from Africa. The United States and Canada represented North America. The organisers also decided to spread the tournament across both New Zealand and Australia. It started in May 1987 at Eden Park in Auckland, with the All Blacks thrashing Italy 70–6.

For trivia buffs, a penalty try was the first-ever score in the World Cup, while the first player to cross the try-line was renowned New Zealand back-rower Michael Jones. The final was also held in Auckland, with New Zealand victorious over France.

Going for Gold: The Trophy

Despite some doubts about whether William Webb Ellis really was the father of the game (see Chapter 1), the inaugural World Cup organisers strengthened the myth by naming the trophy after him.

Every four years, the captain of the winning World Cup team is awarded the Webb Ellis Trophy (or William Webb Ellis Trophy, to give it its full name). Figure 12-1 shows the victorious Wallabies with captain John Eales holding the trophy in Cardiff in 1999.

When the original southern hemisphere delegation of Ivan Vodanovich, Dick Littlejohn and Sir Nicholas Shehadie approached numerous British rugby unions in the mid-1980s trying to get support for the World Cup concept, it was rejected. The Scottish Rugby Union refused to even meet them. Opposition faded when the Australian and New Zealand delegation said they would go ahead with the World Cup anyway. In the end, it was approved when an England delegate at the International Rugby Board (IRB) changed his vote at the last moment, which saw the World Cup proposal voted through.

Figure 12-1: Rugby's Holy Grail, the William Webb Ellis Trophy.

The IRB recommended the late John Kendall-Carpenter to be the inaugural tournament chairman. For diplomatic reasons, the southerners agreed to Kendall-Carpenter's appointment. It was Kendall-Carpenter, a former England player and school headmaster, who suggested the trophy be named after Webb Ellis.

Kendall-Carpenter went about finding an appropriate trophy, purchasing an impressive gold-plated cup for £80,000. Only one minor thing somewhat spoiled the effect: If you look carefully at the lid of the cup, you see a model of a miniature round football supported by garlands. Not a rugby ball. The cup appears to be an old football trophy. But because the two games shared a common ancestor, nobody was too bothered; It's the thought that counts, no matter what shape your balls are.

World Cup Highs and Lows

When you think of World Cup highs, images of the winning teams celebrating inevitably spring to mind. In 1991, when the World Cup was played in Great Britain and Ireland, Australia, who were among the favourites, defeated England in the final at Twickenham. South Africa, the 1995 hosts, revelled in their triumph in their first World Cup appearance, winning the final against New Zealand at Ellis Park in Johannesburg.

And Australia rejoiced when they won the World Cup title for the second time in 1999, defeating France in the final at the newly constructed Millennium Stadium in Cardiff. Figure 12-2 shows the Wallabies in action during that hard-fought game.

You would expect a tournament involving the best teams in the world to produce some wonderful moments – games and tries and teams that remain in the memory for decades. The World Cup tournament has certainly produced some great moments and tries – as well as moments that can only be described as bizarre.

Ignition in the opening game

No-one really knew what to expect when the first World Cup tournament started. The organisation had been rather rushed and it was crucial for the first game to be a success in order to quell the objections of the many critics who thought rugby was going too far too early.

Figure 12-2:
The
Wallabies
heading
for a World
Cup win.

In the first game between New Zealand and Italy, the All Black winger John Kirwan changed everyone's thinking when he bobbed, weaved and danced around practically every Italian player on the field to score the most extraordinary of tries, which started almost 80 metres from the opposition try-line.

Kirwan's try launched the World Cup. His performance shook everyone up and announced to the world that this new-fangled tournament really was something special. The world media and the rugby public already knew that the World Cup was alight.

Gallic glory in Sydney

The Australia versus France semi-final in 1987 is still rated among the greatest Tests played. All due to one of the most monumental team tries that ended a 24-all deadlock.

With injury time approaching, the French kept the ball alive for more than two minutes, testing the Australian defence first on one side of the field and then the other. On numerous occasions, it appeared that the persistent Australian defence would end the French symphony, but they kept backing up, recovering the ball every time it appeared to be lost.

Eventually the ball was delivered to France's masterful fullback Serge Blanco, who ran here, there and everywhere, repeatedly changing direction and somehow evading a tackle from Australian hooker Tom Lawton to lunge over the line for the most cherished of victories, knocking Australia out of contention in the process.

Every dedicated supporter of rugby now claims they were at Concord Oval that day. Many are having themselves on, because the official attendance was a paltry 17,768, showing just how far rugby has come in Australia in a short time.

Take-off in 1991

The 1991 tournament, held in Britain, Ireland and France, was the first to recognize the promotional and commercial potential of the World Cup. It attracted a massive new television audience, and also gained the sponsorship support of big multi-national companies.

This tournament had the added benefit of being extremely close and competitive, and the long overdue re-emergence of England as a genuine force on the field galvanised a big country hungry for sporting success. England's march to the final gained the sport much greater media exposure than it had enjoyed previously, turning players like England captain Will Carling into household names.

The second World Cup did not just shake up the tournament, it also shook Australian rugby out of its slumber. Australians watching on TV experienced drama in the quarter final against Ireland – which Australia should have lost – triumph when they rolled the over-confident All Blacks in the semi-final, and relief when the Wallabies held on in the final against England, who had strangely decided to totally change their game-plan.

When the Wallabies returned to Australia, they were astounded by the reception. On the morning of their ticker-tape parade along George Street in Sydney, the players and management honestly didn't think anyone would attend. Instead the route was crammed with thousands of rugby fans – old, new and converted.

Spiking the tea

Controversy erupted in the lead-up to the 1995 World Cup final between New Zealand and South Africa, when the New Zealand All Blacks believed they had been deliberately poisoned at their Johannesburg hotel. All Black coach Laurie Mains was told later that a woman "with a name something like Suzy" had been sacked by the hotel after she admitted that she had been paid to put a substance in the tea and coffee which was served in the All Blacks dining room.

Because most of the team was struck by illness the day before the final, it seemed unlikely to be accidental food poisoning. Only three members of the New Zealand starting XV were not affected; they had all been late for the lunch where the contaminated tea and coffee was served.

Beware low-flying aircraft

Ask any one of the spectators who were at the 1995 World Cup final what one of their most vivid memories was, and it invariably crops up. Along with the epic drama, which saw South Africa win in extra time, and President Nelson Mandela presenting the trophy wearing the #6 Springbok jersey, what sticks in everyone's memory is the South African Airlines jumbo jet that flew about 50 metres above the Ellis Park grandstands just before the start of the game.

The incident was dangerous, yet it did not seem out of place on an afternoon of great significance for a country which had only recently been on the brink of serious bloodshed. After the plane made its first pass, the electronic scoreboard showed it making a wide loop so that it could take another run at the stadium.

And, no, it wasn't the result of a crazed pilot, but a planned part of the pre-match entertainment. Only in South Africa!

That dinner, that walkout

South Africa had been excluded from the 1987 and 1991 World Cup tournaments because of its apartheid policies. South Africa returned to the fold in 1992. In 1995, with Nelson Mandela as president, South Africa was once again part of the big international rugby family.

The ranks of the South African Rugby Union were still dominated by many from the old guard, who loved to boast about the "good old days". That year, 1995, the South African team, the Springboks, were celebrating their momentous win at the World Cup final dinner.

A South African rugby autocrat, Louis Luyt, soured the evening by making an infamous speech. After presenting Derek Bevan with a gold watch for his "excellent refereeing" in an earlier match won by South Africa, Luyt then totally lost the plot.

To a stunned crowd, which included the English, French and Australian teams, Luyt announced that the 1995 World Cup was the only genuine tournament because the Springboks had been involved for the first time. He said the All Blacks of 1987 and the Wallabies of 1991 couldn't label themselves world champions because South Africa had not participated in those earlier tournaments.

The England team gave Luyt a mock standing ovation, then all three visiting teams made the decision to walk out, such was the indignation at his speech. The next morning most visiting rugby administrators condemned Luyt's speech as disgraceful.

France wheels out the guillotine again

The Twickenham semi-final in 1999 turned out to be a second French revolution, as unwelcome to its victims as was the first. The French team humiliated tournament favourites New Zealand, despite being ranked 15–1 outsiders.

Even the most hardened New Zealand rugby writers were hiding their heads in their hands as the All Blacks totally lost the plot.

New Zealand were ahead 24–10 in the second half when the French suddenly went on a crazed try-scoring spree, which saw them tally 26 unanswered points between the 46th and 59th minute.

All the supporters from the northern hemisphere were in ecstasy, especially as France went on to win 43–31.

Broadcasting to the world

The first World Cup tournament in 1987 was broadcast to only 17 countries and had a cumulative audience of 300 million people. This inaugural tournament finished with a net surplus of £1 million after accumulating gross commercial income of £3 million.

Twelve years later, the 1999 World Cup was broadcast to over 150 countries, reaching a cumulative audience of over three billion people. The net surplus was over £38 million, a figure which exceeded the total revenue generated by the three previous tournaments. An amount close to £70 million was raised from the 1999 World Cup commercial programme.

The aftermath of this revolutionary defeat saw heads roll. Andy Haden, the former All Black forward, predicted the result would "rock New Zealand rugby to the core, absolutely to the core." The first to go was All Black coach John Hart, who announced his resignation before the team returned home. Rob Fisher, the New Zealand Rugby Union chairman, followed shortly after.

Introducing the World Cup 2003

Australia is the first country to host the World Cup tournament for a second time. As with the Olympic Games, countries bid for the right to host the World Cup. The International Rugby Board decides which nation or nations win the right to host the World Cup. Australia and New Zealand, after intense lobbying of IRB delegates, won the bid to co-host the 2003 tournament.

However, because New Zealand could not guarantee "clean" stadiums throughout the country (which means all ground advertising is removed for the duration of the tournament), New Zealand lost the right to be involved in the hosting of the fifth World Cup tournament.

New Zealand was originally to stage about a dozen matches, but after the co-hosting arrangement fell through, Australia instead became the venue for all those games. The IRB World Cup organisers have determined that the 48 games played in the World Cup 2003 are to be spread across Australia, with matches held in ten different cities, in seven states and territories, and in 12 different venues, starting on October 10, 2003.

To ensure that no team, particularly the Australian team, is perceived to have an advantage, all teams play in a number of Australian cities, some cities having more than one venue. Defending champions Australia find themselves on a road show, with pool matches in Sydney, Brisbane, Adelaide and Melbourne, while the 1999 runners-up France play matches in Brisbane, Townsville, Sydney and Wollongong.

Lining up the favourites

The 2003 World Cup is to be a record 44-day tournament, seven days longer than the event in 1999. One of the early favourites to win is the England team, which has dominated northern hemisphere rugby for several seasons and defeated the Australian, New Zealand and South African teams at Twickenham in 2002, as well as then beating Australia and New Zealand on consecutive weekends on tour in 2003.

Lights, action . . . and time to party

Anyone planning to watch the 2003 World Cup from start to finish – pay attention. The most important bit of advice we can give you is to rest up now, because you won't be getting much sleep between October 10 and November 22, 2003.

Rugby supporters in the southern hemisphere can expect long days and nights watching games played sometimes in the afternoon but mostly in the evening, while those in the northern hemisphere are going to be watching games at the same time as having breakfast. If you are going to be one of the thousands of supporters heading to Australia from the UK and Ireland prepare to live on only a few hours' sleep a day while the tournament is on: Rugby fans find themselves unable to stop watching the spectacle of a never-ending avalanche of tries and exhilarating moments.

Above all, expect the unexpected. Each tournament throws up unexpected results and one giant-killing team. Warn your unenlightened friends (if you have any friends who don't follow rugby) that you intend watching every game, so they might as well write you off their social calendar.

If you are staying at home, then holding a rugby party or two for your like-minded friends isn't the worst idea. That way you can watch the games on television to cheer your favourite national side to victory – or oblivion – in the company of friends.

You can easily find out the World Cup schedule by checking some rugby Web sites, such as PlanetRugby (see Chapter 17 for full details and Web addresses for the most rugby-friendly sites around). Check the schedules, find out when your team is playing and start writing the invitations.

The greatest threat from the southern hemisphere is expected to be New Zealand, which has built up well for the tournament and has a large base of players to select from. New Zealand has an added incentive to win the tournament on Australia's home turf – to exact revenge for losing its tournament co-hosting arrangement.

The Australian team is a likely semi-final candidate. Some concerns exist about the depth of the team's squad, the lack of experienced players in several positions, and whether the pressure of playing at home in front of an expectant and unforgiving crowd is likely to overwhelm the players.

France, one of the more unpredictable teams in world rugby, has a relatively comfortable pool and should also make it to the semi-finals. The French often struggle away from home but if they maintain their composure and produce several more match-winning rugby players, which they have a way of doing every season, they could be a surprise winner and the first northern hemisphere country to go home with the World Cup.

Looking at the likely lads

Key players at the 2003 World Cup include England fly-half Jonny Wilkinson, who is probably the most consistently accurate goal kicker in world rugby. Wilkinson could easily win the World Cup for England on the basis of his lethal boot, but he can also play a bit with the ball in hand. England also have a formidable pack led by captain Martin Johnson, and lively outside backs with winger Ben Cohen a constant threat.

Australia is relying heavily on its midfield combination of scrum-half George Gregan and fly-half Stephen Larkham to get the Wallabies attacking in the right vein, with former rugby league internationals and utility backs Mat Rogers and Lote Tuqiri providing the ingenuity out wide in the attack.

New Zealand has an abundance of good players in the back-line, and a young but improving pack, with Chris Jack making his name at lock and Richie McCaw doing the same on the openside flank. New Zealand also has a fine brace of fly-halves in Carlos Spencer and Andrew Mehrtens and in Aaron Mauger, they have an inside centre of genuine class. The calibre of the players that South Africa and France are likely to field is far more unpredictable, but you can be certain that some new superstars emerge during the tournament – they've done so before.

Chapter 13

The International Scene

*R*ugby cannot yet lay claim to the remarkable worldwide popularity of football. After all, you can see kids kicking a football around in almost every country on the planet and there is no point in denying that football is a more accessible and less complicated sport. Rugby's popularity is growing, however, as the game itself develops, and fitter, faster players produce exciting contests that are beamed around the world. Events like the Rugby World Cup have helped take the game to the masses yet the game is growing steadily far from the shop window nations – nearly 100 countries are now members of the International Rugby Board.

In this chapter, we describe the relationships that exist between national teams from the main power bases of international rugby. The rivalry that exists between the northern and southern hemispheres, in particular, ensures that inter-hemisphere games are a real spectacle! We also take you on a tour of some of the world's great rugby grounds and describe memorable games that have taken place. So take your passport and get ready for a journey around the rugby battlefields.

Sizing Up the Six Nations

The annual Six Nations rugby tournament is the bedrock of international rugby in the northern hemisphere. It is the event that underpinned the whole of international rugby before the World Cup, and is the envy of those not involved in it. It took the southern hemisphere countries until the late 1990s to try to emulate the Six Nations, with their smaller Tri-Nations series (we discuss this series below).

The other vital factor is that the Six Nations exists on a level removed from the field of play. Quite simply, it is the most remarkable fans' tournament to be found anywhere in sport. Travelling support for the matches sees up to 30,000 followers attending the host city venue to support the visiting team – when we say they attend the host city venue, we do not mean that they always actually attend the match. Some people are so enraptured by the special atmosphere of a Six Nations weekend that they travel without tickets, take part in the festivities surrounding the game and are quite happy to watch the game itself on a television screen.

The savage dent that would be put in the profits of hoteliers, airlines, restaurants, taxi firms, rosette sellers, ticket touts and bars if the tournament was ever to be abandoned hardly bears thinking about!

When five became six

Since 1883, national teams from England, Scotland, Wales, Ireland and France have been battling it out to determine the best team in their part of the world. From 2000, the hitherto Five Nations tournament became the Six Nations when Italy, after years of good results, was allowed to join the party.

Held annually in the New Year, the Six Nations tournament is contested by each of the six teams playing each other on a revolving roster of games, with teams alternating as hosts each year (so, if England play France at Twickenham in 2004, the match in 2005 would be in Paris). The tournament invariably attracts capacity crowds in an electric atmosphere, especially at Twickenham, the home ground of the English national side but also at the other venues – the Millennium Stadium (Cardiff); Murrayfield (Edinburgh); Lansdowne Road (Dublin); the Stadio Flaminio (Rome); and the Stade de France (Paris).

Competitions within a competition

The winner of the Six Nations is the country that accumulates the most points over its five games. Participating teams also attempt to win the *Grand Slam*, which occurs when they defeat all of their five opponents.

However, some of the participating teams attach special significance to some of the matches played within the series.

The Six Nations Trophy

The fact that the Calcutta Cup is steeped in over a century of history (see "The Contest for the Calcutta Cup" later in this chapter), makes it all the more remarkable that the bedrock of the northern hemisphere game, the Six Nations tournament, had no real trophy to award the winners for 111 years!

From its origins in 1883, when the Home Unions all played each other for the first time, the event was soon dubbed The International Championship by newspapers reporting on the matches.

Then, with the admission of France in 1910, the term Five Nations Championship became increasingly popular. However, the only prizes on offer were verbal accolades, such as "Grand Slam", rather than actual trophies. Even the side finishing last got a fictional award – the dreaded "Wooden Spoon", which still exists to this day (with Wales picking it up in 2003).

The winners eventually got their hands on a real cup in 1994, when the (then) Five Nations committee approved the awarding of the Five (now Six) Nations trophy. And it's been looking great in trophy cabinets ever since.

A *Triple Crown* means that one of the teams from the Home Unions (England, Scotland, Wales and Ireland) has defeated all the others. So, if England defeats Wales, Scotland and Ireland, it has secured the Triple Crown. France and Italy, naturally, cannot win the Triple Crown.

England and Scotland also play for the *Calcutta Cup*, which is a private rivalry between two old enemies (we describe the Calcutta Cup in more detail later on in this chapter). The match they play against each other in the Six Nations tournament decides the winner of the Calcutta Cup.

For many years, England and Wales were the strongest teams to contest the Five Nations. France has overtaken the Welsh in recent Six Nations competitions, while Italy have so far struggled to be competitive. Scotland have lately been in the doldrums, and Ireland are showing signs of revival.

Tracking the Tri-Nations

Although the rugby-playing nations of the northern hemisphere *think* the Six Nations tournament is the best in the world, Australia, New Zealand and South Africa like to think the same about their own event – although "Southerners" coming north to experience the European extravaganza have been taken aback by an intensity they never knew existed. The *Bledisloe Cup*, contested by Australia and New Zealand, is incorporated into the Tri-Nations series.

The Tri-Nations has become one of the southern hemisphere's most eagerly anticipated sporting events since it began in 1996. However, it began in contentious times, and the debate about it continues to this day.

Going professional with Murdoch's millions

In 1995, the Australian rugby league ranks were in turmoil when Rupert Murdoch's News Limited Corporation made a bid to take over the domestic competition. Thus began the Super League saga, with rugby league officials offering big money for players to stay with the establishment in an effort to stop them from signing with Murdoch's breakaway Super League organisation.

Rugby union administrators were naturally nervous that they would lose a lot of their key players to league. To counter any possible exodus to league, the union administrators began consolidating their fortress. First, New Zealand, Australian and South African rugby administrators signed a deal with Murdoch guaranteeing them US$550 million for a decade of television rights. Then, the IRB declared that rugby would switch from an amateur to a professional code, enabling rugby players to be paid openly for the first time.

In return for such a large sum of money – a sum that has financed the game in New Zealand, Australia and South Africa since 1995, Murdoch wanted quality television rugby to show. And so was born the Tri-Nations and the Super 12 tournaments. (The Super 12 is an annual tournament played between the leading provincial clubs of New Zealand, who have five teams entered, South Africa, who have four teams entered, and Australia, who have three teams entered.)

Six Nations versus Tri-Nations

At times, it's a bit like watching two spoilt schoolboys quibbling over who has the better pushbike. Put an English rugby supporter and an Australian rugby supporter together and before long they start to bicker over which is the best – the Six Nations or the Tri Nations.

The Australian says the Tri-Nations is the best tournament because it involves the strongest and most impressive rugby nations and because entertaining the spectators is vital. However, the English argue that the Six Nations tournament is the best tournament because of the tradition, the intensity, and the fact that, unlike the Tri-Nations, it is not all froth and bubble. The pot shots are never ending. Hopefully, at heart they are not spiteful.

Coming of age "down under"

The two innovative competitions didn't solve everything, however. After the deal with Murdoch was signed, a disagreement erupted between the rugby establishment and a rebel organisation called the World Rugby Corporation over control of the sport. The establishment eventually won, and the Tri-Nations and Super 12 have thrived and prospered, becoming the benchmark for quality rugby in the Southern Hemisphere and, occasionally, beyond.

The Contest for the Calcutta Cup

The Calcutta Cup, which is played for annually between England and Scotland (now as part of the Six Nations), is not only the oldest trophy to be played for in international rugby, it is also the most unique in appearance. It was presented to the RFU by the members of the Calcutta Football Club in India after it was forced to disband in 1877 due to the departure of key players, many of them soldiers, to other parts of the British Empire.

The members decided to use the £60 remaining in the club's bank account to purchase silver rupees. They then had these melted down by Indian silversmiths and crafted into the Calcutta Cup. The RFU big wigs were so impressed by the gift that they decided to make it the prize for the yearly set-to with the Scots, beginning in 1879. It has been played for ever since.

The only dip in the Calcutta Cup's fortunes came in 1988, when, after a shockingly poor match (England won 9–6), the players made sure they enjoyed themselves by having a few beers at the post-match dinner. However, two famous forwards, the Scottish flanker John Jeffrey and the English #8 Dean Richards, got so carried away in the revelry that they spirited the hefty trophy out of the room into the Edinburgh night, where they decided to use it as a rugby ball.

At some stage it was dropped, and damaged. When one Scottish official saw the Cup the following morning he was overheard saying: "It looks like we'll be playing for the Calcutta Shield from now on." Fortunately, the Cup was not dented or scuffed too badly, but the quality and detail of the original work by the Indian silversmiths was such that it took their Edinburgh counterparts four months to restore.

The north/south divide

Once upon a time, everyone in the rugby world got on reasonably well. The teams from the northern hemisphere, particularly the teams from England, thought they were the masters of the game and everyone loyally followed them.

However, before long, teams from the southern hemisphere challenged this notion. For many years, teams from New Zealand and South Africa were the dominant forces in the international game. Then came the rise of Australia, which coincided with the start of the World Cup in 1987 (see Chapter 12, which covers the World Cup in detail).

The southern hemisphere's success in the World Cup in recent years has at times sparked a robust rivalry between the two hemispheres, not least because three of the four finals have been contested by northern hemisphere sides.

Something of a slanging match has ensued because the north accuses the south of trying to change the game, and the south responds by saying that teams from the north play an outmoded form of rugby.

When the southern hemisphere administrators, and in particular the South Africa, New Zealand, and Australia Rugby (SANZAR) delegates organised new tournaments, such as the Super 12 and the Tri-Nations, the view of the north was that these events were no more than glorified basketball.

The controversy shows no signs of abating. The north believes it is upholding the essential traditions of the game, and that the south, while hoping to make rugby a more popular international sport, is guilty of too much tinkering with the game's core principles.

Olympic Rugby: A Competitive Dodo

Rugby was introduced to the Olympics in Paris in 1900, when France defeated England. However, it wasn't exactly the most popular event in the Games – only three teams competed.

Rugby didn't make an appearance at the 1904 Games in St Louis. The 1908 event struggled to get off the ground, despite being held on supposedly strong rugby territory, England. Only two teams were involved – Australia, who were touring Great Britain at the time, and Cornwall, who were chosen by English Rugby Union officials to represent the United Kingdom.

The final was played at Shepherds Bush in London. Getting pummelled by an opponent was the least of the players' worries. Bordering the touchline on one side of the field was a swimming pool about 100 metres long, with netting on top to catch flying balls and stray players. Huge mattresses were spread along the rim of the pool in case a player accidentally fell in and injured himself.

Added to this bizarre scene, men with long poles and small nets fished the ball out whenever it went over the top of the netting, into touch and into the swimming pool. The Australian team successfully negotiated the swimming pool and won the final 32–3, receiving Olympic gold medals for their efforts.

The United States won the Olympic event in 1920 and again in 1924, when they defeated France in the final in Paris. The result disgusted the local French crowd, who jeered the Americans. At the medal ceremony, the American national anthem was drowned out by the booing of the crowd and the US team required a police escort to get out of the ground. That was the last time rugby appeared at the Olympics: Olympic organisers decided that individual events were preferable to team sports.

Commonwealth Games Rugby

Adding to rugby's international flavour has been the introduction of the game at the Commonwealth Games. Rugby first appeared at the 1998 Games in Kuala Lumpur, where it was played as a seven-a-side event. As expected, New Zealand won the first gold medal, defeating Fiji 21–12 in the final.

Apartheid splits the rugby world

Matches between South African rugby and the rest of the World have produced some of rugby's finest moments, notably in a tumultuous series of Test matches between the Springboks and the All Blacks, arguably rugby history's biggest rivalry; and between South Africa and the British Lions.

However, contacts and traditions were interrupted because of the policy of Apartheid and the world began to develop a slogan – no normal sport in an abnormal society. There was also a United Nations resolution, which sought to prevent a range of cultural, artistic and sporting contacts with what was becoming an outcast republic. Rugby was caught in the middle of this storm – players and officials who revered Springbok rugby and who had made lifelong friends in previous tours, demanded their own rights – the rights to maintain sporting contacts and friendships. The 1969–70 South African tour of the United Kingdom was marred by demonstrations against the tourists and the 1971 Springbok tour of Australia prompted a series of protests. Far more seriously, the 1981 tour to New Zealand brought civil disorder to New Zealand on a major scale, causing rifts in families and prompting scenes of violence and sporting disaster as the factions in favour of, and against, the tour fought, often literally, for their beliefs. It was a tour that, it is said, brought New Zealand into the reality of the times.

The Wallaby tour of South Africa in 1992, which coincided with New Zealand also visiting the country, had its dramatic moments, especially when the African National Congress protested over match officials playing the banned white anthem *Die Stem* before the Test match between the All Blacks and the Springboks in Johannesburg. (We discuss the rugby ground, Ellis Park, in the section "Fields of Dreams" further on in this chapter). That incident almost led to the Wallabies ending their tour early and heading for home before their Test against South Africa in Cape Town. Peace was eventually restored. Australia remained in South Africa and went on to win the Test by a record 26–3 margin.

These days, the Springboks are back as a staple of world rugby, with Apartheid relegated from the country's politics.

The All Blacks brought out the big names in their quest for gold, with wing Jonah Lomu and fullback Christian Cullen, two All Black giants, contributing heavily to their Games triumph. They also fielded a strong team for the 2002 Commonwealth Games in Manchester, with outstanding attacking players Eric Rush, Bruce Reihana and Roger Randle instrumental, as New Zealand successfully defended their title. They met Fiji again in the final, winning 33–15.

For those of you who like to plan well ahead, the next Commonwealth Games will be held in Melbourne in 2006.

Seven-a-Side Rugby: The Famous Sevens

When people think of *sevens rugby*, they immediately have visions of the famous Hong Kong Sevens event, which has been a highlight of the international calendar since the early 1970s. It is a festival of fast football and cheerful imbibing and enjoyment is the name of the game. The significance of the Hong Kong event has been massive in other ways – before the IRB really began to promote the sport worldwide, the Sevens provided a shop window for the lesser nations to promote their own rugby and to leave an imprint on the union map.

In recent years, Sevens football has become far more serious. The IRB organises a World Sevens series, incorporating tournaments in a variety of cities including Durban, Dubai, Wellington, Hong Kong, Shanghai, Kuala Lumpur, Tokyo, London and Cardiff.

Sevens football attracts a lot of newcomers to the sport, as it is a fast, abbreviated form of the game that is easy to understand. With only 14 players on the field, each team has an abundance of space, enabling attacking players to score a feast of tries.

Those involved in the World Sevens series aren't usually the world's best players as the tournaments often coincide with major rugby events such as the Six Nations and Heineken Cup. England has started to use the Sevens series to blood new, promising players and to see whether they are ready to take the next step.

Going for the Jugular: Great Rugby Rivalries

Many team sports have the effect of generating great rivalries between the teams and their supporters, both nationally and internationally. To give an account of all the great rivalries that exist between teams in the world of rugby would mean writing another book, so, in this section we describe just a few of the more notable relationships.

New Zealand and South Africa

The most intense relationship in international rugby has been between New Zealand and South Africa. For countless decades, the two countries believed that when they faced each other they were deciding who was the best in the world. This belief was justified, because for many years South Africa and New Zealand were on a level far above everyone else. Both were the real trendsetters and intellects of the game.

During the 1930s, 1950s and 1960s, tours by one country to the other were regarded as the ultimate in rugby. While this may not be the case today, at the time the rivalry between the two "market leaders" was ferocious, illustrated by the words of one South African player before the start of the first test of the 1949 series: "When South Africa plays New Zealand, consider your country at war."

Tours were invariably rough and tough. After a tour of South Africa in the 1960s, New Zealand centre Ross Brown confessed, "I wouldn't like to go through that series again. It went beyond sport. We were playing for national prestige. It honestly took me three months to recover. I didn't sleep properly for about three months, those Tests upset me so much."

Wales and England

Probably the strongest rivalry in the northern hemisphere is between Wales and England, especially when Wales were the superpower of the Five Nations tournament (since 2000, the Six Nations tournament) in the 1970s. The sociological differences alone between rugby people in Wales (where it was predominantly a working class sport) and England (where it was mainly a middle class sport), intensified the historical rivalry between the two countries.

In his pep talk before the 1977 clash against England, Welsh star Phil Bennett asserted that the English had a long history of exploiting the Welsh. Nearly ten years later, in 1986, English official Dudley Wood referred to the tension between the two nations. To his way of thinking, the relationship between the Welsh and the English was based on trust and understanding: "They don't trust us and we don't understand them."

Wales and New Zealand

Wales and New Zealand have also had some historic battles on the rugby field, with the All Blacks often finishing on top. Back in the 1970s, celebrated All Black scrum-half, Sid Going was talking about these battles, and said, "You don't beat Wales in Wales – you just happen to score more points than them."

For a century, the two countries have been involved in some of the most dramatic and controversial internationals ever recorded. Their teams seem to be able to rise to the occasion when they are playing each other – though frankly, New Zealand are dominating the series at present, with a 50-point thumping in 2003 the latest humiliation.

Introducing the Fields of Dreams

Because of the passion and commitment shown on the pitch, rugby grounds are often vibrant and exciting places to watch sport. Your average rugby spectator is a devoted and noisy follower of his team and if you immerse yourself in the game, a great time will be had by all. And luckily, most of the best rugby grounds are superb stages for great performances.

Twickenham

What was once a cabbage patch is now a magnificent arena that is headquarters of the game of rugby in England. Twickenham is the home of English rugby, and one of the game's most recognisable and distinguished grounds (see Figure 13-1). Based in the south-west outskirts of London, Twickenham was originally a 10-acre market garden. Following redevelopment, Twickenham staged its first Test in 1910.

Twickenham is a ground that oozes tradition and style. As Welshman John Morgan explained: "an international at Twickenham is more than mere spectacle. It is a gathering of the clan." A Twickenham Test match is a great social occasion, invariably drawing capacity crowds and the social set, who wine and dine on champagne in the car parks before kick-off.

The gaunt old wooden stands were gradually replaced and Twickenham rebuilt in its entirety from the late 1980s to the early 1990s; there are further plans afoot to re-develop the south side of this massive ground and to increase the capacity beyond 80,000.

Australia, in common with all the major rugby countries, has enjoyed a few memorable moments at Twickenham, in particular the narrow 1991 World Cup final victory over England. So intense was the atmosphere that afternoon that Australian coach Bob Dwyer temporarily forgot where he was. During the second half, Dwyer noticed that two of his players – David Campese and Michael Lynagh – were embarking on a speculative backline move. Dwyer leapt to his feet and screamed at the top of his lungs, "Kick the ball to the s**thouse!" It was only after he had sat down that Dwyer realised that the Royal Box, with the Queen sitting in it, was right behind him. Her Majesty presented the World Cup to Nick Farr-Jones, the Wallaby captain, after the match.

Millennium Stadium

This is arguably the greatest sporting stadium in the world. It is massive and soaring and futuristic but also, amazingly homely. No wonder that FA Cup final and other major football occasions take place there while London's Wembley Stadium is being rebuilt. Nothing could better Cardiff Arms Park on match day. Because the old Arms Park was situated virtually in the centre of the city, Cardiff became a rugby mecca in the hours leading up to kick-off. In all the streets, lanes, markets, pubs and shops, everyone talked, ate and drank rugby.

It must be cold out there today ...

Twickenham was also where, in the 1970s, the first-ever rugby streaker first made his appearance. There is a famous picture of the streaker being led away with a policeman's helmet covering his crown jewels!

The most famous Twickers streaker, however, is Erica Roe, who ran onto the field topless during the half-time break in the 1982 England match against Australia. England captain Bill Beaumont tried no less than four times to start his half-time pep talk, but found it impossible because his players kept turning around to watch Erica evading the police.

The one problem is that at present, Wales do not have a team to match their stadium; however, for so small a rugby nation to create such a wonderful monster is testament to the fact that rugby remains in Welsh hearts.

Murrayfield

A picturesque ground in a magnificent city, visiting teams continually say that Murrayfield has one of the best playing surfaces – which is not surprising, considering that the ground boasts rugby's first underground heating system.

In 1958, Edinburgh suffered an intensely cold winter, which froze all the city's rugby and football grounds. Nothing new in that, considering it is in Scotland! However, following a donation from a Glasgow businessman, electric cables were laid under the turf the following year, ensuring that games could be played in any type of weather. Such are the benefits of a ground having its own electric blanket.

While Scotland's rugby fortunes have ebbed and flowed with their Six Nations line-up struggling appreciably in recent times, the locals can always show off Murrayfield. The stadium was rebuilt in the 1990s, and some of the old atmosphere has departed, especially with a wide running track in front of one stand. Safety regulations in Britain mean that the old standing terrace is no more. In some ways, this is a shame – the 1977 match between Scotland and Wales drew over 100,000 spectators, many of them crammed on the vast bank opposite the main stand, and it was an impressive sight to behold.

Still, the place has an historic feel about it still; the skirl of the bagpipes can chill the blood of the opposition as "Flower of Scotland" is belted out.

Stade de France

This wonderful stadium looks, as you approach it, like a giant spaceship which has landed in the northern suburbs of Paris. It is imposing, modern and magnificent, underlining again the fact that rugby stadiums in Europe are cathedrals of the sport. The 1998 football World Cup final took place there, with France winning the title of World Champions. The 2007 Rugby World Cup final will also take place in the stadium.

French rugby moved most of its international matches there from the old, smaller and raucous Parc des Princes in the south-west of Paris. Critics say that the new stadium is too genteel, that the roar has died, and they may have a point. France has become easier to beat at home than they were in the Parc.

But the Stade has an impossible glamorous, Parisian feel to it, and will deservedly be seen as one of the headquarter arenas of world rugby.

Lansdowne Road

Within walking distance of the centre of Dublin, Lansdowne Road is now rather run-down, but still has a unique atmosphere (see Figure 13-2). One of the great delights is to be part of the swarm of humanity heading towards the ground from the City on match days, when everyone gets caught up in a huge cyclone of rugby fans, swaying this way and that.

Unlike most rugby grounds, where everyone likes to get into their seats well before kick-off, the tradition in Dublin is to wait until the last minute before taking your seat. This causes a mad, frantic rush in the final few minutes before kick-off. If you get caught in the middle of it, just pray you survive!

Ellis Park

South Africa has enjoyed many triumphs at the imposing ground at Ellis Park; the 1995 Rugby World Cup was won here, to riotous celebrations. Australia, for one, regards the stadium almost as a graveyard. Situated on the outskirts of Johannesburg, Ellis Park began its life as a brickfield and rubbish dump. The ground has since become a huge, frightening arena, renowned for being invaded by rabid Springbok supporters and large, powerful South African teams.

Figure 13-2:
Hoping for
the luck of
the Irish at
Lansdowne
Road.

Sydney Olympic Stadium

Sydney rugby has had a number of homes. Traditional Wallaby supporters still get misty-eyed about Test matches at the Sydney Cricket Ground (SCG) even if the view from parts of the arena was appalling. Rugby left the SCG in the 1980s and then spent some years at the Sydney Football Stadium. While it was a good, functional ground, the crowd capacity of 40,000 was just too small.

Thankfully, the 2000 Olympic Games gave Sydney the reason to at last build a proper sporting stadium at Homebush. The Olympic Stadium holds more than 80,000 spectators, and it was inevitable that rugby would also head to Homebush too. And, although Wallaby fans have taken their time getting used to the idea of travelling away from Sydney's rugby heartland and their local pubs, they have gradually grown used to the Olympic Stadium being the home ground for the national team.

At first, the view from some sections of the ground was far worse than at the old SCG, especially high up in the heavens behind the goalposts. However, the reconfiguration of the ground in 2002 brought everyone closer to the action, and the complaints have softened somewhat.

Now that Australia has won numerous tight matches there, and after winning a series against the Lions, Wallaby fans have been convinced that the Olympic Stadium is the ground for them, even if they are sitting 1,000 rows back. Some might find the place charmless and access is poor for the unwary. However, rugby now needs these leviathan stadiums to cram in the burgeoning numbers who want to watch.

Ballymore

Although major Tests have been transferred to the larger Lang Park or Gabba arenas in recent years in Brisbane, it is Ballymore, which has a capacity of just over 20,000, which remains one of the favourite grounds of many long-time Wallaby supporters.

The main aim at Ballymore is for rugby fans to enjoy themselves. Bars proliferate. In one bar behind the main grandstand the number of drinkers during a game sometimes exceeds the number of spectators in the grandstand. The Queensland Rugby club has its main bar at the back of the main stand, which adds to the relaxed atmosphere and ensures many long and emotional nights for spectators as well as past and present players.

Australia has savoured some of its greatest victories at the ground, as well as its most embarrassing defeat. In 1973, Australia was beaten by one of world rugby's minnows, Tonga. To add to the humiliation, a group of Tongan supporters, delirious with the most unexpected of victories, jumped on top of the Australian dressing-room after the game and banged away on the galvanised iron roof for ten minutes, laughing hysterically.

Carisbrook

A typical New Zealand ground, Carisbrook in Dunedin has a reputation for being cold, wet and inhospitable. Nearly everyone and everything is open to the elements, in particular the harsh Antarctic wind that whips across the ground.

Carisbrook (shown in Figure 13-3) has one of the few spectator hills left in major sporting arenas. On match day, this area is usually invaded by "scarfies", local university students who invariably wear a scarf to ward off the winter chill.

Figure 13-3:
The hardy
crowd at
Carisbrook
Stadium.

In Dunedin, a South Island city, you discover New Zealand rugby at its most basic, relying on good old-fashioned rucking and running rugby. That's the formula that has made both the local team, Otago, and the national product, the All Blacks, such devastating forces.

Chapter 14

Home and Away

The huge jigsaw of European rugby has finally been pieced together over the last decade, and flagship tournaments like the Heineken European Cup, and domestic championships such as the Zurich (English) Premiership, are unmatched anywhere in the world for their vibrancy, variety and quality.

Elite players from all over the globe have been drawn to participate alongside Europe's best, attracted by the opportunity to play on the biggest stage that there is below the international game. With crowds and television audiences growing, and sponsors keen to renew their association with the sport, the future is bright. Since elite rugby switched from being an amateur to a professional sport in 1995, European rugby has had a few more teething problems with professionalism than the southern hemisphere. This was mainly because, with three times as many different rugby nations and cultures to accommodate, there were three times as many *t*'s to be crossed and *i*'s to be dotted. Now that has been done, the message is clear as daylight – European Rugby Rules, OK.

The Heineken Cup – How Refreshing

Aaah! The Heineken Cup, the tournament that refreshes the parts that others cannot reach. In the eight seasons since it was launched, the Heineken Cup has established itself as the most compelling competition between non-international sides in existence. For sheer drama it has outstripped the southern hemisphere's Super 12 on a regular basis, but it is not just its cliff-hanging finals that give it more edge than a cut-throat razor.

The sheer scope of this annual tournament is breathtaking, bringing together the elite club and provincial teams from the rugby heartlands of England, France, Ireland, Wales, Scotland and Italy to battle for the honour of being Europe's champions.

The Heineken Cup is about capitals of rugby, such as Leicester, Toulouse, Limerick and Llanelli, and the fervour of fans steeped in the traditions and folklore of their teams. It is a tournament that galvanises the rugby towns, cities and regions of Europe like no other. Beer company Heineken have been the title sponsors since the tournament's inception in 1995, and their fore-sight has been handsomely rewarded. From the beret-wearing Basques of south-west France to Munster's Red Army, from England's Roman city of Bath to the wild Scottish Borders surrounding Hadrian's Wall, pulses quicken at the thought of the challenges to come. Whether your tipple is a foaming glass of ale or a glass of fine claret, the Heineken is the Cup that cheers!

The long road to the final

The Heineken Cup is about survival of the fittest. The team that will win is a team that can not only stay among the front-runners during the pool rounds as the 24 competing sides jockey for position, but can also time its finishing burst to perfection as the competition reaches the knockout stages at the end of a long, hard season. The Heineken Cup has no automatic right of entry in the tournament: In the Heineken Cup, each team (reigning champs exempted) has to earn the right to be there by qualifying through its own domestic league or cup competitions. This is unlike the Super 12 in the southern hemisphere, where franchised teams are permanent fixtures whether they finish top or bottom.

Those nations with the most professional clubs, and the largest spectator base, get the biggest allocation. The big boys are England and France, who are allocated six teams each. Then comes Wales with five, Ireland with three, and Scotland and Italy with two each. It is up to each national union to decide on qualification criteria, but, broadly speaking, the domestic league and/or cup champions in each country, and the highest placed teams thereafter, will claim the places.

The national allocation is decided by the tournament organisers, European Rugby Cup Ltd (ERC for short). ERC is run by a board of 12 directors (two from each of the Six Nations), one of whom is elected chairman. It has a chief executive and a small staff to handle day-to-day running, including discipli-nary issues, and is based in Dublin. It is ultimately answerable to the Six Nations and, in turn, the International Rugby Board (IRB).

The format

After 78 matches spread over eight months, the best two teams of the 24 who started out on the Heineken Cup trail in September meet in the final at the end of May. The winner is the rightful king of European club (provincial) rugby.

The tournament is divided into two stages: pools and knockout. There are six pools of four teams, and they play a round-robin of games home and away to decide who will go into the knockout stage. The pool rounds are spread throughout October, December and January, and then there is a break until the quarter-finals and semi-finals which are played in April, with the final at the end of May.

Pool Rules

The pools look simple enough – and they can be – but they can also remind you of maths homework. Here's the simple bit: a team gets two points for a win, one for a draw, and nothing for a loss. The six pool winners, and the two best placed runners-up, qualify for the quarter-finals.

Now for the hard stuff: the mathematical permutations surrounding the winners and best runners-up at the end of the pool stage are sometimes so convoluted that they could give Albert Einstein a migraine – but it all adds to the dramatic tension! If you really want to understand how it all works, take a look at the sidebar on "Separating the Men from the Boys".

Separating the men from the boys

In the Heineken Cup, the pool winner is the club with the highest number of match points earned in its pool. The runners-up will be the two clubs from all six pools with the next highest number of points. The pool winners are ranked one to six, and the runners-up ranked seven and eight.

But if clubs are equal on points and are in the same pool, qualification is based on the two matches played between them:

✔ The club that has earned the most match points from the two matches wins outright.

✔ If equal match points were earned, the club which has scored the most tries in the two matches wins.

✔ If the number of tries is equal, the club with the best points difference from the two matches wins.

If these statistics are all equal, or the teams have not played each other previously in the pools, qualification is based on:

✔ The number of tries in all pool matches

✔ If this is equal, the aggregate points difference from all pool matches is used.

✔ If still level, the club with the fewest number of players sent off in all pool matches wins.

✔ Finally, if there's no other way to separate the teams, the decision is made by the toss of a coin (yes, really!)

The Quarter-finals

The winners of the pools (and the best runners-up) qualify for the quarter-finals. Teams ranked one to four have home advantage.

The quarter-final draw is: 1vs.8, 2vs.7, 3vs.6, 4vs.5.

The Semi-finals and Final

The winners of the four quarter-finals are entered into the draw for the semi-finals. The semi-finals are drawn by ERC, and are played at venues decided by ERC.

The two semi-final winners head off to victory, or oblivion, in the final; the final's venue is again decided by ERC.

Bring on the gladiators – famous Heineken Cup teams

Drawing teams from England, France, Scotland, Ireland and Italy means that there's a lot of rugby talent on display in the Heineken Cup. Although the teams who participate may change each year, a number of teams have indelibly made their mark on the competition.

The English

The English may have opted out of the tournament twice in its eight year history, but they still lead the table with four winners.

Bath

The side from the old Roman spa town (why doesn't some bright spark call them the Centurions?) dominated English rugby before the Heineken Cup was launched. Bath won umpteen league championships and cup titles from the mid-1980s to the mid-1990s. However, just before they suffered the decline that seems to accompany every rise, they managed a glorious last stand. Cast as the underdogs in the 1998 final against the holders, French club Brive, they left the massed ranks of French supporters in the 36,500 capacity crowd at the Stade Lescure, Bordeaux, stunned. A valiant backs-to-the-wall effort earned them a 19–18 victory as they clawed back a nine point deficit, scoring the game's only try through Jon Callard. It also prompted a mass exodus of Brive fans before the final whistle.

Leicester Tigers

The "Toygurs" (that's what a Leicester accent does to big cats) have the best record in the tournament. Leicester made European club rugby history on

25 May 2002, when they made the first successful defence of the Heineken Cup title. Their 15–9 victory over Munster in front of a record 74,000 crowd at the Millennium Stadium, Cardiff, made them the first team to not only win back-to-back finals, but also the first to lift the trophy twice. The previous year they became champions after beating Stade Francais in a thriller in front of a 44,000 sell-out crowd at the Parc des Princes in Paris. The result was in the balance until the closing minutes, when Austin Healey made a searing break to send Leon Lloyd sprinting clear for his second try. However, they have not had things all their own way. In their first final (in 1997), they were blitzed by France's Brive, and in 2003 Munster gained sweet revenge, travelling to Leicester's Welford Road fortress to deliver a quarter-final knockout.

Northampton Saints

The Saints went marching in, winning the club's one and only major trophy, when they beat Munster in 2000 in a final low on points but long on nail-biting tension. Played in front of 64,400 at Twickenham, Munster may have scored the only try through flanker David Wallace, but the hero of the hour was unquestionably Pat Lam, Northampton's Samoan captain and no.8. Lam took the field with a shoulder so badly damaged that he should not have played, yet he was like a man possessed. Suitably inspired, his side gave Paul Grayson sufficient territorial advantage to land three penalties for a 9–8 win. As he received the trophy, Lam's injury meant that he had to enlist the help of another mighty Saints forward, Tim Rodber, to raise it aloft.

The French

France produced the first two winners, but then had five years in the doldrums before winning again through Toulouse.

Brive

They are known as Brive "Le Gaillard", or Brive "The Brave", because the small town in the Correze valley has historically been a centre of national resistance when France has been invaded. However, it was Brive who did the invading in 1997, by hammering Leicester 28–9 at Cardiff Arms Park to win the Heineken Cup final with breathtaking pace, power and precision. After coming unstuck the following season against Bath their fortunes dipped, and they were later relegated to the French second division before returning to the top tier in 2003.

Stade Francais

After lying dormant for half a century, the Parisian side sprang to life thanks to an injection of cash from Max Guazzini, a telecommunications millionaire. Having signed half the French national side, Stade were pipped to the post by Leicester in 2001. They are not short of resources, talent or ambition and are likely to make further bids for the European crown.

A nice tie

In the event of a tie at full-time in the knockout stages of the Heineken Cup, extra time of 20 minutes is played (10 minutes each way).

If the result is still not resolved by the end of extra time, the winner is declared as the club which has scored the most tries in the match, including any extra time tries. If the number of tries scored is equal, a place-kicking competition is used to determine the winner (place kicks are like penalty kicks).

Toulouse

In France they call Toulouse the capital of rugby, and with good reason. Toulouse are the most successful club in the French game by a country mile, and style is as important to them as it is to Pierre Cardin. For the fans of "Stade Toulousain" winning is not enough – it has to be done with flair. Toulouse were the winners of the first Heineken Cup, beating Cardiff 21–18 in the inaugural tournament in 1996 at Cardiff Arms Park in the only final to go to extra time. It was one of two years in which English clubs did not play. In 2003 they repeated the feat, beating fellow French side Perpignan 22–17 in Dublin, and sending Leicester a message that anything they can do, Toulouse can match.

The Irish

The Irish have had the Cup in their clutches just once, when Ulster defied the odds, although Munster have twice come close.

Munster

It takes more than a few sledgehammer blows to break the hearts of Munstermen. They have lost two finals (2000 and 2002) by slender margins, and two semi-finals in similar manner, but still they keep coming. They may not be the most gifted side, but they are among the best organised and hard-working, and at their Thomond Park stronghold in Limerick (scene of their legendary victory over the All Blacks) they are virtually unbeatable. Mind you, the passion of their army of travelling fans could make Munster feel at home in Timbuktu.

Ulster

The men whose jerseys are emblazoned by the Red Hand of Ulster got their clutches on the big prize by beating the French side Colomiers 21–6 in Dublin in 1999. With the English clubs boycotting the tournament due to rugby politics, Ulster had an easier passage than might otherwise have been the case.

The Northern Irishmen made the most of it with fullback Simon Mason kicking six penalties as Colomiers froze.

The Welsh

The Welsh clubs are yet to win the big prize, although they will hope for better things now the talent has been centred in amalgamated sides.

Cardiff Blues

The sleeping giant of Welsh rugby has been snoring loudly since losing to Toulouse in the inaugural 1996 final, and the next season losing to Brive in the semi-finals. They have too much pedigree and history to slumber forever. Time to wake up, boys!

Llanelli Scarlets

The Scarlets, as Llanelli are known, have kept the Welsh flag flying in Europe in difficult times. The Welsh game has been slow to streamline itself to the demands of professionalism, but Llanelli have adapted well, and their Stradey Park home is no place for faint-hearted visitors.

Llanelli have suffered two semi-final defeats to last-gasp kicks by Northampton (2000) and Leicester (2002), with both English sides going on to win the final. The Scarlets are always likely to be in the shaker.

The Scots

In the Heineken Cup, Scottish clubs are not exactly tartan terrors. Over the past seven years, Scottish rugby has been represented in the Heineken Cup by two provincial sides, Edinburgh and Glasgow, and while not pushovers, neither side has so far reached the knockout stages. There are hopes that the introduction in 2003 of a third province in the traditional home of the Scottish game, The Borders, will lead to a sharpened competitive edge.

The Italians

The Italians are the latest to take a seat at the European game's top table, and although they are still on the antipasti – like the Scots, they have yet to get to the main course of the knockout stages – the Italian clubs are hungry to improve. Despite Italy being the poor relations of the Six Nations, neither Viadana or Amatori & Calvisano, their two sides in the 2003 tournament, were on the receiving end of cricket scores, while Viadana beat Neath (Wales) and Bourgoin (France) in the Pool round the previous year.

The European Challenge Cup and Shield – It's All About Aspiration

Don't write it off because it's the catch-all tournament for sides which fail to qualify for the Heineken Cup. Given the strength of English and French domestic competitions, there are usually some tasty teams who are rebuilding and looking to make a statement by progressing in this competition. As an added bonus, this competition splits into two – the Challenge Cup and the Shield – so rugby fans get twice the amount of excitement.

A cup on the up

This may be Europe's second-tier competition, but in 2002 it came of age, because ERC introduced a huge incentive by awarding the Challenge Cup winners a place in the following season's Heineken Cup. In 2003 the organisers improved it further by introducing a straight knockout draw for the 32 teams (nine French, seven Italian, six English, four Welsh, two Spanish, two Romanian, one Irish, and one Scottish), rather than the previously used pools, which frequently resulted in weaker teams being on the end of multiple drubbings.

The format

The knockout system that was introduced in 2003 has a dual benefit. On one hand it provides the less powerful, less wealthy sides (such as those from Spain and Romania) with a chance to measure their progress against the strong. It allows them to weigh their aspirations and gauge what they need to do to improve. On the other, it quickly sets like-against-like in terms of standards:

- In the first round, 16 seeded teams face 16 unseeded teams on a home-and-away basis.

- In the second round, the competition splits into two parts. The winners (on aggregate, and, if tied, on tries scored) advance into the last 16 of the Challenge Cup, while the losers go into the last 16 of the Shield.

The Challenge Cup and the Shield then continue as separate tournaments on a knockout basis, with each round home and away, from 16 to quarter-finals, and semi-finals. The home-and-away element comes to an end with the final, which is a single match played at a neutral venue.

The Zurich Premiership – England's Finest

If successful sport is all about competition, then the English Premiership is pressing the right buttons for success. The Premiership currently consists of 12 teams, and is considered to be one of the toughest leagues in world rugby.

With increasingly close and unpredictable results due to well-matched teams, crowds have grown rapidly. There was a 40 per cent overall increase in the three years from 2000 to 2003, and in the 2002–2003 season over a million people watched Premiership matches live. In that season there were also 37 sell-outs, and Sky Sports, the competition's main broadcaster, screened 28 games live (you can read more about televised rugby in Chapter 16).

At the time of writing, Premiership teams field players from 25 different countries, proving that the league has admirers from both near and far. Certainly, few competitions are as gruelling. For a number of years, the club at the top of the league table after all of the teams has played their 22 games were champions. That changed in 2003 when a play-off system was introduced, culminating in a winner-take-all Premiership final.

The format

All Premiership clubs have a schedule of 22 matches. They play each of the other 11 Premiership teams both home and away, starting in late August and finishing in early May. 4 points are awarded for a win, 2 for a draw, and 0 for losing.

There is also 1 bonus point for a team that that loses by 7 match points or less, and a further 1 bonus point for a team that scores four tries or more in a match – so a losing side could still come away with a maximum 2 points.

The new play-off system means that the club that finishes top of the league qualifies automatically for the Premiership final. The second and third clubs play a semi-final to decide the other finalist – with home advantage going to second-placed club. The winners of the Premiership final at the end of May are the Premiership champions.

The team with the competition's worst record is relegated at the end of the season, and replaced by the winner of the league directly beneath the Premiership (see the section "One Man's Ceiling is Another Man's Floor" for more on relegation).

To Play-Off, Or not to Play-off, That is the Question...

Opinion is divided on whether play-offs are the right way to determine a championship.

Many fans believe that a side that wins the league is worthy of winning the championship outright for its consistency throughout the season. They believe that this is undermined if a johnny-come-lately with an inferior record over the 22-match season beats the top team to the title in a one-off game. Others take the view that a champion side is one that is not only consistent, but can also rise to the big occasion – as London Wasps did in thrashing Premiership leaders Gloucester 39–3 in the inaugural final to become the 2003 English champions.

One Man's Ceiling is Another Man's Floor

Promotion and relegation remains a vexed issue, with some of the clubs within Premier Rugby – the umbrella organisation responsible for the management and promotion of the 12 elite clubs in England – taking the view that it makes professional rugby non-viable economically.

This view does not have popular support. The broad base of opinion in the English game is that there must be the opportunity for aspiring clubs in the semi-professional National Division One, and below that, to progress to the highest level. At the moment, the Rugby Football Union (RFU), which is the governing body of English rugby, is committed to that principle. In 2003 it was one-up, one-down, with the club that finished bottom of the Premiership, Bristol Shoguns, and the winners of National Division One, Rotherham, changing places.

Nor is it possible to deny the sheer sporting theatre of relegation battles. The biggest Premiership attendance so far was recorded by Bristol Shoguns for their relegation showdown against local rivals Bath which attracted almost 21,000 to Ashton Gate in May 2003.

Wild on Europe

The first three teams in the Zurich Premiership – the champions, the runners-up, and the beaten semi-finalists – qualify automatically for the Heineken Cup (see earlier in this chapter for details about this competition). The next four teams play off in the Zurich Wildcard for the fourth English Premiership slot in the Heineken Cup. The other two places go to the winners of the European Challenge Cup (again, see earlier in this chapter) and the Powergen Cup (you can read about this competition later in this chapter, in "Everyone's Up for the Cup!").

It's a banker

You might ask what the pinnacle of English club rugby has to do with a Swiss city famous for its bankers. The answer? The English Premiership has been sponsored by the financial services giant, Zurich, since 2000, and in 2003 the company (which, surprise, surprise, does actually have a Swiss headquarters in the city it's named after) renewed its backing for a further three years.

The Premiership clubs

Here are the sides that will do battle for the Zurich Premiership to determine which club is the champion of England in the 2004 season.

Bath

Bath have won six Premiership titles, making them the most successful side in English league rugby alongside Leicester. However, their last title was in 1996, and in 2002 and 2003 they came within a whisker of relegation.

Private Godfrey of *Dad's Army* was once the club chairman, and recently they've been playing like him. Things should improve.

Gloucester

Way out in front in league points in 2003 (15 clear), the "Cherry and Whites" were easily the most consistent side in the Premiership. This is a real rugby town with a strong support base, especially those in the hardcore fans in The Shed, who invariably give the opposition the benefit of their west-country wisdom, when they visit Gloucester's Kingsholm ground.

Leeds Tykes

The Tykes have consolidated their place in the Premiership after being granted a stay of execution when they finished last in 2002. They were not relegated because Rotherham, who had won promotion, failed to meet stadium criteria. In 2003 they finished mid-table.

Leicester Tigers

With six Premiership titles to their name – including four in succession from 1999 to 2002 – the Tigers have been the team to beat. In 2003 they stumbled, finishing in mid-table, but with stars like Martin Johnson and Neil Back they remain the best supported side in the country.

London Irish

The Exiles have an Irish flavour to them – particularly when celebrating St Patrick's Day at their Madejski Stadium home in Reading – but their cosmopolitan side has been drawn from all over the shop, especially the southern hemisphere. They did well in 2002, but a limited game plan was laid bare in 2003 and their fight to avoid relegation went to the final game.

London Wasps

Wasps moved from one football stadium to another in 2003 setting up in High Wycombe after leaving Loftus Road in west London. The move to the Thames Valley did them no harm, as they finished second in the league. Despite an itinerant history since professionalism (they have had three grounds in six years) they have won the Premiership twice (1990 and 1997).

NEC Harlequins

"The Quins", as they are known, had a reputation as the toffs of the English game in the amateur era. Their quartered shirts – including the unusual colours chocolate and magenta – are amongst the top-selling rugby brands, but on the field they have not been among the market leaders in the professional game.

However, a mid-table finish in 2003 indicates they might be getting their act together at The Stoop, which nestles in the shadow of Twickenham.

Newcastle Falcons

A bastion of the game in Geordie-land, the Falcons won the Premiership title in 1998. Since then the exciting young side coached by former England fly-half Rob Andrew, has failed to fulfil its potential.

Northampton Saints

The Saints have earned the reputation for being under-achievers. It probably has something to do with the fact that, despite a fine custom-built stadium at Franklin's Gardens (capacity 12,500), the trophy cabinet has been bare since 2000 when they won the Heineken Cup.

Saracens

Saracens have built a loyal fan base despite being based at Vicarage Road, the home of Watford Football Club. However, they have found it harder to hang on to their players than their fans. Saracens have discovered the hard way that big-name signings does not necessarily mean big team spirit, and they have not troubled the leaders in recent seasons.

Sale Sharks

One of the Premiership success stories. They moved in 2003 from their humble Heywood Road ground to Edgeley Park, which they purchased from Stockport County Football Club. The Sharks have bought wisely to strengthen their squad, and they could be on their way to becoming a power in the Premiership.

Rotherham

The battlers from South Yorkshire won the National Division One title twice in succession, but were denied promotion in 2002 in controversial circumstances: they were deemed to have failed stadium requirements for the Premiership. In 2003 they won again, and this time they were not to be denied, going up to replace Bristol Shoguns who were relegated.

The Celtic League – The Gathering of the Clans

This competition was launched by the Celtic unions in the summer of 2001 to give teams from Wales, Ireland and Scotland a competitive structure to rival the Zurich Premiership. It has had a couple of different formats, but is now played on a 22-game basis with all 12 participating teams appearing in one league. The team allocation is four teams from Ireland, three from Scotland, and five from Wales, following the restructuring of the professional game in Wales on a regional basis in 2003.

The format

A conventional league played home and away from September to May, with the team at the top after 22 games declared champions. The Welsh, Scots and Irish teams are all professional and are effectively regional franchises, as with the southern hemisphere's Super 12. There is no promotion or relegation into this tier in the respective countries that participate.

Celtic League competitors

The Celtic League format has been developed to give professional sides in Wales, Scotland and Ireland a competition to rival the English Premiership.

The Irish

It's still early days in the history of the Celtic League, but so far, the Irish clubs have stolen a march on their opponents.

- **Munster:** Reigning champions of the Celtic League, and a handful home or away.

- **Leinster Lions:** Sparked by brilliant centre Brian O'Driscoll, the Dublin-based side are a growing force.

- **Ulster:** Hard to beat at their home ground of Ravenhill, but not the greatest travellers.

- **Connacht:** The poor men of Irish rugby, maybe, but not poor in spirit.

The Scots

Scottish rugby is desperately in need of a boost, and this competition could provide it.

- **Borders:** A newly-formed side from the Scottish rugby heartland with a mission to restore a great tradition.

- **Edinburgh Rugby:** Given the number of international players in their ranks, Edinburgh have seriously underperformed in the Celtic League.

- **Glasgow Rugby:** Better known as a football city, and disappointing for their rugby so far.

The Welsh

The five Welsh regional franchises are newly formed at the time of writing, so there is no track record to speak of. The teams that have a clean slate to write their own records on are:

- **Celtic Warriors:** the Bridgend/Pontypridd Region

- **Cardiff Blues:** the Cardiff Region

- **Gwent Dragons:** the Ebbw Vale/Newport Region

- **Llanelli Scarlets:** the Llanelli Region

- **Neath/Swansea Ospreys:** the Neath/Swansea Region

Everyone's up for the Cup!

Nothing matches the thrills and spills of sudden death contests, and there is a strong tradition of knockout cup competitions in England, Wales, Scotland and Ireland, with the senior English and Welsh Cups dating back to 1972. The

English Cup is thriving under the sponsorship of Powergen, and the introduction of the Celtic Cup (in 2003) promises to keep knockout rugby high on the agenda in the rest of the British Isles.

The Powergen Cup

Since the early 1990s the cup final has frequently filled Twickenham to its 75,000 capacity, with Bath unrivalled as a cup side after winning it 10 times between 1984 and 1996. The competition starts with 44 teams drawn from the leagues below the Premiership in Round 1, and these are whittled down to four non-Premiership clubs by the end of Round 5. They go into the draw for Round 6, when the 12 Premiership big boys join in. Just as in the previous rounds there is a draw for the quarter-finals and semi-finals, with the first out of the hat getting home advantage. The final is played at Twickenham, with the Powergen Cup winners not only playing for glory, but qualifying for the Heineken Cup.

The Celtic Cup

The format pitches the bottom eight clubs from the previous year's Celtic League against each other. The four winners go into a quarter-final draw with the four semi-finalists from the previous year, and then to semi-finals and final (at a venue decided by the Celtic League).

Chapter 15

The Domestic Scene

*L*ike most sporting codes, the upper echelons of rugby wouldn't and couldn't exist without the help and support of the grass-roots, the lower echelons where promising young players are encouraged and helped to progress as far as their talents will take them.

In this chapter, we explain how the amateur club system works, producing the players that eventually represent their country on the world stage. Club rugby in England, Wales, Scotland, and Ireland has many levels. Those who don't have the time, or perhaps the dedication, to pursue the game seriously and become an international star, can still enjoy a competitive game of rugby. Clubs are also where youngsters and women receive their initial education in the ways of the game.

Enjoying Rugby at Every Level

Getting started in rugby is easy, especially if you live in a town or city, although in the British Isles the chances are that you will never be more than a few miles from your nearest rugby club. Training opportunities abound, and, as you become more proficient in the game, you can move up to the next level to continue developing your talents. Wherever you live in England, Wales, Scotland, Ireland, or Northern Ireland, you will almost always be near to a big club or provincial side with a dedicated following.

In most parts of the British Isles you will have the opportunity to play, or support, rugby at a level that suits you. You can play onwards and upwards through the club structure if you have the requisite ability; you can play at a more relaxed social level and, if you are female, you can play rugby in a women's team.

Rugby for Kids

While international and elite club rugby, such as the Zurich Premiership and Heineken Cup, may get all the media exposure, as well as the big crowds and a lot of the money, they owe their very existence to the grass-roots club system. It is the solid base on which a strong, vibrant, rich pyramid is built.

Nearly all the great players have relied on the grass-roots club system to get started – and to give them the basic skills, the experience, and the confidence to make their names.

Easy does it – a graded approach to physical contact

In England the RFU has introduced a graded process to introducing young children to the rugby, which stipulates that in the early stages it is a non-contact sport.

At the ages of 6 and 7 it is essentially a non-tackling, running, handling game of tag rugby. Initially it is played seven-a-side, and then nine-a-side, and there is no kicking.

Then, at Under 9 level, tackling is introduced, as is a three-man scrum. At Under 11 level, the team numbers increase to 11, with 5 forwards and 6 backs, and kicking is introduced for the first time.

At Under 14 level teams increase to 15-a-side, and play full contact rugby. This continues up to Colts level (ages 17–19), although, for safety reasons, there is an important difference between age grade and adult rugby: in age grade rugby the scrum can never move more than 1.5m either way.

This system is replicated, with some variations, in the rest of the British Isles.

Getting started in Mini or Age Grade rugby

Although some schools play rugby at both a social and competitive level (there are 3,020 affiliated to the RFU), many others don't.

So, the first contact that many aspiring rugby players make is with a club. However, school sports teachers can also be a useful source of information, and whether or not the school plays the game, they can usually tell you where your nearest local rugby club is.

For those who are really motivated there is nothing to stop a youngster from playing for both his school and a club. Many of the great players in the British Isles started that way. One of rugby union's great advantages is that it is well organised at Mini and Age Grade level. Over the decades, rugby has been able to create a strong network with the help of the national unions in England, Wales, Scotland and Ireland, ensuring that if youngsters want to play rugby, a club or organisation will be close at hand.

Children can start playing from around the age of 6 – although the age at which they start depends a great deal on just how keen they are, and how enthusiastic their parents are to spend their Saturday or Sunday mornings on a wet and windy touchline!

Because rugby is a winter sport in the British Isles, the season for Mini and Age Grade rugby usually starts around September and continues until May.

Making the transition from Mini and Age Group rugby to Colts

From Mini and Age Group rugby (the latter going up on a yearly basis to age 18), the next step is joining a Colts team. As under-19s, they will be closely watched by the senior coaches at the club, and they generally have the advantage of having coaching staff of their own who have had considerable experience.

Signing up with a grass-roots club

Grass-roots clubs advertise for prospective players through local newspapers, schools or websites around August each year, giving details of practice days.

At these practices the aspiring player (or his parents) will give his personal details, such as address, age and playing level. The grass-roots club will provide information about where and when it trains, when it plays its matches or tournaments, and what equipment is required for the season.

Parents keen to try their hand at coaching, or helping around the club in other ways, can also sign up at the start of the season. Any grass-roots club worth its salt is sure to greet you with open arms, because, as self-help societies, they are usually on the look out for new helpers as well as new players. (To find out more about coaching, turn to Chapter 11).

All the grass-roots clubs in the British Isles are affiliated to one of the national unions, so, if you want to find out who plays in your area, your first point of contact should be the national union. Most clubs can be accessed on the Internet through the listings on the national union Web sites.

Easing into training

When players join a grass-roots club, they are invited to training sessions, which are generally held on weekday evenings. At the first few training sessions the coaches determine whether the players are ready to actually play the game, and at what level they should play. Factors such as age, weight and skill level are taken into account.

The way of the dragon

Play the Game was created in 1996, by the Dragons Rugby Trust, which is the part of the Welsh Rugby Union dedicated to age grade rugby. *Play the Game* is an educational package to support the teaching of rugby within the national schools curriculum for 7–14 year olds.

Play the Game was developed by a team of teachers, curriculum specialists and WRU coaching experts, and was designed to meet the needs of non-specialist teachers in primary schools and those of rugby coaches in secondary schools and kids sections at grass-roots rugby clubs.

Its teacher friendly format of bi-lingual, weather-proof, step-by-step illustrated lesson cards, supporting video and skill based activity cards for pupils, was widely acclaimed throughout Wales and further afield.

Play the Game has subsequently been adopted by the International Rugby Board to support the development of the game worldwide. The Board commissioned the Dragons Rugby Trust to adapt, translate and produce it in ten languages. Multiple copies have since been distributed to all 93 IRB member countries.

An A5 pocket version is available from the WRU (Appendix C has their contact details) and is aimed at players of all ages who wish to develop and measure their individual and team skills. It is a user-friendly aid for teachers, coaches and parents to support them in doing so.

At training sessions, coaches teach the aspirants the basics of the game. It is significant that the laws that apply in Mini rugby and at the lower age group levels are different to the laws for the senior levels of the game (for players aged 18 and upwards). These modified laws have a greater emphasis on safety, and focus on the amount of force used in tackles and scrums. For example, the amount of tackling in a Mini rugby game can be restricted so that newcomers can learn the basics, in particular running with and catching the ball, without fear of getting hurt. Youngsters, such as 6-year-olds, tend to retain their enthusiasm for the game when they know they are unlikely to get injured. Generally, a youngster should not be pushed too hard, or too quickly. It is important that children's coaches recognise the importance of giving youngsters plenty of time to decide whether rugby is the sport for them.

Grass-roots cup competitions

The introduction of Intermediate and Junior Vase cup competitions for grass-roots clubs alongside the elite Powergen Cup (see Chapter 14 to find out more about this competition) and has brought about a community of competition within the English game which is virtually unrivalled. The Powergen Cup final sees not only two elite clubs (invariably from the Premiership) play for the main prize but it allows clubs throughout England to compete in three other grades of competition:

- ✔ The Powergen Junior Vase final for grass-roots teams
- ✔ The Powergen Intermediate Cup final for middle tier grass-roots clubs
- ✔ The Powergen Shield for the National Division sides (professional and semi-pro) who have fallen in the sixth round of the Powergen Cup.

The coming together on cup final day at Twickenham gives players from every level and region the chance to compete on the hallowed turf. The competitions involve hundreds of clubs battling it out on pitches up and down the country, in the hope of competing in the showpiece final. In 2003 it was estimated that more than 23,000 players took part in the cup competitions, bringing about a genuine equality of opportunity.

The County Championship

Forty years ago the County Championship attracted the best players in England, but today it is very much a grass-roots tournament. It is played mainly by amateurs and a few semi-pros with strong county allegiances, and starts in group stages before progressing to a knock-out format, with the final played at Twickenham.

At one time this was the most prestigious competition in English rugby – and, if Cornwall make it to the final, you can still bank on 30,000 Cornishmen turning up at Twickenham – but the role of county rugby has changed.

Now, instead of being a showcase for the top rugby talent in the country, it has been supplanted by the elite club leagues (see Chapter 14). However, a strong county identity remains among the grass-roots clubs of areas such as Lancashire, Gloucestershire, Cornwall, Yorkshire and Cheshire, and it is keenly contested.

Rugby for Adults

Nearly all clubs play in a league – although there are still a few clubs who only play recreational friendlies – and these are split into four major regions in England – North, Midlands, South-West and London and South-East. These regions can run anything up to 34 leagues (as is the case in the area with the highest population, London and South-East). If you're good at the game, there's always a chance that you'll end up playing at one of the top levels:

- ✔ **National Division Teams.** The sides in the four leagues below the Zurich Premiership are largely semi-professional, but very few of the players at this level are likely to be selected to play international rugby.

- ✔ **Test or International Rugby.** Playing for your country is the absolute pinnacle of a rugby player's career, but remember that most stars of the game began their careers at a grass-roots club.

But of course, there's absolutely nothing to stop you playing and enjoying rugby at a much lower level than at these heady heights (we tell you about the Community Game in the next section).

Playing club rugby

In England, club rugby is called the *Community Game*. This title applies to the rank and file of clubs below the elite tier of clubs, and there is unlikely to be any significant payment for playing. A similar distinction is made in Wales, Scotland and Ireland.

In England, which has the largest number of rugby players in the world – an estimated 634,000 players at all levels – the elite level incorporates the Zurich Premiership and then National Divisions 1, 2 and 3 North and 3 South. That elite level accounts for just over 40 out of 1,800 clubs, so you don't need to be

Einstein to work out that the Community Game accounts for the vast majority of English players, with some clubs, particularly those in densely populated traditional rugby areas, fielding several teams from 1st XV down to fourths and fifths, as well as veterans sides.

Similar structures exist in Wales, Scotland and Ireland. Below the provinces or regional teams in the Celtic League (see Chapter 14), a series of club leagues feed into one another. In Wales there are 17 leagues from Division 1 to Division 7, and in Scotland the BT-sponsored league structure is topped by a Premier League. In Ireland there are nationwide AIB Divisions 1, 2, and 3, and below that grass-roots club leagues in each province.

Joining your local club

So, you're thinking of joining a rugby club? Whether you want to play rugby, or want to support your local club from the sidelines, an exciting experience awaits you.

To become acquainted with the local league structure, scour the local newspapers during the season and learn the names of the leading clubs. Information on local teams can usually be found on the sports pages of the local press, especially on a Monday when the results of the weekend's games are published. Club rugby is alive and well throughout the British Isles, so you shouldn't have to search too hard to find an outfit that suits you.

Whether you want to join a club at playing, coaching or administrative level – or just burn a few burgers on the barbecue on match day – don't hesitate to contact them. The telephone numbers of rugby clubs are easy to find, either through the Internet, or in the good old-fashioned phone book. (Appendix C lists key organisations in British and Irish rugby.)

A good way to introduce yourself to a club and get to meet the members is to offer to help out at Mini and Age Grade rugby level, either by coaching (if you are qualified) or by doing some of the myriad tasks needed to get them organised.

Becoming a club player

If you are an aspiring player, all rugby clubs have secretaries and on the ground organisers who can tell you when and where training sessions are held, and which team official you need to contact.

Get in contact with the club you want to join early in the summer, so that you find out as soon as possible when and where pre-season training starts. Grass-roots clubs usually start getting themselves organised in late June or early July. Pre-season training gets under way before August so that coaches and team managers can work out the numbers of players available for the season, and decide in which teams to select the various players.

The actual playing season starts around the beginning of September. If you are not quite ready for the level of rugby played at the club you have selected, they can usually put you in touch with another club which may be more your speed.

Soaking up the atmosphere as a social member

A social membership, which usually involves a small annual subscription, enables you to enter the club, use its bar and other facilities, and become involved in its various activities.

If you are passionate about rugby, social membership of a rugby club gives you the opportunity to swap stories at the bar with those of similar mind. You will often find that those propping up the bar are also the life and soul of the club in that they are the unpaid secretaries, sponge-men, workers, and social organisers who keep their club going. They are from that special tribe known irreverently by players as "Alickadoos", but without them everyone knows that club rugby would grind to a halt.

Club Rugby is played at a number of levels: at the top end, in National Leagues 1, 2 and 3 North and South, it is highly competitive, and clubs with wealthy backers may be able to afford professional or semi-professional squads. However, the further down the leagues you go, and the smaller the resources, the less competitive the game becomes. It is these lower leagues that attract players who haven't the time or energy to train several times a week, or who don't want to spend most of their Saturdays getting psyched up for the big match. That's not to say that the rugby is not competitive – as a hard, physical contact sport, rugby can never be anything less than competitive – but it means that winning is not the be all and end all, and that the game has a greater social touch. Most members of clubs at the bottom end of the leagues probably train only one night a week, and sometimes the clubhouse could be the bar of the local pub.

However, they are still likely to rely heavily on a strong sense of identity and club spirit. Clubs rely on people volunteering their time and their administrative qualities, and it is these stalwarts of the amateur game who enable hundreds of matches to be played each weekend.

Living the dream

One recent story that illustrates just how strong the link between club rugby and the elite international and Premiership tier remains, is that of the Sale Sharks winger Mark Cueto. Cueto's story shows just how far a player can progress from club rugby in a very short time. When Cueto ran out in front of 65,000 fans at Twickenham to take his place on the England right-wing against the Barbarians at the end of the 2003 season, he did so having left his Cheshire club, Altrincham Kersal, who play in North 2 West, only two years previously. The breathtaking progress made by Cueto, 23, stands as a beacon of hope not only to all aspiring youngsters at grass-roots clubs, but also to any newcomer to the game.

Coaches who are teaching youngsters with little or no rugby background, take note: Cueto didn't play any rugby from the ages of 8 to 17, he played no national Age Group rugby, and he didn't even dream of getting a sniff of an England shirt during his time at Stelfox Avenue, Timperley, the home of Altrincham Kersal.

However, Cueto got the chance because of the remarkable way in which he made up for lost time. In the 2002 season he finished as the Zurich Premiership's top try scorer, and his reputation as arguably its deadliest finisher was enhanced when he was again among the top try scorers in 2003.

Cueto got the rugby bug after being asked to play in a friendly game in his final school year at St Thomas More, Crewe. As a result, he headed for his nearest union club, in his case Altrincham Kersal. Then, having embarked on a degree in sports science at Crewe and Alsager College, his rugby career took off, when, in his third season at Kersal, Sale invited him to play midweek for their second team, the Jets.

Cueto's story is not as rare as you might imagine, and it clearly illustrates, that even in these days of academies and talent scouts, that you can still discover stacks of talent in club rugby.

Women's Rugby

Women's rugby has become one of the fastest growing female sports in the British Isles since it started in the 1980s. In England alone there are now some 6,500 players in 300 teams affiliated to the RFUW (Rugby Football Union for Women) for players aged 16 and upwards.

There is a thriving domestic championship comprising Premier Divisions 1 and 2 at the elite end, as well as a National Women's Cup competition. Many of the leading women's teams, like Saracens, Wasps and Clifton, are affiliated to men's clubs, and England field one of the world's best national women's sides.

England reached the World Cup final in 2002, losing to New Zealand, but then bounced back to win a Six Nations Grand Slam the following season. With that sort of competitive edge, the women's game has not lacked publicity, and, as a result, there has been a significant take-up of the sport among women students in particular.

Like its men's counterpart, the leagues below elite level in women's rugby are structured along regional lines (North, Midlands, South West, London and South East).

The Women's Rugby Football Union is affiliated to the RFU, and the women's game got belated recognition when, in 2003, the England women played their first international at Twickenham, against France, as a curtain-raiser to the Six Nations game between England and France.

There are those who believe that the women's game is a purer version of rugby than its men's counterpart. Unlike men, women tend to focus on playing the ball more than trying to knock ten bells out of their opponent.

The game in Wales has also got a firm foothold, although in Scotland and Ireland it has not yet achieved the same exposure or popularity.

Local Clubs with National Ambitions

There's no shortage of clubs throughout the country who are striving to reach the top and establish themselves among the professional elite. Some have wealthy backers, some have a strong asset-base in terms of grounds, but all of them have ambition.

London and the South-East

There are more people playing club rugby in this part of England than any other, and there are plenty of aspiring clubs out there. Here are some of the notable ones.

Rosslyn Park

Once one of England's top clubs, "The Park" refused to take the pay-for-play route at the start of professionalism and tumbled down the leagues. Having produced English rugby legends over the decades of the calibre as Prince Obolensky, Andy Ripley and Paul Ackford, they are now clawing their way back up the leagues. In 2003 they won National 3 South, winning 24 out of 26 games. The Park prides itself on being an open, friendly club but they still steadfastly refuse to pay players. The club insists that their ethos is a major attraction because it embraces the spirit of the amateur era where people played for the sake of the sport and the friendship it engendered.

The clubhouse at Priory Lane in Roehampton is pretty unpretentious despite housing club history books that stretch back to 1879, the year in which it was founded. However, Rosslyn Park are not stuck in the past in all respects and their women's side, the Slingbacks, are going great guns.

Esher

A relative newcomer on the block, Esher have earned their place in National 2. They're a side committed to a stylish running game under the guidance of coach Hugh McHardy, a former Harlequins and Scotland B scrum-half. The irrepressible McHardy has also recruited one of England's most renowned forwards of recent years to coach his pack, in the shape of Peter Winterbottom.

Founded in 1923, the Surrey club have just built a new clubhouse and McHardy is very much an all-for-one, and one-for-all type of manager. It is this selfless approach and his lack of tolerance for prima donnas, that has seen the club shoot up the rankings.

Blackheath

Having been among the English elite since its formation in 1858 – it claims to be the first rugby club ever founded – "The Club" has fallen a long way since the game went professional in the 1996 season. Successive relegations has left it clinging on for dear life to remain among England's top 40 clubs.

Thankfully, the decline has been halted and this famous outfit has stabilised sufficiently to hope for better things. The Rectory Field remains one of the most famous grounds in the game for historic reasons. It has been played on since 1883, and before that matches were played on the nearby heath from which the club takes its name. Supporters still sink a pint or two of bitter at the Princess of Wales pub, which acted as the original clubhouse.

Worthing

The Sussex club is often held up as a prototype of how to run a successful rugby club. Worthing field five adult teams, an academy side, a women's team and 12 Age Group and Mini rugby sides from under 18 downwards.

The Rugby Park at Roundstone Lane, also doubles as a facility for conferences, weddings and other social events, boosting the club's turnover to £400,000 per annum. Worthing is synonymous throughout both senior and club rugby for its Mini rugby and Age Group sections and also for organising the Worthing Festival, a yearly event in April which attracts 1,500 young players from all over the country.

Worthing can boast justifiably that many of England's current stars have trodden the turf of its six pitches as Mini rugby players. These include the likes of Jonny Wilkinson and Kyran Bracken.

The South West

Always a traditional rugby bastion, competitive rugby is alive and well in the West country.

Penzance and Newlyn

"The Pirates", as they are known, are English rugby's most westerly National League club, and they are doing their best to return Cornish rugby to its former glories of the 1950s and 1960s.

Penzance and Newlyn won National 2 in 2003, making it their fifth promotion in eight seasons – so it looks as if their goal is within sight. They deserve it, not least because of the thousands of miles they have had to travel in pursuit of their holy grail. Cornishmen have started to share the vision of the club's millionaire backer Ricky Evans (he is the UK's biggest importer of overseas green vegetables!) with crowds of 1,600 regularly attending games at the Mennaye Field.

Exeter Chiefs

A top three finish in 2003 in National 1 indicates that not only are Exeter's sights set on the Premiership, but they have the desire to match their ambition. All their players have jobs outside rugby, but with the flexibility for them to train in a professional manner.

At the time of writing, the Devon club were about to build a Premiership specification 10,000-seater stadium and conference centre on a 21acre site in Devon at Junction 30 off the M5. This is a joint venture with the construction firm, Mowlem, who have permission for a housing project at the club's old County Ground near Exeter city centre. Now that's what we call building for the future.

The Midlands and the North

Unheralded they may be, but the clubs north of Watford Gap know how to blow their own fanfare.

Nuneaton

Chris Tarbuck's first training session as the newly appointed coach in 2000 drew just seven players to Nuneaton's Liberty Way ground. Three years later Nuneaton deservedly gained promotion to National 2 after the Warwickshire club won National 3 North, and, it goes without saying, Tarbuck's training sessions are now well attended. The club has a strong Colts section, which has resulted in many of its first team squad being home grown.

Orrell

This club, whose Edgehall Road ground was once described as "a lay-by off the M6", have had their ups and downs since forcing their way into the top tier during the 1990s. However, despite slipping into National 1 since then, the support of Dave Whelan, a multimillionaire sports retailer has given this village side, founded in 1927, hope of a revival.

Orrell beat Exeter Chiefs 26–20 in an ebb-and-flow Powergen Shield final at Twickenham in 2003, to indicate that the union code is alive and well in the rugby league heartland around Wigan. Orrell had been among the big boys, and, despite their humble beginnings, they want to get there again. In the short term, much will depend on whether Whelan continues to back them.

Worcester

After being relegated to North Midlands 1 in 1988 Worcester began their rise and rise, achieving what amounted to seven promotions in 10 seasons to their current position as almost perpetual promotion candidates in National 1.

The overhaul of the club was completed, when, helped by local businessman Cecil Duckworth and a £1.3m National Lottery grant, they invested £5m in making their Sixways ground one of the best in the country. Although the capacity is currently 5,300, there are plans to double this if Worcester Warriors gain the promotion to the Premiership that, so far, they have missed out on narrowly. However, for all their aspirations, Worcester are still very much a community rugby club, running six senior teams, three women's teams and a thriving Mini rugby and Age Group section.

Part IV
Following the Game: The Informed Fan

"Remember the streaker who tried to cross the pitch in the Barbarians game and got mixed up in a rolling maul?"

In this part . . .

You know the basics, and you know where you want to fit into the rugby food chain. So now you want to know exactly where you can get more rugby information, what media outlets can improve your knowledge of the game, and how to get the most enjoyment out of watching it being played.

We explain the impact that television has had on the game and recommend the best channels to watch. Then we tell you about the best sources of rugby information through such media as radio, newspapers, magazines, books and Web sites.

This part ends with the kind of advice you need to totally enjoy your day out as a spectator. From what to wear to what to say and when to say it, every base is covered.

Chapter 16

Compulsive Viewing: Rugby on the Screen

- -

In This Chapter

▶ Tracking the surging popularity in televised rugby

▶ Knowing the television channels that broadcast the games

▶ Listening in to the referee

▶ Understanding what the commentators really mean

- -

Lights, camera, action! These days, no self-respecting rugby player would ever leave home without one vital item in the kit bag. Forget the tape, mouthguard, lucky underpants, or gentleman's protector – the number one requirement in the modern game is the make-up kit. Okay, rugby union players may not yet be big stars like Russell Crowe or Tom Cruise, but increased exposure on television has made many of them household names. The modern-day passion for celebrity players has also created greater awareness, enthusiasm and understanding of the game among the general public, many of whom have been sufficiently enthused to forsake their armchairs and watch the game live in the stands.

Those who prefer to stay close to home comforts and watch the game on television are equally happy. Coverage of rugby union on television has grown, and so has the audience watching – not only at stadia around the world, but at home in their living rooms too.

The Wonderful World of TV Rugby

Television executives have finally learnt what the rest of us have known for years – that when it's played well rugby union is hard to beat. Horse racing may be called "The sport of kings", but for most of us rugby union fans, ours is the king of sports. A thunderous, free-flowing game of union has few equals, and even when it fails to hit all the high notes it usually provides a spectacle to rival anything served up by its round-ball cousins.

Viewing figures for the Six Nations (you can find out what this is in Chapter 13) which is the jewel in the crown of northern hemisphere rugby, prove the point that rugby is becoming an ever more popular televised sport. In the 2003 championship, 12 out of 15 games attracted audiences of more than 3 million in the UK, with the Wales versus England game peaking at 6.7 million. The UK broadcasters for the event are currently the BBC, who secured a three-year deal worth in the region of £70m to the Six Nations.

The high ratings achieved by televised games make the point eloquently enough. In this chapter, we look at how television has boosted rugby's profile as a national and world sport.

Keeping Up with Current Rugby Channels

Although "The Beeb" still retains a strong interest in the sport (for example, in 2003 they had the broadcast rights not only to the Six Nations but also to the Heineken Cup, Europe's most prestigious club tournament), they have not had the field to themselves. The Zurich Premiership in England is televised by Sky TV, a pay-per-view channel, as are England's autumn internationals against southern hemisphere opponents. Sky also have the UK rights to the annual Tri-Nations tournament between New Zealand, Australia and South Africa, as well as to the Super 12, the southern hemisphere's biggest provincial tournament. In addition, Sky bid successfully to cover the Lions tour of Australia in 2001, and they also have the rights for the tour of New Zealand in 2005.

With rugby dispersed over several channels, your most valuable asset as an armchair rugby fan is a reliable television guide, because screening times for matches are unpredictable and change week by week. Television rights do change hands and so stations can vary from season to season in terms of the tournaments they show. So, you need to have a reputable television guide to find out where your favourite team is next appearing on the old goggle box.

Consider this section your guide to what's what and who's hot among current national and pay television channels.

Switching on to pay television

For the rugby nut in the British Isles, subscribing to pay television is obligatory. In recent seasons this has been highlighted by the thoroughness, depth, and technical expertise shown by the newcomer in the field, Rupert Murdoch's Sky TV. There is a general consensus that this pay-per-view channel's coverage has put pressure on the BBC and ITV to raise their game. Sky's weekly magazine programme, *The Rugby Club*, is infinitely more thorough than *Rugby Special* ever was, and it provides quality interviews with the main movers and shakers of the week, as well as detailed match analysis from the previous weekend's games and well-researched previews of up-coming matches.

Reach for the Sky

Sky's main pundits are former England internationals Stuart Barnes (England fly-half 1984–93) and Dewi Morris (England scrum-half, 1988–95). Barnes is not everyone's cup of tea, but then, with the notable exception of McLaren, very few commentators meet with universal approval. We like him. He's an informative, opinionated summariser, and a good technical analyst who is prepared to stick his neck on the block (make sure the cheque's in the post, Stuart!), as sharp off the field as he was on it. Morris adopts more of a straight-man role in the studio, but their failures or successes as Premiership tipsters are good for a laugh, if not for your pocket! Sky's main commentator is Miles Harrison, and his measured tones are offset well by Barnes's more forthright observations. They are a decent double act, irrespective of whether their live weekend game is an autumn international or a Zurich Premiership match.

In production terms, Sky have also stolen a march – or at least a camera angle or two – thanks to their increased number of match cameras (a whopping 21 for international matches). Their leading director, Martin Turner, is recognised as one of the best in the business because of his understanding of the game and his ability to strike the right balance between tight and wide shots.

Southern comfort

Sky also shows a southern hemisphere Super 12 game live once a week, plus a highlights wrap of the other matches, ensuring that followers of the tournament get good value for money. The same is true for Tri-Nations matches during the annual round-robin between New Zealand, South Africa and Australia. The Super 12 coverage also gives an insight into the broadcast values of the other nations involved because it uses local broadcast feeds from each of the three countries, enabling viewers to get different viewpoints and analysis on teams and issues.

The shaky start of televised rugby

Once upon a time, watching a rugby match on television required enormous patience – and a fast eye. Although the Six Nations (previously the Five and Four Nations), has been a fixture on BBC television since the tournament was broadcast for the first time in 1938, the game below international level in England, Scotland and Wales was sketchy in its coverage until the introduction of professionalism in 1995.

For many years the rugby rations on offer from broadcasters left followers of the game feeling starved. Outside the Six Nations, and truncated footage of Lions tours – often due to technical limitations in transmission technology from countries like South Africa and New Zealand and the high costs of sending outside broadcast units – there was very little television promotion of rugby union.

From 1966 through to the 1990s all that was available was *Rugby Special*, a highlights pro-gramme produced by the BBC, and even then it failed to find a regular place in weekend sched-ules. Thankfully, rugby got a better deal when the game went professional, and that, combined with the growth of cable and satellite sports channels available to viewers in the UK, has ensured that rugby fans get plenty of access to their favourite product these days.

The New Zealand broadcasters, in particular Grant Nisbett and Tony Johnson, are classy performers, as is Australia's Gordon Bray, and although the South African callers struggle at times, they come up with some lines that are as puz-zling as they are amusing.

The BBC – playing catch-up

The terrestrial networks hold the whip hand over Sky in one overwhelming respect. When it comes to the numbers game, they can reach far bigger audi-ences: and rugby administrators the world over want to get their product into the most homes possible.

Yet, the BBC still appears to be playing catch-up when it comes to camera work and technical expertise. The men behind the cameras sometimes suffer from a lack of rugby awareness (probably because they are football men), and so fail to capture important cameos within the game, while on the pro-duction side they have a habit of screening replays instead of transmitting crucial live action. The BBC's failure to use graphics as effectively as Sky also doesn't help the commentators come across at their best.

BBC commentators face a major challenge: Bill McLaren's shoes are hard to fill (see the section "The Voice of Rugby" later in this chapter for how this origi-nal BBC rugby commentator made his mark). His successor, Eddie Butler, acknowledges as much. However, Butler's more laid-back delivery has its own fans, while Nick Mullins is a promising newcomer with a lively turn of phrase.

Another plus for the BBC is that Brian Moore, Jonathan Davies and Jerry Guscott are no shrinking violets, and, as summarisers, are all capable of making acute observations about the match in front of us. All of them are worth listening to, however, The Beeb's coverage may need an injection of pace – and more of the enthusiasm that McLaren was so famous for.

Sadly the BBC has also failed so far to turn *Rugby Special* into a programme that rugby fans consider to be special. Despite a commitment to schedule the programme regularly in the 2002–2003 season, it has flitted in and out of the scheduling. Now you see it, now you don't.

ITV's mixed bag

ITV is in the weird position of being a bit-part player, where the other two rugby broadcasters are full-timers. They currently appear on the scene once every four years – in other words, whenever a World Cup is on. As a result, they have one big problem – access to little or no recent rugby action, making their preview attempts look dated. Although John Taylor is a respected commentator, ITV's World Cup record has been mixed. While it was generally reckoned that they had been innovative in 1991 when they had no experience of rugby, and produced a good product, by the time the 1999 tournament came round, they had lost much of their gloss.

Relations between ITV and Rugby World Cup Ltd reached a low point with a blistering attack by Leo Williams, the then RWC chairman, at the end of the 1999 tournament.

Williams condemned their decision not to broadcast the third place play-off between Australia and New Zealand nationally a "disgrace", and said that the channel's consistent scheduling of their highlights package after midnight showed a lack of commitment to the tournament. However, peace was made in the aftermath of the tournament, and ITV are in harness again for 2003 and 2007. There is plenty to improve on, but now that ITV's second channel ITV2 is accessible in 10m homes in Britain, they certainly have the scope to do so.

Sadly, in 2003, the Six Nations was not shown live on either public service or cable television in Australia, which was extraordinary considering it was a World Cup year and that England and France were among the tournament favourites. Bizarrely, a private concern bought the rights and forced punters to pay exorbitant prices to watch the games live from a limited number of Australian pubs. Hopefully that situation will be rectified quickly because Six Nations rugby has a following around the world.

The World Cup boom

ITV currently have the UK broadcast rights to the tournament of tournaments – The Rugby World Cup. The World Cup is the single biggest factor in the game's increased popularity over the past few years because of the way it has given television broadcasters, newspapers, radio, magazines and Internet sites, an unrivalled opportunity to cover and project the game.

The growth since the inaugural World Cup in 1987 (played in Australia and New Zealand) has been phenomenal. For instance, the 1999 World Cup was broadcast to 209 countries and was watched by 3.1 billion viewers. That sounds like everyone on the face of the earth was watching and that seems unlikely given that not every human being has a television. Fair enough, but

in television terms, viewer figures are calculated on 1 minute segments of a sport being watched, and these include repeat viewers. So, if one viewer watches 10 games, for statistical purposes he becomes 10 viewers. Complicated enough for you?

Let's make it simpler. Putting aside the arithmetic involved in calculating numbers of viewers, the figures tell us one thing. There's a massive appetite for rugby union out there!

As a result, the UK broadcasting rights alone are worth their weight in gold. ITV have paid in the region of £40m for the rights to the 2003 and 2007 tournaments, and it is this sort of income which funds the International Rugby Board's (IRB) development of the game worldwide.

Never on a Sunday?

In Europe there is an increasing trend towards games being played on both Saturday and Sunday, whether they are club or international. This trend is television inspired. Broadcasters, having paid handsomely for the rights, are experimenting with kick-off times to see whether they can increase their audiences. Whereas traditionally kick-offs have been at 3 p.m. on a Saturday afternoon, they are now scattered the length and breadth of the weekend, with the France vs England game in the 2004 Six Nations scheduled for a Saturday evening kick-off. Sunday rugby has sparked fierce debate, with some rugby fans, particularly the travelling variety, arguing that the rhythms of the rugby season – where, for instance, you travel Friday, watch your Six Nations match Saturday afternoon, return home Sunday, and are back to work on Monday – are being seriously disrupted.

Whatever the rights and wrongs of the debate, if you stay at home you could find yourself spoilt for choice. It was, for instance, possible on one weekend in late May 2003 for British viewers to tune into coverage of the Super 12 final from Eden Park, Auckland on Sky early on Saturday morning, and then watch the Heineken Cup Final from Lansdowne Road, Dublin on BBC in the afternoon. Then, on Sunday afternoon, you had the choice of watching England play the Barbarians at Twickenham on Sky, or watching Wasps against Bath in the Parker Pen Challenge Cup Final at the Madejski Stadium, Reading on British Eurosport, another pay-per-view channel.

So, British and Irish rugby is reasonably well served in terms of television coverage, with BBC Wales and S4C in Wales and RTE in Ireland tailoring their output to the demands of their own audiences.

Becoming a Rugby-Savvy Viewer

Knowing which channels to watch rugby on is one thing, but knowing what to watch out for – and who to watch out for – are just as important if you really want to get the most from watching matches in the comfort of your armchair. Listening to the experts can sometimes be as entertaining as watching the game itself.

Enjoying memorable television insights

Rugby on television can get you up close and personal. Excellent camera angles, especially those from the sideline, or from hand-held cameras, give you an intimate look at exactly what's going on in line-outs, scrums, rucks, and mauls. Watch closely and you can learn a great deal about correct techniques – and what some teams do to upset the opposition.

Don't forget to turn the volume up on your television set because the referee now wears a tiny microphone, enabling viewers to actually hear what his decisions are for. It also gives you the chance to eavesdrop on the referee's conversations with players, and vice versa.

This is illuminating, because usually referees do not hold back in what they are saying, especially to players who are trying to referee the game themselves. Several referees, including England's Tony Spreadbury ("He knows what he was doing", is a Spreadbury favourite) and South Africa's Andre Watson, are very entertaining. You also discover which players possess a "rich" vocabulary, which ones crawl to the ref, and which ones have no idea what's going on.

However, while television provides an excellent view of the action, it doesn't always provide you with the full picture. Sometimes it's not quite as good as actually being there, because the angle of the television shot or a directorial glitch means that you will not always be able to see everything that's going on. For instance, if a team has an attacking overlap (four players to the defence's two) some of the players might be outside the television's frame.

Voices and faces that popularised rugby

For many people, their first contact with rugby union has been through the television screen. Because a well-produced and well-annotated televised game can really help you understand what's going on, fans frequently develop loyalties to their favourite commentators and television channels that are almost as deep as their loyalties to their favourite clubs and players!

Early rugby commentators made lasting impressions on how the game is perceived today. You may still see footage of classic games, or hear references to the commentaries on those games, so it's helpful to know a bit about who they were – and the challenges they faced. In Britain, the government-backed television company, the BBC, had the field to itself in both television and radio coverage of rugby in the immediate aftermath of World War Two.

From the 1950s through to the 1970s the game in the British Isles was well served by commentators like G V Wyn-Jones, ("Geevers"), with his wonderfully-rich Welsh tones, Jock Wemyss in Scotland, Fred Cogley of RTE in Ireland, and Peter West, with his very correct "pukka" English pronunciation.

However, it wasn't until the early 1970s, with the growth in popularity spurred by two successful Lions tours of the southern hemisphere (1971 to New Zealand, and 1974 to South Africa), that television commentators became linked inextricably with the game.

What a score!

Nothing demonstrates the way in which a commentator can bring a game to life on TV more than Cliff Morgan's commentary when the Barbarians played New Zealand at Cardiff Arms Park on 27 January 1973. Morgan, who had been the fly-half on the 1955 Lions' tour of South Africa, captured the drama of the Barbarians' early score as if he was living every shimmy, pass and sprint himself: "This is great stuff. Phil Bennett covering, chased by Alistair Scown. Brilliant! John Williams, Bryan Williams...Pullin...John Dawes, great dummy...David, Tom David. The halfway line...Brilliant by Quinnell...This is Gareth Edwards...A dramatic start! What a score!"

Morgan's commentary has been immortalised because his breathless delivery and his sheer thrill as the great move unravelled captured the moment so perfectly.

Morgan was followed by a host of former internationals turned commentators, including the BBC's Chris Rea (Scotland centre, 1968–71), Nigel Starmer-Smith (England scrum-half, 1969–71), John Taylor, ITV's lead commentator (Wales flanker, 1967–73), as well as Ian Robertson (Scotland centre, 1968–70), Alistair

Hignell (England fullback 1975–79), Eddie Butler (Wales no.8, 1980–84) and Phillip Matthews (Ireland flanker, 1984–92). It is a trend that has continued with recent high-profile players like Jonathan Davies (Wales fly-half, 1985–97), Brian Moore (England hooker, 1987–95) and Jerry Guscott (England centre, 1989–99) joining the BBC as match summarisers in recent years.

"The Voice of Rugby"

Perhaps the most renowned commentator of the lot was not a former international – although he might have been but for contracting tuberculosis at the end of the Second World War and being hospitalised for the best part of two years. That commentator is Bill McLaren. When Bill retired from commentating after the Wales vs Scotland game at the Millennium Stadium, Cardiff in April 2002, there was a sense of loss felt by rugby fans throughout the British Isles – and further afield too. "The Voice of Rugby" had called a halt.

They'll be dancing...

Here are a few McLarenisms to be going on with. A good try was often greeted with the words, "They'll be dancing in the streets of (substitute try scorer's home town or village) tonight." Or, following a heated exchange between a couple of no-neck props, "There's a bit of argy-bargy, but nothing too serious...".

Even better, if a player had produced a searing break, McLaren would pipe up, "And there he goes like a demented ferret," or, in the case of Ireland winger Simon Geoghegan's super-charged running action, "He's got more arms and legs than a mad octopus."

"The voice of ... Latvia?"

There's one anecdote above all others that illustrates McLaren's command of his trade. During the World Cup Sevens tournament at Murrayfield in 1993, McLaren's BBC colleague Ian Robertson decided to play a prank on him during a match involving Latvia, one of the lesser-known participants. McLaren was taking a well earned breather during his commentary when Robertson sold him a verbal dummy: As the Latvians, who were not exactly household names even in their own households, broke away in attack, Robertson turned to his fellow commentator with the words, "I see that a Latvian is about to score, and I'm sure Bill McLaren can tell you all about him."

The master craftsman did not so much as pause, finding not only the words but the information to provide a seamless link. "Thank you Ian," he said, "And this is Silovs, the 24-year-old from Riga, six foot two and all 15 stones of him: a bank official. He scored three tries in the qualifying round against Russia . . .". Now, that's what you call a real pro.

His description of Wales winger Ieuan Evans's try against Scotland in 1998 is another that lingers in the memory: "Magic, magic all the way...Merlin the magician could not have done it better." The same applies to McLaren's gift for commentary.

Translating television gobbledegook

When you listen to commentaries on rugby games on TV, you will often hear phrases or catchphrases with a strange ring to them. Usually, these phrases are kept to a minimum because commentators are aware that some of their viewers have only a limited knowledge of the game, and that there is no point in alienating them by speaking a foreign language! Interesting phrases you may hear while watching television include:

- ✔ **"Aaaarrgghh!":** Used when a player makes a particularly blatant mistake, like fumbling a pass, or allowing one to be intercepted.

- ✔ **"He's gone blind":** This doesn't mean a player has suddenly lost his sight, but instead that he's decided to attack the blind side, or short side, of the field (for more on tactics, see chapter 9).

- ✔ **"He's hoisted a Garryowen":** No, this isn't running an Irish flag up a mast. Instead, it's used when a player kicks a high ball towards the opposition in the hope that their fullback, or someone else, drops it. Why Garryowen? It's the name of the Irish club which developed the tactic (for more about kicking skills, see chapter 6).

- ✔ **"That's got snow on it!":** A particularly high altitude Garryowen.

- ✔ **"It's high enough, it's long enough, it's straight enough":** This phrase often accompanies a successful long-distance penalty kick for goal.

- ✔ **"Look at him pick and go!":** A player rushes to the breakdown, quickly picks up the ball from behind the feet of his tackled team-mate, and speeds off in the hope of taking advantage of the unsuspecting opposition (for more about these tactics, see chapter 7).

- ✔ **"He's seagulling":** This is used to describe a forward who has a habit of hanging around in the back line looking for glory, rather than doing the hard work at rucks, mauls and tackles.

- ✔ **"He's getting a bit of a shoeing":** usually applies when a player who prevents the ball coming back in a ruck is removed by being scraped out backwards with the studs on the boots of the opposing forwards.

> ✔ **"That's high!":** We're not talking about mind-altering substances here, but about a dangerously high tackle which has risen above the shoulders to the neck and head.

Referees have their own subtle language, as well, of course, and it helps if you can recognise their hand signals. Table 5-1 in Chapter 5 is a handy checklist of referees' signals. For unfamiliar words and phrases, you can turn to Appendix B, a glossary of rugby terms.

The all-seeing eye and the match commish

TV cameras have had a significant impact on the game in other respects. Among the most controversial developments are the procedures surrounding television Match Commissioners and their powers to cite players for otherwise unseen misdemeanours, and the increased access given on tours to fly-on-the-wall video documentary makers.

The television Match Commissioner's job is to study footage of the game for any misdemeanours which have gone undetected by the referee or his touch judges. If the Match Commissioner, or the officials of either of the teams involved in a game, find a serious incident that merits further investigation they have a 48-hour "window" after the match in which to cite the perpetrator.

But Commissioners are not always up to speed. For example, South Africa's record defeat by England at Twickenham in November 2002 highlights some commissioners' unwillingness to review new footage that could help determine foul play. After a series of off-the-ball incidents, Sky TV's *The Rugby Club* pinpointed acts of South African foul play running into double figures. Most of these incidents showed Springbok players going for the man rather than the ball, and yet the Commissioner considered only one incident worthy of scrutiny.

Although the South African captain, Corne Krige, was shown appearing to stamp, elbow, and punch opponents, as well as accidentally concussing his own fly-half with a swinging arm aimed at an England player, the Springboks were, initially, unrepentant. Krige claimed afterwards that he was being unfairly victimised.

Given that the Match Commissioner failed to be as vigilant as Sky's commentators, Krige's alleged skulduggery went unpunished. It was not a good day for television match commissioning or South African rugby.

Videos – Seeing Is Believing

The consolation is that whatever live action you miss you'll probably be able to get hold of on video. Take your pick! There is a huge variety of videos available on any area of the game that grabs you. They range from the historic to the quirky, and from sensational tries or "big hits" (as in tackles), to more sober coaching compilations.

Here are a few handpicked favourites to whet your appetite:

- ✔ *Living With Lions*, which is the story of the first Lions' tour of the professional era which ended in glory with a 2–1 series victory over South Africa in 1997. This was the first of rugby's "fly-on-the-wall" documentaries, and it showed the tour warts and all. Warning – if four-letter words are not music to your ears, buy some earmuffs!

- ✔ *All Blacks vs Springboks* is as illuminating as it gets. This video is subtitled *The Toughest of Rivals* and it doesn't take long to find out why. New Zealand and South Africa dominated international rugby in the amateur era, and there's bruising, compelling action from this clash of the giants, starting in 1956, and ending with the Springbok tour to New Zealand in 1981 that almost sparked a civil war (see Chapter 13 for more about this incident).

- ✔ *Bill McLaren: Rugby At Its Best* is a video bursting with classic action from the 1970s and 1980s in particular, with the great Welsh teams of the 70s, the 1984 Wallabies, and the bewitching French featured heavily.

- ✔ *Grand Slam Heroes* is one of a host of videos featuring England's 2003 Grand Slam. It must be a bit of a relief to get this on the shelves, given the amount of time it took England to make a clean-sweep of their Six Nations opponents and reflect their dominance in northern hemisphere rugby.

- ✔ *101 Best Tries* can only be described as a "try-fest", which shows off all the great northern hemisphere touchdowns over the decades, including several which defy belief.

You can also select from a host of good coaching and instructional videos, most of which are available from national unions such as the Rugby Football Union (RFU) in England. A good basic coaching guide is provided in *Understand the Game: The Winning Edge*, an hour-long compilation by Don Rutherford, the former RFU technical director. If you are interested in more coaching information the Web site of the national unions in the British Isles are the best place to start (and you can find these in Appendix C).

Flies on the wall

The rifts between management teams and players could not have been demonstrated more clearly than in the behind-the-scenes documentary of the 2001 Lions tour of Australia titled, *Up Close and Personal with the Lions*.

Although the Lions eventually lost the three test series in the closing moments of the final test in Sydney, the tone of frustration is present throughout.

Austin Healey and Matt Dawson, the two players whose newspaper columns criticising Lions coach Graham Henry caused a massive stir, reveal why they were so critical. In a sound bite at the beginning of the video, the friction is highlighted when a shot of Healey and Henry on the training field is accompanied by the player's pointed statement that he wanted to play for the shirt more than he did for Henry.

The footage underlines that some players were uncomfortable with the unrelenting intensity of the training regime during the tour. The idea that less can be more on the motivational front was illustrated in Willie John McBride's short, softly spoken, but galvanising address to the Lions before the First Test at the Gabba. McBride reassured them that the gut-twisting anxiety they were feeling should be there, and that each of the players would need to reach into the depths of their inner beings during the game. The Lions were suitably inspired, winning 29–13, but McBride's lesson was not heeded and thereafter it seemed that they were subjected to verbal overkill before every match by their coaching and management team.

Chapter 17

Keeping Up with the News

*Y*our search for the fount of all rugby knowledge should not be too taxing. While rugby union may not get the massive amount of space and coverage that football commands in the British Isles (and in most of the rest of the world), there are plentiful sources from which rugby fans can get their daily fix of news and views.

The rise in the game's popularity has coincided with a dramatic increase in the coverage it receives in newspapers, and other forms of print media, as well as through the Internet, in sports literature, and on the radio.

Newspapers have been an excellent source of rugby information ever since England played their first rugby international against Scotland at Raeburn Place, Edinburgh, in 1871. That game was covered by *The Times* and by the end of the nineteenth century coverage of rugby in most national newspapers was extensive. In fact, the challenge issued by Scotland to England, which led to that first international match, was published in a Victorian sports newspaper called *Bell's Life*.

Whatever it is you are looking for, whether it's an entertaining read, analytical match report, comment, gossip, facts and figures, or simply results, the written press – national, regional and local – should be able to give you the answers you need.

The pen is mightier than...the All Blacks

The influence of the press in rugby has been evident from the game's early days. The origin of the name the All Blacks is a great example of this influence: The story goes that the New Zealand tourists of 1905 – considered to be the first of the great sides to tour the British Isles – came to be known as the All Blacks due to a meddlesome typesetter changing the headline from "All Backs" which had been intended as a tribute to the running and handling skills displayed by the whole team. Another explanation is that they were dubbed the All Blacks by the rugby correspondent of the *Daily Mail*, JA Buttery, because of their black strip. Whether the name was of Buttery's making, or a typesetting error, the press certainly played a part in creating this famous nickname.

While newspapers remain the most popular and authoritative forum for commenting on the game, Web sites have become another popular, and more immediate, place to find out information – as long as you have access to a computer and know which Web sites provide accurate news (you can find some good examples listed in this chapter).

There are now a host of Web sites which put the wide world of rugby at your fingertips. These range from information packed specialist rugby sites, such as PlanetRugby, as well as those of all the national unions (the English, Welsh, Scottish, and Irish unions all have their own sites), all the major clubs and provinces, both UK and worldwide, as well as a host of smaller clubs. A large percentage of the amateur rugby clubs in England have Web sites. So don't think you only boot up if you want to train or play – if you want to find out more about rugby, boot up your computer, and have a browse!

Rugby union is well served on the radio, too. Although the game does not dominate radio chat shows in the way football does, international match commentaries have been broadcast since 1927 on the BBC, and today the network of local stations, both BBC and independent, ensure that you won't miss out on following your team.

This chapter aims to guide you to the media sources that best meet your needs. So, if you want to read a paper or check a Web site, check statistics, scores and match analysis, or turn on a radio commentary; or if you want to read an interview with one of your favourite players, buy a rugby magazine, or delve into some rugby books for some in-depth information, read on!

Nosing Around in Newspapers

Most national newspapers in Britain and Ireland have a rugby correspondent as well as columnists and freelance reporters covering the sport. This ensures that coverage is broad and extensive, particularly in the broadsheets, which have traditionally devoted far more space to rugby union than the football-dominated tabloids. Some of the tabloids have responded to the increased popularity of the game, and are often first with news stories, but they are less likely to give you big, in-depth rugby features. However, whether you are a rugby union beginner or something of an expert, newspapers provide an authoritative perspective.

Rugby coverage always becomes more extensive around the time of World Cups, Lions tours, the Six Nations, major test matches against the southern hemisphere unions, or the climax of important club competitions such as the Heineken Cup and Zurich Premiership (Chapters 12–14 tell you more about these competitions). Newspapers are also mindful of rugby supporters wanting to plan their year, and regularly provide the latest in fixture lists.

Don't think that newspaper coverage is all dry and serious – rugby union is often a humorous game, attracting the most bizarre characters. Some of the funnier incidents get an airing in off-beat gossip columns, such as the "Rugby Shorts" column in *The Sunday Times* written by Nigel Botherway.

Here's the breakdown of the UK's leading rugby newspapers.

The Nationals

These are the big boys of the newspaper world; these papers cover rugby in the whole of the UK, but invariably focus on only the biggest teams. The broadsheets provide the most consistent coverage, with the tabloids (the *Daily Mail* apart) tending to focus only on rugby's big international matches. Most broadsheets produce special supplements for World Cups and Lions tours, as well as lift-outs each season for tournaments such as the Six Nations, the Heineken Cup and the Zurich Premiership.

National newspapers provide match reports, technical analysis, previews, interviews with top players and coaches, news stories and "celebrity" columns on the game (you can read who writes for which paper below). Nor is coverage centred purely on rugby in the British Isles: Rugby events in Australia, New Zealand and South Africa also get their fair share of column inches.

The Sunday papers

Although you can find rugby coverage in the newspapers every day, the biggest days are usually Sunday – when the Sunday broadsheets provide reports of Saturday's big matches, and preview Sunday's games as well as providing features and news stories. Sunday broadsheets almost always devote a double page spread to rugby union in a dedicated sports section, and when internationals are played they will run to five or six pages with rugby on the front page of the sports section. Sunday broadsheets that report on rugby include:

✔ *The Sunday Times* (Circulation: 1,397,154 Source ABC). Call us biased, but with Stephen Jones – considered the doyen of British rugby correspondents – Nick Cain (that's right – one of this book's authors!), and columnists of the stature of former England and Lions centre Jerry Guscott, England no.8 Lawrence Dallaglio, and former Wallaby coach Bob Dwyer, this is informed rugby writing at its most revealing and entertaining. The biggest of the Sunday broadsheets, it also runs separate Irish, Scottish and Welsh editions.

✔ *The Sunday Telegraph* (Circulation: 753,319 Source ABC). Former England and Lions lock Paul Ackford is a rugby correspondent never short of an opinion, and he is ably supported by Rupert Bates and columnists Ieuan Evans and Tim Horan.

✔ *The Observer* (Circulation: 469,414 Source ABC) Eddie Butler keeps his writing skills honed writing for this paper alongside his BBC commentating duties.

✔ *The Independent on Sunday* (Circulation: 221,158 Source ABC). Rugby correspondent Tim Glover is a good wordsmith, while Harlequins coach Mark Evans and Jonathan Davies are challenging columnists

The tabloids are catching up (when it comes to reporting on rugby at least – some of the other news stories in the Sunday tabloids are enough to make even the bawdiest rugby player sit bolt upright). Here are the better reads for rugby fans:

✔ *The News of the World* (Circulation: 3,915,609 Source ABC). Chief rugby writer David Norrie doesn't miss many tricks, and England winger Dan Luger is a columnist.

✔ *The Mail On Sunday* (Circulation: 2,381,631 Source ABC). Not a huge amount of column inches devoted to the game, but when the big games come along, Patrick Collins and Ian Stafford do the business for this paper. England and Lions captain Martin Johnson also has a column.

✔ *The Sunday Express* (Circulation: 954,149 Source ABC). Stephen Bale and Neil Squires have re-established this paper as a required rugby read. England's top try-scoring winger Ben Cohen is a columnist.

The daily papers

Daily newspapers include match reports, as well as features and news. Nearly all the broadsheet dailies will devote a good spread on Monday to analysis of the weekend's action.

As with Sunday papers, the broadsheets still offer more column inches to rugby than their tabloid equivalents:

- *The Daily Telegraph* (Circulation: 946,343 Source ABC). Although the space devoted to rugby appears to have shrunk, rugby correspondent Mick Cleary, and his team of Brendan Gallagher and Rob Wildman, cover all the bases. Sky TV's Stuart Barnes writes a spiky weekly comment, and columnists include former England coach Dick Best, while England scrum-half Matt Dawson provides the line from inside the England camp.

- *The Times* (Circulation: 674,756 Source ABC). Rugby correspondent David Hands and reporter Mark Souster have restored this as the paper of rugby record in recent seasons. Their main columnist is England's golden boy Jonny Wilkinson.

- *The Guardian* (Circulation: 405,858 Source ABC). A sound mix from rugby correspondent Robert Kitson and reporter Paul Rees, with Gloucester coach Nigel Melville and Saracens and France centre Thomas Castaignede giving the inside track as columnists.

- *The Independent* (Circulation: 221,700 Source ABC). Rugby correspondent Chris Hewett writes with verve.

The tabloids are the papers that find the latest rugby news, fast. Here's a breakdown of them:

- *Daily Mail* (Circulation: 2,441,560 Source ABC). It has devoted an increasing amount of column inches to rugby union, and correspondent Peter Jackson is a tireless news gatherer with a sharp eye for a story. Columnists include England winger Jason Robinson and Newcastle Falcons coach Rob Andrew.

- *The Daily Express* (Circulation: 966,211 Source ABC). Rugby correspondent Stephen Bale and his assistant Neil Squires keep the information and insights flowing. England winger Ben Cohen is the paper's columnist.

- *The Sun* (Circulation: 3,533,643 Source ABC). Rugby correspondent Tony Roche has managed to carve himself a niche in a paper in which space is at a premium. Jason Leonard, England's most capped player, writes a column.

✔ *Daily Mirror* (Circulation: 2,061,241 Source ABC). Rugby correspondent Alex Spink keeps rugby on the map in a football dominated tabloid. The main columnist is England flanker Neil Back.

✔ *Evening Standard* (Circulation: 426,849 Source ABC). Rugby correspondent Chris Jones keeps Londoners and commuters in touch with the capital's teams, players and news.

The Celtic connection

Ireland, Wales and Scotland all have extensive rugby coverage in their own newspapers, focussing on the game in their own regions.

Ireland

Ireland has a vigorous tradition of rugby writing with correspondents like Tom English (*Sunday Times* – which is the Irish edition of the national paper of the same name), Brendan Fanning (*Sunday Independent*), Peter O'Reilly (*Sunday Tribune*), Gerry Thornley (*Irish Times*), Tony Ward (*Irish Independent*) and Barry Coghlan (*Irish Examiner*) carrying the torch.

Wales

The Western Mail (correspondent, Simon Thomas) has been traditionally the most influential rugby paper in the mountains and valleys, while the *South Wales Echo* and *Wales on Sunday* (correspondent, Simon Roberts) give the game plenty of column inches.

Scotland

The Scotsman (correspondent, David Ferguson), *The Herald* (correspondent, Kevin Ferrie), and *Scotland on Sunday* (correspondent, Jeff Connor) carry the rugby flag north of the border.

Most of the national tabloids produce Welsh and Scottish editions, which give more space to regional teams than national coverage.

Northern Ireland

The Belfast Telegraph (Gavin Mairs) keeps Ulster's rugby in the public eye.

The English regionals

Rugby is widely reported by papers from the *Western Daily Press*, *Bath Evening Chronicle* and *Gloucester Citizen* in the west, to the *Leicester Mercury*, *Birmingham Post* and *Northampton Chronicle & Echo* in the Midlands, and the

Manchester Evening News, *Yorkshire Post* and *Newcastle Journal* in the north. All these newspapers provide rugby union coverage, some more extensively than others. The focus is mainly on Zurich Premiership teams in their region and their stars, in particular their England players.

Whiling Away with Web Sites

Rugby is blessed with some excellent Web sites, so it isn't hard for the rugby addict to get a daily fix of information, latest news and detail on virtually any aspect of the game. Most leading Web sites also have excellent archive sections, where you can easily access background information on a wide variety of rugby subjects. You can also find a balanced view on what is going on in international rugby. There are good sites located not just in the British Isles, but in a number of different countries such as New Zealand, Australia and South Africa, and this enables you to get a variety of opinions on the latest breaking news.

All national unions, all the Zurich Premiership clubs, and a large number of the other clubs in the British Isles at all levels of the game, have their own Web sites – check them out in Appendix C.

The number of Web sites that explore all areas of the game is impressive, and here are a few worth having a look at:

- **Gwlad** is an independent Welsh Web site (www.gwladrugby.com). It has been both a lively forum for debate and has, at times, operated as an effective pressure group, allowing fans dissatisfied with the running of the game in Wales to get their views across to WRU administrators. It also has a wide-ranging menu and a good archive section but it could do with more regular housekeeping to make sure everything is up to date.

- **PlanetRugby** (www.planet-rugby.com) is the leading Web site in the British Isles, and is a near-encyclopaedic source of information. Although it provides an excellent focus on the game in the northern hemisphere, there is also a huge amount of information on the game south of the equator. While the site offers a good balance of news, analysis, opinions and background, its greatest strength is its database, which provides a huge amount of information on players, countries, matches played, historical facts, and the background to most issues.

  If you want to check up on a player and find out his full name, age, number of international appearances – any information almost down to which side of bed he gets out of – PlanetRugby provides the lot. This site is also useful to the enthusiast who wants to know how a team performed in previous years, as match reports on all the leading games are stored on the database. PlanetRugby also has a string of correspondents around the world, who report on what is going on in their part of PlanetRugby – hence the name.

✔ **Rugby Heaven** is the leading Australian rugby website, and can be found at www.rugbyheaven.com.au. For several years, this site has been the baby of Ben Kimber, who, with the help of Rob Murray, has turned it into a hive of activity. It relies on the resources of the *Sydney Morning Herald*, the *Daily Telegraph* in London, and various news agencies, enabling it to provide news from around the globe. The site boasts numerous interesting sections, such as World Cup, Six Nations, Tri-Nations, Super 12, and provincial and off-the-field stories. It also has tipsters competitions, polls, and many interactive services. Revamped at the start of the 2003 season, it now has a cleaner, more authoritative look with easier access to information.

✔ **Scrum.com** (www.scrum.com) provides good news, features and guest columnist services, although its database is not extensive as that of its main rival, Planet Rugby.

✔ **The Rugby Football Union Web site** (www.rfu.com) is the place to look at if you want the latest news from the England bunker. In addition to providing the official line, this site features the latest press releases from the Rugby Football Union (RFU) and official team announcements. If you are trying to find out nuts-and-bolts details, such as when matches are being played, or how to contact various rugby bodies both at professional and amateur level, this is a great site to start at. One criticism is that it could do with offering a simple, step-by-step starter pack for those wishing to become involved in the game.

Getting Your Rugby Fix over the Radio

There have always been those who prefer radio's vivid commentaries to those on TV, and turn the volume down on the box while turning it up on their radio. Rugby union's radio heritage is as rich as it is diverse.

Radio has unquestionably slipped from the pole position it enjoyed in sports coverage from the 1920s to the 1950s, but even now some people prefer the urgency and descriptive qualities of radio commentators over their television counterparts, turning the television volume down and the radio up during rugby internationals. And if you're out and about when a big game is on, the radio is still a welcome companion, particularly if you're stuck in a traffic jam!

BBC Radio remains the market leader, with rugby correspondent Ian Robertson and commentator Alistair Hignell leading a team which provides live match coverage on all the big games on Sport on Four (Radio 4), while Radio 5 Live provides regular bulletins.

Rugby's radio "first"

Radio and rugby union have been joined at the hip since January 1927 when the England vs Wales game at Twickenham became the first ever outside broadcast of any live sporting event in the British Isles. The man behind the microphone was Captain Teddy Wakelam, who had played for Harlequins before serving in the First World War. When commentating, Wakelam used to invite someone who was blind to sit in his commentary box so that they could assess whether his words painted the picture well enough. He also had a poster next to him emblazoned with the words, "Don't Swear!"

Another pre-television innovation was a plan of the rugby field printed by the *Radio Times*. This plan was divided into eight squares, and, as Wakelam described the action, his assistant would call out "Square 3!" or "Square 8!" to pinpoint where the ball was. On one occasion, during the pre-match parade by the band of the Royal Welsh Regiment, which was accompanied by the regimental mascot (a goat), Wakelam's sidekick got ahead of himself, shouting "The goat is in Square 2!".

Jock Wemyss was another First World War veteran who became a famous BBC radio commentator. Wemyss was capped by Scotland before the war, lost an eye during active service, and resumed his international career against France in Paris in 1920. In the changing room before the match, Wemyss was nonplussed when a selector presented Scottish jerseys to everyone bar him in what was virtually a new side. When he asked whether he could have a jersey the selector told him, "You've already got one." He was referring to the Scotland jersey given to Wemyss before the outbreak of war six years before, and the selector only relented when Wemyss was about to run onto the pitch bare-chested. Who said the Scots were tight?

With characters like Wakelam and Wemyss to start the ball rolling, rugby and radio have been a permanent fixture ever since.

Independent Radio News (IRN), also provide summaries from all the major games, and there are an abundance of local radio stations, both BBC and independent, such as BBC Radio Gloucestershire and Leicester Sound, which provide live commentary of matches involving their local heroes.

Bringing on Some Books

There can be few better ways of getting to know the game than by delving into its literature, both ancient and modern. Rugby union is well catered for in terms of literature, particularly in the British Isles where publishers have discovered that, like football, most things written about rugby have the potential to sell.

Here is an eclectic selection to give you a taste of what rugby is all about.

- **The Art of Coarse Rugby** by Michael Green (Arrow Books, 1960). When this was first published in 1960 it was a sensational success, with four editions printed before the end of the decade. Its magic was that everyone in grass-roots rugby suddenly realised they were part of a great shared experience. Forget the superstars at the top end of the game, this is rugby from the perspective of Green's "Bagford Vipers Fourth XV" – ordinary blokes playing for the fun of it on a mud patch in the middle of nowhere. Although this is now a bit of a period piece the humour still shines through.

- *Goodbye to Glory* by T P McLean (Pelham Books, 1976). McLean is the most authoritative rugby journalist New Zealand has produced to date and his story of the 1976 All Black tour to South Africa does not disappoint. According to McLean, this was the tour when New Zealand woke up to the fact that the Springboks would do anything to stop them, leading to plenty of bad blood between the camps. A searing expose of an explosive tour.

- *Barbed Wire Boks* by Don Cameron (1981). Cameron is not only a gentleman but also a died-in-the-wool New Zealand rugby man. This is a riveting account of how the 1981 Springbok tour almost started a civil war in his green and pleasant homeland. He recounts his disbelief as the tear gas and police truncheons were used to disperse anti-apartheid activists with New Zealand plunged into widespread civil disorder.

- *Endless Winter* by Stephen Jones (Mainstream Publishing, 1993). Jones presents the inside story of "New Rugby" in one of the finest state-of-the-game books ever written. He portrays the story of rugby as a game on the cusp of professionalism, focussing on a 1992–93 season which began with the return of the Springboks to the international fold after apartheid, and ended with the British Lions tour of New Zealand. Jones, who is one of the world of rugby's leading commentators, goes in search of rugby's soul – and finds it.

- **The Rugby War** by Peter FitzSimons (Harper Collins, 1996). A dramatic account of the clandestine battle for power that gripped the rugby world after the 1995 World Cup when Kerry Packer, the Australian magnate, tried to wrest control of the world game from its traditional guardians, the national unions and International Rugby Board.

- *Fields of Praise: The Official History of the WRU, 1881–1981* by David Smith and Gareth Williams (University of Wales Press, 1993). The Welsh Rugby Union (WRU) commissioned two historians rather than specialist rugby writers to produce this learned tome for its centenary. They came up with a great social document on the place of rugby in Welsh life.

✔ *The History of the British Lions* by Clem and Greg Thomas (Mainstream Publishing, 1998). This is the definitive history of the Lions, the greatest of touring sides. It is written in the main by Clem Thomas, himself a famous Lion and captain of Wales. When Clem passed away his son Greg updated the book to include the 2001 tour of Australia.

✔ *The Great Fight of the French XV* by Denis Lalanne (translated by E J Boyd-Wilson) (1960). Lalanne's account of France's first overseas tour in South Africa enthralled the French public. The tone is heroic which is fitting given that France won the two test series against the Springboks (one win, one draw), and it rapidly became a bestseller.

✔ *Total Rugby* by Jim Greenwood (A&C Black, 1978). Subtitled *Fifteen Man Rugby For Coach & Player*, this technical book by the former Loughborough Colleges coach has stood the test of time. It is one of the best coaching manuals written and is now in the fourth reprint of the fourth edition.

Scoring with Magazines

Although specialist rugby magazines are generally focussed towards the enthusiast, readers dipping into them for the first time needn't worry that it's going to be like reading an advanced chemistry manual. As rugby caters for an ever-broadening market and Rugby union wins new fans, rugby magazine editors are smart enough to realise that their publications need to appeal to all their readers, ranging from experts to newcomers, and from armchair fans to aspiring players.

If you are a newcomer to rugby, magazines can provide you with a wealth of detail and information to improve your breadth of knowledge about the game. There is something in there for everyone, and the more your read, the more you become intimate with the special language that is rugby.

Rugby gets a fair amount of shelf space on the newsagents' stand:

✔ *Rugby World* appears monthly and provides a host of guides and companions to the major events in the game such as the Six Nations. Editor Paul Morgan and assistant editor Alan Pearey have carried on a proud tradition – the magazine dates back to the 1960s – and during its lifetime *Rugby World* has cultivated a vast array of writers who provide a broad view of the game.

The team includes Frank Keating, one of Fleet Street's most celebrated columnists, as well as regular pieces from England no. 8 Lawrence Dallaglio, Scotland and Lions coach Ian McGeechan and Wales captain Marty Williams.

✔ ***International Rugby News*** is more of a feature-based magazine and is edited by a Wales based Kiwi, Graham Gillespie, with Hugh Godwin as its main correspondent and player columnists such as England flanker Lewis Moody, Irish centre Rob Henderson, Aussie winger Joe Roff, and former All Black no.8 Zinzan Brooke. Although it has a smaller circulation than *Rugby World* it is a survivor, and recently went "International", publishing Australian and New Zealand editions.

✔ ***England Rugby*** comes out six times a year, and is dedicated mainly to features on the England team. This is not surprising as it is published by the RFU.

✔ ***Rugby Times*** is in tabloid newspaper format and has only been available for one season at the time of writing. It's main thrust is towards English international and domestic rugby.

There are a number of overseas magazines that can be obtained in the UK through subscription, notably those from New Zealand (*NZ Rugby News*), Australia (*Australian Rugby Review* and *Inside Rugby*) and South Africa (*SA Rugby*).

There are also small circulation magazines in Scotland (*Scottish Rugby*) and Ireland (*Irish Rugby*).

Chapter 18

Spectating and Sobriquets

. . . .

In This Chapter

▶ Taking your seat at a rugby match

▶ Doing the right thing by your fellow spectators

▶ Staying warm and comfortable whatever the weather

▶ Cheering on your favourite team

▶ Making dazzling comments on the game

▶ Globe-trotting with your national side

. . . .

*W*elcome to the chapter in which we discuss, among other things, some of the colourful language you may hear at a rugby match.

In this chapter, we give you tips on how to get the most from your visit to a rugby match and become the perfect rugby spectator. While it may sound pretty simple – you pay your entrance fee, take your place on the sideline and watch the action unfold – like most sports, there is an art to blending in at rugby games. Knowing what to do and what not to do is important; we even give you some tips on the best kind of clothes to wear.

Spectating at a rugby game can range from standing on the sideline, cheering on your local club side, or sitting way up at the back of the grandstand, urging your national side to victory. This chapter not only helps you track down tickets to international matches, it also includes a gourmet's guide to rugby food!

For those of you who want to get into the real spectator spirit, we provide some hints on how to impress those around you with your incredible rugby knowledge. And for those who are absolutely passionate about the game, we end the chapter with information on touring overseas with your national team.

Finding Your Place in the Crowd

Congratulations – you're about to take the plunge and actually attend a rugby match. Rugby is one of the most user-friendly sporting events, generally attracting an intelligent, passionate crowd who believe that the only rugby worth watching is good rugby.

Crowd violence is not part of the rugby scene, so have no concerns on that score. The spectators in the stands and on the sidelines tend not to get completely carried away. On the occasion when emotions bubble over, the crowd generally has the good sense to calm down quickly.

The best place to watch a game is in the stands near the halfway line. A spot here gives you a good view of the whole field. At many games at grass-roots club level, where seats (or standing room) is on a relaxed first-come, first-served basis, you have no problem in getting a spot near the halfway line. For elite club games and international matches, it's a different matter – seats at the halfway line are the most expensive.

Not all is lost, however. Other good places that afford a good view of the action are near the 22 metre lines. Some fans love sitting behind the goalposts because of the tactical perspective, in spite of the fact that when the players are all down the other end of the field, not a lot can be seen.

Blending in with the Crowd

Unlike football in Britain where fans from opposing sides have to be segregated to prevent violence, spectators at a big rugby match will be safe from everything but a bit of banter, even if they find themselves seated right in the middle of rival supporters. The game may have made a radical change from amateur to professional, but the atmosphere in the crowd in most parts of the rugby world is still civilised and committed to seeing fair play.

In this section, we give you a few suggestions on rubbing shoulders with your fellow spectators. Then we move on to the right kind of clothes to wear. Other spectators won't care much if you are wearing last season's fashion, but with the 10 month long European rugby season now stretching from summer to winter, if it starts snowing and you are wearing a light cotton shirt, you are not going to be happy.

Following rugby etiquette
(not an oxymoron)

So that you know what's done and what's not done at a game of rugby we have put together a few words of wisdom that may save you from embarrassment. Basically this section is all about minding your manners!

- **Don't wave huge flags emblazoned in your club colours:** Rugby audiences regard themselves as more genteel than fans of certain other sports and get very testy if their view is constantly impeded by the enormous flag you are waving.

- **Speak up only when you're pretty sure you know what you're talking about:** Spectators who make remarks about the game without fully understanding the situation immediately find themselves in the rugby equivalent of Siberia – no-one else talks to you. Your comments should at least sound well-informed. You don't need to spout Shakespeare. Your immortal lines could include phrases like "Go wide!", "They don't like it up 'em!", or "Time for a Garryowen" (the section on television gobbledegook towards the end of Chapter 16 can enlighten you on the meaning of these phrases). The section on how to sound like an expert later in this chapter can also give you some ideas for comments that sound deep and meaningful.

- **Call the ref "Sir":** In other codes, referees are called all sorts of horrible names, but in rugby, the referee is a figure of respect, hence the use of the word "sir" when addressing the man in charge. Even international players call referees "sir", but then they have an ulterior motive – they don't want to get on the wrong side of the whistle-blower. Showing regard for the referee indicates that you are not just a fan but someone who understands the traditions that make rugby the noble game it is. Not least, that without respect for the ref, there is no game.

- **Eat your burger properly:** If you're eating a burger or hot-dog, remember to spill the ketchup over yourself and not the huge bloke standing next to you. Don't be inhibited about licking up the steaming concoction that dribbles down your arm. If this sounds uncouth, don't worry. Look around and you discover that you are not alone in this activity. Eating on the hoof is one of the great joys of rugby spectating. And in most games, remember to avoid the pies unless you have a sturdy stomach!

- **Buy someone a beer:** If you go off to buy a beer, ask the person next to you if they want one. You instantly make a friend. Having friends around you at a rugby match gives you a great feeling of companionship and gives you the opportunity to exchange views on the game.

✔ **Show respect for the opposition:** The good rugby fan applauds the opposition when it does something impressive. Friendly, civilised behaviour makes the occasion more enjoyable – even if your team is losing.

✔ **Don't Be A Boo Boy:** When an opposition player is taking a shot for goal, be silent. Don't imitate the idiots who try to distract the goal kicker. Such antics are frowned upon because most rugby spectators believe that, while rugby is a hard, physical game, it is one which should not be made harder by total disrespect for the opposition. Rugby people believe it is a thinker's game, not a trip to the panto!.

✔ **Get There Early:** Don't wait until the last minute before you take your seat, particularly if you are lucky enough to get tickets to an international match. The pre-match build-up adds to the atmosphere, and you are able to watch the players limbering up for the contest. Sometimes the sheer emotion of the occasion, especially when the national anthems are sung, can reduce players to tears, including the most gnarled warriors.

✔ **Criticise the ref:** Because everyone else does!

Dressing for the occasion

You may have the idea that all rugby fans wear Barbour jackets, and although a fair number do because they are useful all-weather gear, there is no uniform you have to put on to be a rugby fan. However, an increasing number of fans believe the height of fashion is to deck themselves out in clothes that scream out their rugby allegiances (see Figure 18-1). This is almost always a national team or club jersey, and they have become so popular as leisure wear that those manufacturers who saw the trend have made a fortune.

Rugby is a game for all people, and the old class distinctions of the Victorian era which led to the split between rugby union and rugby league over the latter's decision to pay for play, are dead and buried (see below, The Great Schism). Remember, whether you are in Saville Row suit or a pair of shorts and a t-shirt, you are welcome.

The best clothes to wear to a rugby match are those that are functional and rainproof. You need to be wearing something that keeps you warm and staves off the worst weather a rugby afternoon or evening can bring.

Rugby is still primarily a winter sport and you often have to confront horrible, often very wet and cold weather. Dressing appropriately for the weather conditions usually means more clothes rather than less. If you go prepared for something akin to a day spent standing in a car wash, you won't end up with the shivers at 2 a.m. and a trip to the local hospital suffering from a bout of pneumonia.

Figure 18-1:
Showing
their true
colours,
rugby fans
cheer their
team on.

Don't forget that, as a spectator, it is easier to take off layers of clothes if you get too warm than try and get warm when you haven't got anything else to put on. If in doubt about the weather, at the very least take an umbrella and a waterproof coat.

As for those accessories, you are not going to a high-society garden party. Leave the big hats at home or be prepared for a considerable amount of flak from those forced to sit behind you in the terraces. But some warm headgear is certainly a good idea, as are gloves and woollen socks.

If you want to take a thermos of coffee or cocoa to the match, you might want to check the ground rules beforehand. Security guards can get finicky about what you take into a ground, primarily because of agreements with the ground caterers about what spectators are allowed to take in.

The Great Schism

If you spend any amount of time around rugby grounds, it won't take too long before you hear some reference to the other rugby code, rugby league.

Over the decades, the relationship between rugby league, which is 13-a-side game, and rugby union, has been strained.

The rift was often bitter, and was not improved when the professional code repeatedly bought union's best players, with working-class Welshmen from international half-backs David and Evan James in the 1890s, through to gifted fly-halves like David Watkins in the 1960s and Jonathan Davies in the 1980s, all lured north. Now the boot is on the other foot with rugby union attracting rugby league heroes like Jason Robinson and Henry Paul to switch codes in 2001.

Neither union nor league covered itself in glory during the 100 year divide, and even though union became professional in 1995, the rivalry between the two codes remains fierce, even though rugby league is a much smaller game. Where union has a genuine international base, league is still essentially confined to Lancashire and Yorkshire in England, and New South Wales and Queensland in Australia.

It was these limitations that led England's 1980 Grand Slam scrum-half Steve Smith, a northerner who had travelled the world with England and the Lions, to respond famously to a rugby league owner who offered him a contract, quipping that the team's annual tour would probably be to Wigan Pier. Over the decades, union administrators have not behaved well, particularly in their treatment of union players who have been lured to rugby league.

The story of Mike Gilbert, who played for the All Blacks in 1935 and made the switch to league, joining the English club Bradford Northern in 1938, is a case in point. The New Zealand rugby community turned their backs on their one-time hero, and several years later, when Gilbert went to Athletic Park in Wellington to meet an old All Black team-mate, he was ordered out of the ground. The snubbing continued for almost 50 years, and included refusing Gilbert an invitation to the New Zealand Rugby Union's 75th jubilee celebration. Finally, in 1995, Gilbert was accepted back into the fold.

Spectating in Style

As a general rule, rugby fans are excitable wherever you go in the world. Argentine followers sometimes throw flares onto the pitch. French fans double-up as brass bands. English and Welsh fans start singing. Irish fans party on until all hours of the morning, no matter who wins the game.

Sometimes the players get in on the act and stir the emotions of the crowd before the game has even begun. Before kick-off, the New Zealand All Blacks do a war-dance that is a challenge meant to boost their fighting spirit and intimidate their opponents. Figure 18-2 shows the All Blacks performing the haka before a Test match (more information about the haka is given later in this chapter).

Figure 18-2:
Trying to
scare their
opponents,
the All
Blacks
perform
the haka.

England fans have taken to drowning out the haka with their own anthem "Swing Low Sweet Chariot", while the Welsh bard, Max Boyce, does his own version of the haka to the nursery rhyme "Humpty Dumpty". You may come across some great wags in a rugby crowd – if you attend a local game, be prepared for fun and frivolity.

For most rugby fans, the outcome of the game is not a matter of life-and-death, and the day is usually tinged with humour.

Going to watch an international

The pinnacle of spectatordom in Europe is to attend a Six Nations international, or an international against an incoming southern hemisphere touring side, or even travel overseas to support the Lions. The days when attending international matches was a relatively cheap venture are long gone. These days most of England's matches in the Six Nations are oversubscribed two-times over, and your only means of getting a ticket is through being a member of a rugby club. To get a reasonable seat at an international match – and this doesn't mean somewhere near the perfect spot on the sideline at the halfway mark – expect to pay anything from £50 upwards at grounds like Twickenham. While children's tickets are often half-price, usually they are only available for matches against teams that are not at the top of the rugby drawer, such as Japan, Romania, Canada and the USA.

If you are not a club member, you must be prepared to pay big for the experience, by going to one of the corporate hospitality companies. Packages for a day out, including wining, dining and entertainment from an after-dinner speaker will cost anything from £350 to £500.

For the biggest international matches, such as Six Nations deciders, enthusiasts heavily into rugby are prepared to pay upwards of £1,000 to ensure that they have the best vantage spot. In a situation where demand exceeds supply, general admission prices can only go up.

For some international matches, there is a small public allocation, but they sell out within minutes of going on general sale. For major games, your first course of action should be to contact the national union of the country you live in to find out about ticket availability. (see Appendix C for contact details.)

For major rugby events such as the 2003 World Cup, tickets are very hard to get, being distributed through a ballot system.

If you buy from a ticket tout there is no guarantee that the ticket will be genuine, and you could end up not only seriously out of pocket, but seriously disappointed because you are turned away at the gate. Also, if you are a club member who sells a ticket to a tout for a profit, you could get your club blacklisted by the likes of the RFU, who buy tickets from the touts to trace serial numbers. Be warned.

Start saving your money well in advance of the game: Looking the part at an international match can be an expensive exercise because rugby merchandising has become serious business in recent years.

Fans are prepared to buy virtually anything and everything in order to look like the dedicated supporter. Pretty much everything is available for the right price. You can buy jerseys, scarves, beanies, track suits, flags, cushions, socks and shoes, and stacks more.

You can't miss the merchandising stores at the grounds, because they are everywhere. Just find a queue of people who look as if they have money to burn and you are probably in the right spot. If not, you have probably joined the queue for the bar, so you can't lose either way, really.

Another expensive exercise on the day of the match is to keep fully fuelled. Food and drink outlets at rugby grounds have generally improved in recent years, with increasing variety in the food on offer. While you can still get the rugby fan's staple diet of hot chips, hot dogs and hamburgers, meat pies, pizzas and hog roasts, most big grounds also have restaurants where you can have a sit-down meal.

Sadly, the prices for food and drink at rugby games are not in the budget range. So don't forget to take plenty of money with you when you attend the big games because you are bound to be lured into buying something to eat or drink, and it won't be cheap.

Being a fan without breaking the bank

If attending international matches is just a bit too expensive for you, you can enjoy a game at one of the numerous other alternative venues that don't hit you in the pocket as much.

Having a ball at the Heineken Cup

The ticket prices for Heineken Cup, Zurich Premiership, and Celtic League matches are less expensive than for international matches. (If you don't know what these competitions are, then take a look at Chapter 14.) If you take a family of four, expect it to cost at least £120. You may have some difficulty securing tickets for big club matches, but you can still get a reasonable seat for most games if you plan ahead and contact the club ticket office or supporters club.

Getting a close-up view of the action at club level

A great way to learn the game and enjoy rugby in its essence is to go along to your local club. The crowds at local club rugby grounds are not usually overflowing. You have no difficulty in finding yourself a good vantage point and it is not at all expensive – you usually get plenty of change from £10 when you walk through the entrance gates.

Standing close to the action, you soon realise that the standard of play is relatively good. The smaller grounds are the perfect places to learn the referee's signals, discover what players do under pressure, what the different players actually do, what is required for each position and how players react to different tactics. Overall, being close to the sideline helps you get a good feel about the game.

The haka

Just before the start of a game, the All Black team gets into formation and conducts an elaborate, ritual war dance called the "haka". This Maori challenge has been a highlight of New Zealand Test matches for almost a century. The first haka was conducted by the New Zealand team that toured Britain in 1905, but it was not until the 1970s that it was first demonstrated at a home Test match.

The aim of the haka is to strike fear into the hearts of the opponents of the All Blacks, while at the same time inspiring and motivating the New Zealand team. When done correctly, as it is by modern All Black sides, the haka is very inspiring. When done incorrectly, as it was until the mid 1980s, it looked more like the hokey-cokey.

In an attempt to counter its effectiveness at intimidation, some players have defied the haka. England hooker Richard Cockerill went eyeball-to-eyeball in a snarling confrontation with Norm Hewitt, his New Zealand counterpart, before the first test at Old Trafford in 1997. Sometimes whole teams defy it. At Lansdowne Road in 1989 there was nearly all-out warfare before the kick-off when the Irish line, led by lock Willie Anderson, advanced on the haka. This incensed Wayne Shelford, the confrontational All Black captain who was responsible for restoring the haka as a fearsome challenge, and often led it towards the opposition. As a result of these flashpoints it has been agreed that the All Blacks should perform the haka on one 10 metre line while their opponents line-up on the other. So far, so good.

While the haka is usually conducted before the kick-off, in one match during the 1978 All Black tour of the British Isles, it was attempted during the game – with bizarre results. New Zealand captain Graham Mourie wanted to lighten the seriousness of the tour by conducting the haka late in the game against the Barbarians. Mourie thought that if the opposition was distracted by watching a group of mature men who had suddenly started dancing, one of his players could sneak off and score a try.

All the players were primed to do the haka mid-game, in front of more than 50,000 spectators at Cardiff Arms Park. Mourie chose the signal that would indicate when to start doing the haka, a signal that revolved around the halfback passing to a certain forward. This happened, but the forward then dropped the ball, forcing the referee to call for a scrum. So while some forwards set up the scrum, four other forwards started dancing the haka, to the stupefaction of everyone else there that day. Realising that they must look stupid if not totally mad, the jigging forwards stopped their dancing mid-leap.

Enjoying the camaraderie of local clubs

At the smaller grounds you find the really passionate rugby supporters who follow their club through thick and thin. Club rugby relies on volunteers, and at the canteen, or behind the bar, you are probably served by the girlfriend, boyfriend, mother, aunt or father of a leading player.

Clubs rely on good community spirit and volunteers for their very existence. Quite apart from the outcome of the game a successful match day means money has been raised for the club and playing costs are kept down.

The atmosphere at club games is generally amiable, and you quickly feel at home. Faster than you can say "kick for touch", someone goes past selling raffle tickets or tempting you with snacks and drinks to help make money for the club. Pitch in and buy a ticket or two, because in your own small way you may be helping to develop a club which produces a couple of internationals.

Keep an eye on the weather. Many club grounds don't have the best facilities around and when it rains you are unlikely to find anywhere other than the clubhouse to shelter. Don't leave your umbrella and raincoat at home.

Sampling the local fare

You don't really need to take food or drink to a club ground because the food you can get there is often better than the fare at the big stadiums. You can find anything from bangers and mash to hamburgers, steak sandwiches or meat pies and, although it may not be cordon bleu, it will keep the wolf from the door. Some clubs take great pride in the beer they keep on tap in the club-house and, if yours is one, then not only will you get a pint better than that in many pubs, you will get it cheaper.

Sounding Like a Rugby Expert

You really only need a few phrases to sound like a rugby genius. After the first scrum, turn to your neighbour and say, "That tighthead will have to watch himself, because he's pushing in at an illegal angle." We guarantee you that the person next to you turns, looks at you as if you're a rugby guru and nods his head. You get this reaction even if what you say is not happening because no-one really knows if the tighthead prop is pushing into the scrum at the wrong angle other than the opposing loosehead! (We discuss scrums in detail in Chapter 7, if you want to find out more about them.)

Another crucial phrase to remember is the age-old chestnut, "They're offside, ref!" No matter which team you are following, or whether the opposition is offside or not, every person in the crowd believes the opposition is offside and just loves telling the referee about it. If you shout, "They're offside, ref!" at various well-timed moments of the game, you are sure to get knowing nods from those around you. (Chapter 5 explains the offside law.)

If you are watching an international match and England are losing, it is always smart to make out you're a bit of a rugby historian, or a proud traditionalist. If England suddenly drop the ball, or mess up a driving maul close to the opposition line, mutter to yourself in a fairly loud voice, "It wouldn't have happened in Deano's day, would it?" This will earn you nods of heads and grunts of assent from all around. Every English rugby fan loves Dean Richards, the bear-like no.8, who single-handedly saved England on many occasions during the 1980s and 1990s with his extraordinary capacity to be in the right place at the right time. Two decades on, England fans still reminisce for hours about their favourite Richards moment. Similarly, fans in New Zealand grow misty-eyed when they remember how Michael Jones would play, and fans in Wales hark back to the heydays of Gareth Edwards and Barry John.

If you like the idea of donning your historian's cap, you can read up on some of the greatest British players of all time in Chapter 19. But if in doubt about the kind of reception your comments may attract, just applaud when everyone else applauds and you're safe.

Touring the World

Most international teams on overseas tours have groups of supporters following them around. In fact, an estimated 15,000 Brits followed the 2001 Lions to Australia, drawn from the British Isles and all points in between Blighty and the Antipodes. At times, given that influx mixed with the British already domiciled in Australia, the locals felt that their own stadiums had been hijacked.

Tours for rugby fans are usually organised by travel agents who often get a former player to be tour leader for a group of 40 to 50 supporters. These groups usually include veterans of previous tours, the occasional celebrity, and players' relatives, as well as the ordinary fans who have saved for years having dreamt of watching the Lions playing and winning at the great rugby venues of the world.

No touring team has come close to attracting the travelling support of the Lions, although large contingents of fans will follow the likes of England, Wales, Ireland, France and South Africa to the 2003 World Cup. Most will go on organised tour packages which include travel, accommodation and match tickets, and will cost in the region of £2,750 for 16 days, rising incrementally depending upon how much of the tournament you want to see.

Pack your bag wisely before you head off. For many rugby supporters, the first item that gets thrown in the suitcase when they are about to head off on a rugby tour is a hangover cure. Any hangover cure known to man – it's worth its weight in gold.

For players, rugby tours are the ultimate way of bonding as a team – and for spectators it's a great way of letting their hair down. Those who go on tour as a spectator usually come home delighted that they made the effort to watch their team play in some of the world's major grounds. Most overseas venues have famous rugby stadiums and it is something special to be there, singing your country's national anthem.

If you attend social functions on tour, don't pester the players for dozens of autographs or bore them with your own rugby reminiscences. Instead, enjoy the free drinks on offer.

The tour to distant lands is a great rugby tradition that does not begin and end at international level. Due to the strong international flavour of the game, any club – no matter what level – is usually able to find plenty of overseas clubs willing to offer them a match. So if the club secretary is up to the task, a fascinating itinerary can be organised, enabling players to discover the delights of playing in destinations throughout the world, including the exotic and unexpected. Take it from us, from the Canadian Rockies to the sun-kissed beaches of Tobago, from the Pampas of Argentina to the high veldt of South Africa, the rugby world is your oyster.

Part V
The Part of Tens

"There he goes, our best player
-Born in the Outback
-raised by kangaroos."

In this part . . .

*E*very *For Dummies* book includes a Part of Tens, chapters that each contain ten or so interesting pieces of information. For this book, our choices should get you debating. Who were the greatest English, Welsh, Scots and Irish players of all time? When exactly were rugby's greatest moments? Not everyone is going to agree with our choices, especially the best of British and Irish players, but you have to admit that those we've picked are straight from rugby union's top drawer.

We finish this part with a collection of facts that record some of the great moments in rugby. A ready reckoner for the best, the beautiful and the most bizarre, this chapter is sure to raise a laugh or two.

Chapter 19

The Ten Best British Players of All Time

*B*less them all, bless them all, the long and the short and the tall! Or, at least, that's how one rugby song sees it. To that verse we should add the quick and the sharp and the strong, because those virtues define the rare talents who feature in this chapter. They are a group of men who, irrespective of their varied physiques, had the footballing gifts, the athleticism, the iron will, and the innate ability in the heat of battle to know what to do, and when to do it, that set them head and shoulders above us mere mortals.

Gerald Davies

Thomas Gerald Reames Davies? More like Merlin the Magician! The Welsh sorcerer with the right-angle side-step off either foot was one of the most deadly finishers the game has seen. Tough, very fast, and with a whiplash change of direction, Davies was a winger for Wales during their glory years in the 1970s. Davies was at his blistering best during 1971 Lions victory over New Zealand, scoring three tries in the tests. Along with Gareth Edwards (be patient – he's next on this list), he shares the distinction of being the third highest Welsh try scorer with 20 in 46 appearances.

Davies was a miner's son, and his first language was Welsh. He was born in the Carmarthen village of Llansaint, was bright enough to go to grammar school, and from there went to Loughborough College and Cambridge University, where he studied English and played rugby, initially at centre before switching to the wing in 1969.

For all his plaudits as one of the greatest international backs of all time, the game that Davies considers to have been his greatest was a club match: when he captained Cardiff to a 16–11 Welsh Cup victory over Pontypool in 1978. Davies had fought hard to turn Cardiff back into a side that played attacking rugby, and the fact that they stayed true to that philosophy in the face of Pontypool's power – and almost total domination of possession – brought him great satisfaction.

What brought satisfaction to those lucky enough to be in the crowd for that game was the way in which Davies, despite touching the ball only four times, scored four tries – two of them when receiving the ball from 35 metres out. Davies has since become a respected rugby journalist, and yet, despite all his achievements, his humility is humbling.

Gareth Edwards

Welshman Gareth Edwards was once voted the greatest player of all time – and we're not arguing. His genius was encapsulated in a turbo-charged sprint for the line to score the Barbarians opening try against the All Blacks in Cardiff in 1973. This try is one of the most replayed moments in the history of the game, but, even after endless replays, it still sets the pulse racing like nothing else. Edwards is still amazed that the move came together at all, describing it as an impossible try.

Edwards was a scrum-half who combined bundles of energy with a phenomenal combination of power, pace and footballing skills – skills honed by kicking a tennis ball around the streets of Gwaun-cae-Gurwen, the village near Swansea where he was born and raised. Edwards' father was a miner, but thanks to donations from an anonymous sponsor he was sent to Millfield, an English public school which specialised in developing kids with sporting prowess. He won the English Schools hurdles title, and Swansea Town was interested in signing him as a soccer apprentice before his rugby career took off.

Although just 5ft 8in. high and 12st. in weight, Edwards was a giant in every other sense of the word, spearheading the golden eras of Wales and the Lions in the 1970s. His razor-sharp opportunism was a hallmark, and his uncanny strength made him virtually unstoppable if he got a sniff of the line at close range. He is Wales' joint third highest try-scorer of all time with 20 in 53 tests – an extraordinary feat for a scrum-half.

Edwards was a pivotal player in the Lions successes of 1971 and 1974, playing in all eight tests in New Zealand and South Africa. On top of those overseas series victories, he won every honour for Wales that the (then) Five Nations had to offer, including three Grand Slams, five Triple Crowns, and five out-right Championships. Outside of rugby, Edwards has a successful career as a company director and a TV and radio rugby commentator. He is also a devoted angler and at one time held the British pike record having landed a 45lb monster – which is fitting, because Edwards was never a small fish in a big pond.

Jeremy Guscott

If Guscott's combination of languid grace, superb balance and searing speed isn't enough to mark him as one of the greatest backs ever, he was also a big match-winner. Guscott had an almost otherworldly knack for being in the right place at the right time.

On the 1989 Lions tour of Australia it was his little chip kick and gather for a last-gasp try in the second test in Brisbane that paved the way for a 2–1 series victory. In South Africa in 1997 it was his perfect drop-goal three min-utes from time in the second test in Durban that gave the Lions an unassail-able 2–0 lead. Guscott won almost everything there was to win, including three England Grand Slams, the Heineken Cup, and umpteen league and cup titles with his beloved team, Bath.

Guscott was a wayward youngster, and was expelled from school after a series of incidents culminating in abusing a referee in a football match. Bath rugby team helped him to expel his demons and in doing so unearthed a rare sporting talent. The one-time bricklayer, and sometime model, radio and TV host, has almost as interesting a background as his relative, Reginald Teague-Jones, one of Britain's most famous spies.

Jeremy's life even seems a little sedate by comparison. He now commentates on the sport for the BBC and has a column in *The Sunday Times*.

Barry John

Any fly-half who had the confidence to say to Gareth Edwards, "You throw it, and I'll catch it" had to be something special. Known as "The King" in his native Wales, John's ghosting running, superb kicking and laid back style was touched by genius and underpinned the Lions success against the All Blacks in 1971. The New Zealanders did not know what to make of John: They were used to physical, stocky fly-halves, but John was a will-o-the-wisp figure. He proved to be suitably elusive, and his superb tactical kicking throughout the series had the New Zealanders in a spin. John's kicking was so good in the first test in Dunedin that it effectively ended the career of Fergie McCormick, the dangerous All Black fullback, whose veteran legs were found wanting. 1971 was a great year for Barry John, as he also helped Wales to win a Five Nations Grand Slam during that year.

John's self-confidence was inspirational according to Mervyn Davies, the Lions and Wales no.8, who thought that John played rugby in such a relaxed state that you'd think he was going for a stroll.

John's success brought pop-star style adulation in rugby-mad South Wales. John was overwhelmed by the reaction, and retired a year after the tour, aged 27. Barry John is still remembered as the golden boy of a golden age, and has worked as a broadcaster and newspaper columnist since then.

Martin Johnson

"Captain Colossus" has won just about everything there is to win. The 6ft 6in. leader of the Lions, England and Leicester has the most famous scowl in rugby and as a second row forward Johnson has been peerless for the best part of a decade. Johnson is the ultimate competitor, and his sideboard must be groaning under the weight of winners medals. He has won two International Championship Grand Slams with England, he captained the Lions to victory in South Africa in 1997, and has led Leicester to two Heineken Cup triumphs and four successive domestic Premiership titles.

Like many players with a ferocious will to win, Johnson's disciplinary record is not untarnished. Despite his responsibilities as captain, he has served bans for throwing punches and "over-vigorous play" twice in recent seasons (2001 and 2002) and is no stranger to the sin-bin.

Johnson's will to win shows in more than just his disciplinary record though: up to and including England's 2003 Grand Slam, he had been on the winning team in 25 of the 30 tests in which he had captained his country. That 83 per cent success rate is even better than that of such esteemed southern hemisphere skippers as Australia's John Eales (78 per cent), New Zealand's Sean Fitzpatrick (77 per cent) and South Africa's Francois Pienaar (68 per cent). This little statistical sideshow is right up Johnson's street. He is a fount of knowledge when it comes to sports quiz questions and is the England squad's very own "Statto". Johnson takes a special interest in American Football, even to the extent that he joined a San Francisco 49ers training camp on his way back from the 2001 Lions tour.

Johnson's success is based on the principle that he leads from the front, never asking his team-mates to do what he won't do himself. He is an astute tactician, but is also a great believer in not overcomplicating what he sees as an essentially simple game. He has also adapted his own game to fit the shifting demands made of the front five: Already adept at the grunt-and-grind skills required at line-outs, scrums, mauls and rucks, he worked on improving his mobility and handling skills to the extent that he has become a complete player.

A man of few words, Johnson is unwaveringly focused. So much so that in the 2003 Grand Slam decider against Ireland in Dublin he nearly provoked a diplomatic incident. When England lined-up in the wrong position prior to being introduced to Irish president Mary McAleese (he claimed no-one had shown them where they should stand) the glowering Midlander told Irish officials, "We're not moving." He proved similarly immoveable after the kick-off.

Willie-John McBride

"Tell them Willie-John is here." If that sounds like gunslinger's line from a western, it's not out of place. The brawny Ulster and Ireland lock Willie-John McBride had a hard start in life. He lost his father when he was 4, and was one of six children raised on a smallholding in County Antrim by his mother.

Not one to back down on the pitch, and not a stranger to a bit of hell-raising off it, McBride was a born leader. He was one of the greatest captains ever produced in the British Isles, scaling rugby's highest peak by leading the 1974 Lions to an unbeaten tour of South Africa – the first side to win a series on Springbok soil.

McBride's was a leadership forged in adversity. In the 1960s Ireland was not setting the rugby world on fire, and nor were the Lions (for whom McBride played in the losing tours of 1962 and 1968 in South Africa, and 1966 in New Zealand). However, by the time of the 1971 Lions tour of New Zealand, he had had his fill of being pushed around by southern hemisphere forwards and was determined to do something about it. McBride became as uncompromising as the cold north wind having learned the hard way that South African and New Zealand forwards went for the jugular if they sensed weakness.

In 1971 he was part of a Lions pack that met the All Blacks and the New Zealand provinces head-on during an often violent tour losing just one match. McBride knew what had to be done when he returned to South Africa in 1974. His pre-test team talks reflected this, usually beginning with the words, "We will take no prisoners."

Ian McLauchlan

Ian McLauchlan was nicknamed "Mighty Mouse" on account of his ability to fork-lift opposition props out of the scrum despite being considerably smaller than most international front-rowers (he was 5ft 8in.). This superb technician was playing against Hawkes Bay on the 1971 Lions tour when his opposite number suggested he would make him look more like Mickey Mouse. It was a costly jibe. The man with the mouth ended up looking like a contortionist. Soon afterwards, the ultra-competitive McLauchlan proved that the no.1 on his back was no accident, scoring the first try of the first test in Dunedin. Neither the Lions nor McLauchlan ever looked back. The stocky Scotsman played eight successive tests for the Lions at loosehead prop in the two land-mark winning series in 1971 and 1974.

McLauchlan's story is a classic tale of overcoming the odds. As a young flanker he was told that he lacked the size and strength to play top level club rugby in that position. As a result, he took up weight-training and switched to loosehead prop. Although he put on nearly three stone, and made rapid progress, he had to wait six years from his first Scotland trial before he was selected, because he was considered too small.

By the time he got his chance he was more than capable of holding his ground against monsters such as Jazz Muller, the 19 stone All Black prop he had to contend with in 1971. McLauchlan eventually won 42 caps for Scotland, 19 of them as captain.

Dean Richards

"Deano" is the rugby player's rugby player. The bear-like former Leicester traffic policeman was not a great one for training regimes – he probably thought a coach was something with four wheels on it that took him to matches.

Renowned for enjoying a few pints the night before a big match, Richards was not the most mobile no.8 in the world. Socks habitually round his ankles, the Englishman compensated by having radar for the ball superior to any satellite tracking system, the grappling strength of a Mongolian wrestler, and the tactical awareness of Alexander the Great.

Richards became a cult figure because he flouted the received wisdom about what a no.8 should be. He was not an athlete with a ground-eating stride, nor was he a towering line-out forward. He was, however, a rock-like player of immense power with steadier hands than a safe-picker who hoovered up the loose ball and turned it to his own team's advantage.

In his heyday in the early 1990s, England won three Grand Slams, and he was also a bulwark of the 1989 Lions side that won in Australia. He has continued his winning ways as director of rugby at Leicester.

Wavell Wakefield

Wavell Wakefield was one of the aristocrats of the game – quite literally. Lord Wakefield of Kendal was schooled at Sedbergh and captained Cambridge University in the immediate aftermath of the First World War before having an illustrious career with the RAF (on and off the rugby field), Leicester, Harlequins and England. While "Wakers" (as his friends knew him) may have been born with a silver spoon in his mouth he was worth his weight in gold as a great tactician and as a no.8 or lock.

Powerful and fast, he was an inspired strategist, recognising that if a backrow trio maximised its defensive and attacking capabilities, it could dominate a game. Wakefield's initiatives to maximise the backrow's capabilities required the backs to hound the opposition's midfield backs; while the forwards, who previously ambled from one set piece to the next with the sole intention of gaining possession of the ball and then standing by, were required to tackle and chase in the loose exchanges.

Wakefield brought order and direction to the game, and played a leading part in England's Grand Slam triumphs of 1921 and 1923 before captaining them to a third in 1924. He went on to become a successful businessman, spent 40 years in Parliament as an MP, and was eventually president of the RFU.

In 1930 he turned his hand to writing a book on tactics, called *Rugger*. In it he advocated a limitation on touch-kicks because they were too negative and were stripping the game of its enjoyment. He was ahead of his time. A mere 37 years later a rule was introduced – the so-called Australian dispensation – outlawing touch-kicks on the full outside the 22. (This meant that rather than simply hoofing the ball into touch, players kicking outside the 22 now had to ensure that the ball bounced on the field of play before crossing the touch-line if the line-out was to be awarded where the ball went out. If not, it was taken back to where the kick was taken.) When he heard about it Wakefield saw the humorous side commenting, "That's about the length of time it takes to get a law changed in rugby football."

Jonny Wilkinson

Jonny Wilkinson, MBE, has admitted that he needs to lighten up a little and get a life outside rugby. The only hitch is that his obsessive pursuit of perfection has paid off big time: the 23-year-old English fly-half is a phenomenon.

Jonny doesn't drink, smoke or party and he goes to great lengths to steal a march on the opposition. Not only does he practice his goal-kicking for hours after his team-mates have packed up and gone home but he has even constructed special assault courses to improve his game. To sharpen his footwork he enlisted the help of Steve Black, his trainer at Newcastle Falcons, to rig-up lines of swinging sandbags for him to dodge through.

The result? The Hampshire lad, who made his international debut at 18, is already England's record points scorer and key player. It is not just his goal-kicking which is extra-terrestrial. Wilkinson is the complete package, a clever runner, a pass master, and a devastating tackler in a position in which defensive duties are usually considered optional.

He made a remarkable 22 tackles – twice as many as his nearest team-mate – in the 2003 Grand Slam game in Ireland. And when he hits, they stay hit. But that is just skimming the surface of the Boy Wonder's contribution. In the same game against the Irish, he kept the scoreboard ticking over with two drop-goals, three conversions and a penalty. He finished as the Six Nations top goal-kicker for 2003 with an 89 per cent success rate (25 from 28), and was the leading off-loader out of tackles (9).

England do not have another fly-half who comes close to matching Wilkinson – but then nor does anyone else. The question pre-occupying England coach Clive Woodward is that with Wilkinson's incredible work ethic, how do they save the boy wonder from peaking too soon?

Chapter 20

Ten Matches Made in Rugby Heaven

*I*n everyone's life, certain times and events are etched indelibly in the memory. For rugby fans those momentous memories have been the days when their chosen rugby team fought a great opponent in a magnificent contest and emerged victorious. These are the memories we savour, the moments when you can say "I Was There!" In this chapter we relive ten of the greatest matches in rugby history, and look at the landscape that made them so special.

When talking about what transpired on the field of play on these momentous occasions, we use the shorthand of some rugby terms explained in other parts of this book.

Australia 14 England 25, Melbourne 2003

Despite being at the end of a gruelling ten month season (two months longer than their southern hemisphere rivals), England arrived in Australia on a high. Not only had they embarked on their two test summer tour of Australia and New Zealand with a Six Nations Grand Slam under their belts, they had negotiated the first hurdle of their journey Down Under by beating the All Blacks 15–13 in Wellington, holding out despite being reduced to 13 men through yellow cards.

England had never beaten Australia on Australian soil in ten attempts stretching back to 1967, but this time they were at full strength against the reigning World Cup champions and on the brink of an unrivalled 13-match unbeaten run. They did not let the opportunity slip. Led superbly from the front by Martin Johnson, England dominated Australia in the forward battle, gaining a 100 per cent return on their lineouts and knocking the Wallabies backwards in almost every phase of play.

They were rewarded with first half tries from Will Greenwood and Mike Tindall, and Ben Cohen speared through after the interval to press home England's superiority. Although Wendell Sailor scored a consolation try for the hosts, the damage was done. In the process England recorded their tenth victory in succession over Tri-Nations opponents and became the first northern hemisphere side to win back-to-back away victories over southern hemisphere opponents.

Ireland 6 England 42, Dublin 2003

Under coach Clive Woodward, England had beaten New Zealand, Australia, and South Africa at Twickenham in the autumn of 2002. And yet, they were seen as "bottlers" away from their imposing Twickenham fortress; despite finishing top of the Six Nations, England had failed to win a cherished Grand Slam, falling at the final hurdle on three occasions, all away from home. 2003 represented the last chance of a Grand Slam for some of the veteran warriors in Woodward's pack, like Martin Johnson, Neil Back, Lawrence Dallaglio and Richard Hill.

England gradually gathered momentum during the course of the Six Nations, beating France (25–17), Wales (6–29), Italy (40–5), and Scotland (40–9), before going to Dublin to take on the Irish, who were also undefeated, in a Grand Slam decider.

England showed steely resolve soaking up early Irish pressure to edge ahead 13–6 at half-time courtesy of a fine try by Lawrence Dallaglio and two Johnny Wilkinson drop goals.

Then, on the hour, came the clincher as Mike Tindall burst through to score from a short pass by Will Greenwood. In the last quarter of the match, with their pack pounding forward, England scored three more tries, through Greenwood (twice), and Dan Luger. The ghosts of Grand Slams lost were finally laid to rest – and in emphatic style.

South Africa 15 British Isles 18, Durban 1997

The first Lions side of the professional era were unheralded and unfavoured yet they became only the third side to win a series in South Africa. Their hosts adopted an arrogant stance, with some local critics suggesting that the tourists were more "Pussycats than Lions" after the England forwards failed to steamroller provincial opposition.

However, the Lions scored a resounding 25–16 victory in Cape Town in the first of the three Test series. The second Test at Kings Park, Durban, saw the series on the line as the thin red line of the Lions was stretched to breaking point by a ferocious South African onslaught. Despite a heroic defensive effort, spearheaded by centre Scott Gibbs and back-rowers Tim Rodber and Lawrence Dellaglio, South Africa scored three tries in the middle of the game through Joost van der Westhuizen, Percy Montgomery and Andre Joubert, but wasted 15 points due to poor goal kicking. The Lions' kicker and the makeshift fullback, Neil Jenkins, fared much better, landing five out of five penalties to level the score at 15 all with six minutes remaining.

With the outcome of the match in the balance, the Lions forced a lineout, and Gregor Townsend darted for the line. When the ball came back it fell to Jerry Guscott, who added the winning touch: his drop-kick flew between the uprights, and the series was won for the Lions.

South Africa 15 New Zealand 12, Johannesburg 1995

This was more than a game of rugby, it was a validation of the way that sport can help to heal the wounds of political strife. In South Africa's case it was about a combination of the "One-team, One-nation" campaign wholeheartedly supported by the country's president, Nelson Mandela, in the build up to the 1995 World Cup. It aimed to break the association between rugby and apartheid and make it a sport that all South Africans, no matter what their ethnicity, could support.

Before the final there was a portent of the drama and excitement to come when a Boeing 747 screamed over the Johannesburg skyline, passing just 50 feet above the Ellis Park stands with the words "Good Luck Bokke" painted underneath its wingspan.

The game itself was a juddering confrontation as South Africa strove to overturn the tournament favourites, New Zealand, who featured the mighty Jonah Lomu. The 6 foot 5inch, 18 stone Polynesian winger had scored four tries in New Zealand's 45–29 semi-final blitz of England, and in the week before the final the greats of Springbok rugby had been canvassed for their views on how to stop him. Their advice worked – neither Lomu nor the All Blacks could escape the vice-like grip of the South African defence. The match became a duel between two great goal-kicking fly-halves, New Zealand's Andrew Mehrtens and South Africa's Joel Stransky. Stransky's two penalties and a drop goal saw South Africa to a 9–6 half-time lead; Mehrtens kicked two penalties for New Zealand. After the interval the All Blacks dominated possession but they could not break the Springbok defence and had to settle for a Mehrtens' drop goal to tie the score. With the match locked at 9–9 on the final whistle, the teams faced each other in extra time. Mehrtens put New Zealand ahead in the first minute, but Stransky restored the status quo at 12–12 with a penalty in the last minute of the first period. Then, with eight minutes remaining, South Africa won a scrum wide on the New Zealand 22, and with the composure that is a hallmark of great fly-halves, Stransky slotted the drop goal as calmly as if he was kicking a ball about in the park.

As the match ended and the Springboks huddled in prayer, Mandela made his way onto the pitch to present the World Cup to Springbok captain Francois Pienaar. He was wearing the green and yellow jersey of the side once seen as a symbol of the oppressor; on his back was Pienaar's number 6.

The stadium erupted, and as Mandela handed over the trophy he thanked Pienaar for his efforts on behalf of South Africa, to which Pienaar replied that no one had done more for South Africa than Mandela himself.

France 43 New Zealand 31, Twickenham 1999

The pre-match forecast was for the All Blacks to give the off-colour French a roasting, but in rugby, no-one is ever quite sure which France will turn up – very good France or very poor France. Initially it seemed like the jaded version as Jonah Lomu scored twice to give New Zealand a 24–10 lead. But then the French flipped the switch, scoring 33 points in a burst that smashed New Zealand to smithereens.

Christophe Lamaison kicked two penalties and two drop goals as the French forwards turned up the heat. Then the electric Christophe Dominici scored a long-range try, and Richard Dourthe scored another, following-up a Lamaison chip. The *coup de grace* came when the turbo-charged flanker Olivier Mangne hacked the ball to the New Zealand try line from his own 22, where the grey-haired speedster, Philippe Bernat-Salles, touched down. It turned a Twickenham crowd that had started the match anti-French into loud supporters of an entente cordiale. France were that good.

England 21 France 19, Twickenham 1991

England won the Grand Slam (denied them the previous season by the Scots) thanks to the clear superiority of their mighty pack. Nevertheless, France, who were also unbeaten, marked the occasion with one of the greatest tries in international rugby, also finishing ahead 3–1 on the try count.

With Paul Ackford and the back row of Mike Teague, Dean Richards and Peter Winterbottom bludgeoning France onto the back foot, England gained tactical control with Richard Hill and Rob Andrew calling the shots at half-back. The pressure yielded a steady haul of points from the boot of full back Simon Hodgkinson and there was a deadly strike from England's record try scorer, Rory Underwood.

The French refused to buckle, and after Hodgkinson missed with a penalty attempt France counter-attacked brilliantly. Pierre Berbizier caught the ball in-goal before finding Serge Blanco looping behind him. The French break-out continued with Jean-Baptiste Lafond and Didier Camberabero carrying the ball up the field, before Philippe Sella tore down the right wing. Sella fed the ball inside to Camberabero, and the French fly-half chipped ahead, gathered his own kick, and then cross-kicked for the middle of the field. Winger Philippe Saint-Andre had read his mind, and as Camberabero's kick bounced he latched onto it to score under the posts.

England did not ignore the warning. They tightened their grip up front and, although Camberabero and Franck Mesnel scored further tries, England's pack kept France under the cosh and Hodgkinson's goalkicking translated the pressure into the winning margin.

Scotland 13 England 7, Murrayfield 1990

The first of England's Grand Slam showdowns of the early 1990s resulted in a defeat as resounding as it was unexpected. England had dominated the Five Nations Championship, winning in expansive, convincing fashion with an all-court game. Where England had got to the winner-take-all match in style, scoring bucket loads of tries, Scotland had scraped past both Ireland and Wales by narrow margins.

However, England had not banked on the Murrayfield factor, and the Scottish stadium was a bear-pit of hostility, fuelled by historical differences with the English.

David Sole, the Scotland captain, sensed the mood. So, rather than sprint onto the field, Scotland proceeded onto the pitch in a slow, deliberate march, as if to say, "This match is ours, and you have no right to it."

Scotland proceeded to make England equally unwelcome once the game got under way. Although England scored an excellent early try through Guscott, Scotland were 9–4 ahead at half-time thanks to three Craig Chalmers' penalties. Scotland extended their lead early in the second half with a kick-and-chase try touched down by Tony Stanger, and then held on grimly until the English giant was felled.

South Africa 9 British Isles 26, Port Elizabeth 1974

There are some who argue that the 1971 Lions touring side that went to New Zealand were the greatest, but the Lions side with the greatest record is the 1974 team who visited South Africa. Under the captaincy of Willie John McBride, and coached by his fellow Ulsterman Syd Millar, they were undefeated in the four test series and saw off all their provincial opponents.

McBride had been on four previous Lions tours, suffering three hammerings, but then securing victory in 1971. It had taught him what he needed to know. The success of the 1974 Lions was built on intimidating forward power, with his 1971 henchmen, lock Gordon Brown, prop Ian McLauchlan and no.8 Mervyn Davies, bolstered by pugnacious Welsh hooker Bobby Windsor, two English powerhouses in prop Fran Cotton and craggy blindside Roger Uttley, and a fearless Irish openside in Fergus Slattery. With abundant possession, a gifted back line of Gareth Edwards, Phil Bennett, Ian McGeechan, Dick Milliken, Andy Irvine, J P R Williams and J J Williams made no mistake of putting the Springboks to the sword.

When the first two tests were won, 12–3 (in Cape Town) and 28–9 (in Pretoria), the South Africans were reeling. In a panic-stricken bid to arrest the slide they made 10 changes to their team.

With the Springboks desperate to salvage lost pride there were running fist fights amongst the forwards, with the Lions employing their notorious "99" call. This call meant that if one Lions player was involved in a fracas, everyone would step-in. The early scoring was limited, but in injury time at the end of the first half the Lions went ahead 7–3 through a Brown try from a lineout. After the interval a 50 metre penalty by Irvine and a drop goal from Bennett gave the Lions a 13–3 cushion.

Enter Lions winger J J Williams, a former Commonwealth Games sprinter, with the touch of a fly-half. When the Lions won a line out inside the South African half, Bennett threw a miss-pass to J P R Williams, who came into the line from fullback. An exchange of passes with Milliken saw J J Williams burst clear for his first try. Although Snyman kicked two penalties to reduce the deficit to 19–9, J J then buried the Springbok hopes with a chip over the top of two defenders for his second try – and a score that put the series beyond doubt.

Barbarians 23 New Zealand 11, Cardiff 1973

Fergus Slattery, the Ireland and Lions openside flanker says that the final game of the 1973 All Blacks tour, which pitted New Zealand against a Barbarians invitation side with a virtual 1971 Lions line-up, gave the best players in the British Isles the chance to confirm their superiority over their great rivals.

The gloss still shimmers. Gareth Edwards' try for the Barbarians three minutes into the showdown against the brutally efficient New Zealanders, has been hailed by some as the greatest ever. The sheer flair and unstoppable momentum of the move makes the try unforgettable. From Phil Bennett's jack knife side-steps (the Barbarians coach Carwyn James had suggested to

Bennett before the match that he could sidestep the opposition off the park), through the handling of John Pullin, John Dawes, Tom David, and Derek Quinnell, to that supercharged final surge by Edwards from 35m out, it was the ultimate statement of the Barbarian's desire to win.

The Barbarians built on their amazing start with a second try through Slattery, and then a third through John Bevan, for a 17–0 half-time lead. After the interval the New Zealanders fought back with typical tenacity to 17–11, thanks to two tries from Grant Batty, their small firebrand winger, and a Joe Karam penalty.

However, the Barbarians finished as they started, as David Duckham, the long-striding English winger, capped a superb performance by weaving through the All Blacks ranks, passing the ball to Quinnell, Dawes, Mike Gibson, then Slattery, and finally to J P R Williams to score the try. Bennett's conversion gave the Barbarians a 23–11 winning margin, and rugby in the British Isles was on top of the world.

New Zealand 3 British Isles 13, Wellington 1971

Context is everything. The Lions as they are better known, had never won a series in New Zealand. What's more, despite traditionally having exciting backs they had invariably been pummelled by New Zealand in the forward battle, consequently losing games they should have won.

In 1971 New Zealand went about sorting out the Lions in time-honoured fashion. Their provincial sides used the boot and fist liberally in an attempt to subdue the tourists before the four match test series began. The "Battle of Canterbury" (prior to the first test) saw Sandy Carmichael and Ray McLoughlin (who broke a thumb retaliating), the two first choice Lions props, sidelined as a result of the brutal Canterbury assault.

However, the Lions refused to be softened up, and won the first test 9–3 thanks to a superb defensive effort, and the kicking of Barry John, who effectively ended the career of Fergie McCormick, the New Zealand full-back, with his pin-point tactical kicking. However, the All Blacks came storming back to square the series, winning the second test 22–12 in Christchurch.

The series was up for grabs in the third test in Wellington, and the Lions, inspired by the brilliance of fly-half John and the tactical genius of coach Carwyn James, were up to the task. The Lions produced an opening quarter of such control and authority that the All Blacks never recovered. The pack, led by McBride gained parity, and the superb Lions backs did the rest. They scored 13 points in the first 13 minutes, with Gerald Davies diving over in the corner for the first try, and John collecting a second, gifted to him by Gareth Edwards, who burst through and made a hand-off which lifted the All Blacks fly-half Bob Burgess off his feet. John converted both and dropped a goal, and from there the Lions shut New Zealand out to ensure that, at worst, the series would be shared.

And if you were wondering: The Lions drew the last test 14–14 to make history and fulfil manager Dr Doug Smith's uncanny pre-tour prophecy that the Lions would win the series 2–1, with one test drawn.

Chapter 21

Ten Peculiar Facts about Rugby

"**T**o play rugby union, you need three things: a good pass, a good tackle and a good excuse." Though we wish we could claim to be the people who said that, we have to hand the credit to that ubiquitous person, Anon.

This chapter is a good excuse for me to tell you about some of the strange, odd, even bizarre things that can happen in the world of rugby. While most stories centre on the players, some are about the officials of the game. If you are a collector of rugby trivia, you are in for a treat.

Rugby Attracts Some of the Unlikeliest People

Rugby players come in many political stripes. Just take a look at the names of some of the famous (and in at least one case, infamous) men who once wore rugby jerseys before rugby jerseys became fashion statements:

✔ **Che Guevara:** Best known as a failed exporter of revolution and guerrilla leader, Ernesto "Che" Guevara was also a passionate rugby player. Che was a medical student at the University of Buenos Aires in Argentina when he developed a love of the game. An enthusiastic fly-half , Guevara played several seasons of club rugby before being distracted by a belief that he had to change the world.

✔ **Idi Amin:** They didn't know it at the time, but when the Lions squad touring Africa in 1955 prepared to take on East Africa, they almost played the man who became one of the most despised dictators of the 20th century. Before becoming the president of Uganda and an infamous despot, the all-imposing Idi Amin was not only a keen heavyweight boxer, he was a better-than-average rugby forward, playing the occasional representative match. He didn't take the field against the Lions, remaining on the reserves bench, but became well known for his horrific acts when president several decades later.

Amin was educated in Britain. In 1964, the British Dominion Office described Amin as "…a splendid type and a good rugby player…he is virtually bone from the neck up and needs things explained in words of one letter."

East Africa has a rich rugby history and before World War Two fielded particularly strong teams. The Uganda Rugby Union, founded in 1955, has its home ground in Kampala and now boasts 4,500 players, 12 clubs and 20 referees – but none as notorious as Idi Amin.

✔ **Bill Clinton:** When American officials claim rugby is gaining a foothold in their country, they bring up the fact that at least one of their most recent presidents has played it. Yes, it's true. Bill Clinton, the king of the cigars, did actually play the 15-man game. His rugby career was fleeting, but real enough.

After completing college in 1968, Clinton won a Rhodes Scholarship, which allowed him to study at Oxford University. Clinton, a big believer in doing what the locals do, was soon lured into trying his luck on the Oxford rugby fields. He didn't make much of an impression, but he did run around in several third or fourth team games.

✔ **George W. Bush:** The presidential successor to Bill Clinton went one better than the sax-playing leader. In 1968, George Dubya, allegedly a wild man at college, played in the Yale First XV. The American magazine, *Sports Illustrated*, even has pictures to prove it.

Rugby is Played in Extreme Weather and in Strange Locations

Since the modern game was developed in England in the 19th century (see Chapter 1), rugby has turned up in some rather unexpected places. Equally unexpected are the settings of some rugby-playing fields and the extraordinary range of climate and weather in which the game is played.

- **Bahrain:** Some countries, such as Bahrain, play rugby on desert sand, often in the highest temperatures imaginable.

- **England:** Australian teams touring England have often discovered the delights of playing in the fog. The England 18 Group played the 1978 Australian Schoolboys teams at Twickenham in a fog so thick that the players could not see more than a metre in front of them. The spectators couldn't see a thing, so they were allowed to stand on the sidelines near the dead ball lines in the hope that they might be able to follow the game.

- **Indonesia:** One of the main rugby grounds in Indonesia is found deep in a jungle, while another is almost at the summit of a mountain, near a tea plantation.

- **Jordan:** Few grounds can beat the Amman Rugby Club, whose players play on the floor of the Dead Sea. The pitch, whose surface is soft sand, lies 385 metres below sea level.

- **Russia:** Some of the coldest rugby venues are in Russia. In 1978, Krasnoyarsk played Polyechnika Alma when the temperature was minus 23 degrees Celsius. No-one even contemplated calling the game off – the team from Krasnoyarsk had travelled 2,000 kilometres in order to play. To overcome the chill, the players wore balaclavas, gloves and several pairs of tracksuits.

- **The Seychelles:** Going back to warmer climes, rugby players in the Seychelles play on a ground that was created from the earth of a landslide that followed the passage of a cyclone.

- **Western Samoa:** Rugby legend has it that when Western Samoa began playing internationals, their home ground had a large coconut tree growing on the halfway line. Sounds apocryphal, but then again the Samoans have always prided themselves on their relaxed style.

The Samoans' relaxed style is also reflected in the way they report their rugby. In 1926, the local newspaper missed out on covering the epic Samoa versus Tonga international. *The Samoan Times* explained that its rugby writer "has failed us this week…owing to a previous engagement at a hopscotch match near the Market Hall on the same afternoon, we did not see the Rugby game."

Players Injure Themselves in Bizarre Ways

Much as we would like you to believe otherwise, it is a sad fact of life that, yes, players do sometimes get injured while playing rugby. Some of the better-known accidents – better known because of the utter embarrassment of most of the players concerned – include players who were:

- ✓ **Gored in the Achilles heel:** Northern Transvaal centre Pieter Nel missed the 1990 Currie Cup final when he injured his ankle while running onto the Loftus Versfeld pitch in Pretoria. Nel tried to get around a photographer with a side-step then slipped on some dung left behind by a bull that happened to be the local mascot.

- ✓ **Stretched out while waiting:** Dickie Lloyd was to have played in the 1914 Ireland team against Wales, but while jogging around as he waited for the kick-off, he strained a muscle and had to be replaced.

- ✓ **Blinded by the sun:** In 1969, French flanker Jean-Pierre Salut could not contain his excitement as he prepared to face Scotland at the great Parisian stadium, Stade Colombes. To calm himself down, he decided to be the last player to run onto the field. To get to the ground from the dressing rooms, the players had to run down a very long corridor and negotiate several flights of stairs before emerging into the sunlight. Salut was going really well – until he tripped on the final step and broke his ankle.

- ✓ **Kneecapped in midair:** After struggling with a string of injuries, Scottish halfback Andy Nicol was delighted he had returned to full fitness and was able to lead his country on its tour of South Africa in 1997. He was happily sleeping away on the flight to Johannesburg when an errant drinks trolley smashed into his knee. Nicol was sidelined for several weeks.

- ✓ **Flattened by a pie:** New Zealander Jack Finlay was picked for an international series against Australia in 1946. Unfortunately, Finlay had to miss the second international because of an incident with a flying pie. On his way to Auckland, a hungry Finlay hopped out at a railway station to buy himself a meat pie and ate it while standing on the station platform. While Finlay was engrossed in his pie, a train accelerated out of the station and Finlay was hit by an open carriage door. Shortly afterwards, Finlay announced his retirement.

Sometimes Officials Make Unofficial Calls

Sendings-off occur when a player violates an important rugby law and cannot play for the rest of the game. Sometimes even the officials are not safe from the wrath of other officials. For example, at a Plymouth club game in England in 1967, the referee ordered off the touch judge after he was involved in a mêlée not just with players but also some spectators.

Yet even the most serious rules can be taken too seriously with amusing results. For example, the strangest sending-off wasn't actually meant to be a sending-off. In 1988, former Irish international front-rower Gerry McLoughlin was playing for Welsh club-side Gilfach Goch when he was involved in a mêlée. According to Irish and Welsh lore, when referee Roy Rees had sorted the fight out, he looked at McLoughlin and told him, as a general warning, "Push off and let's get on with the game."

About 15 minutes later, when a scrum was set, Rees discovered that the local club was minus their tight-head prop – Big Gerry. McLoughlin had misinterpreted what Rees had said and thought "push off" meant that he had been sent from the field. By the time Gerry was told of his error, he was in his street clothes. Gilfach Goch had to make do with 14 men for the rest of the game. Somehow Gilfach won.

Rugby Blunders into Multicultural Minefields

When a player is sent off, he usually has to front a judiciary committee, which is a rather formal occasion. Unfortunately, formal occasions have a habit of being undermined by human folly, especially in cross-cultural exchanges, and sometimes result in embarrassment all round.

One of the more entertaining judiciary committee incidents occurred in Australia while Malcolm McPhee was chairman of the Sydney Rugby Union Judiciary Committee. As Neil Marks wrote in his book *Tales from the Locker Room* (Ironbark Press), McPhee and his committee had to interview two players, both recruited from overseas, who had been reported by referees. One was a large Samoan second-rower from the Drummoyne club in Sydney, and the other an even larger Fijian second-rower from the Sydney club of Hornsby.

The Hornsby player was the first to arrive, wearing a Fijian lap-lap and sandals. Accompanying him was his wife, a very large woman dressed identically to her husband. The player introduced himself as Charlie Levula from Hornsby.

"How do you do, Charlie", the chairman replied, politely shaking the big forward's hand. McPhee then noticed Levula's wife standing in the background. Thrusting out his hand, he said, "And you must be from Drummoyne!"

Rugby union may need to introduce a new law – for sending judiciary officials to the sin bin when they make social blunders.

Players Score in Unorthodox Ways

The aim of rugby is to score more points that the opposition. No surprises there. However, over the years, some rather unorthodox methods of scoring have been observed on the field. (You can read about the orthodox scoring system in Chapter 2.)

- ✔ **The unlikeliest try** was scored during a game in Builth Wells in Wales about a century ago. The visiting fullback kicked the ball into some tree branches that were overhanging the pitch. Surprise, surprise – the ball got stuck. While officials went off to find another ball and the players had a rest on the pitch, the ball suddenly fell from the tree. A quick-thinking player grabbed the ball and scored under the posts. The opposition naturally complained but the referee awarded the try because, under local rules, the ball had not gone out of play.

- ✔ **The world's longest try** goes to a team from the Powerhouse Rugby Club in Victoria, who, some time in the 1970s, ran the ball around the Albert Park Lake in Melbourne for ten days. The team covered more than 2,200 kilometres, with no knock-ons or forward passes. Why they did it, however, is anyone's guess.

- ✔ **The fastest try in international history** is an honour claimed by Scotland's New Zealand import, John Leslie. Leslie scored with only nine seconds played in the international against Wales at Murrayfield in 1999.

- ✔ **The only jointly awarded international try** was scored by the Welsh players Howie Jones and Harry Peacock in a Test match against Ireland in 1930. The referee was unable to work out which player grounded the ball, so the only joint try in an international game was awarded.

- ✔ **The accidental try** occurred in the late 1950s. George Nepia, recognised as probably New Zealand's greatest fullback, was well into retirement but continued to play in social matches. In one of these games, the ball hit him perfectly in the chest. Noticing a gap straight in front of him, he sprinted for the line and grounded the ball right under the posts. Only one problem – he was the referee.

The Game Must Go On: From Inane to Canine

The game goes on in spite of the weather. The game also goes on in spite of the sometimes bizarre behaviour of players and officials, and things that happen off the pitch as well as on it.

✔ **Williams vs Randall (1909):** In 1909, two Welsh families decided to play each other in a Sevens game, with £100 in prize money to the winners. Seven brothers of the Williams clan from Pembrokeshire met seven from the Randall clan of Llanelli on neutral ground at Carmarthen. Several thousand spectators crowded the ground to watch the match degenerate into a wrestling bout. The Williams boys won the money.

✔ **East Midlands vs Barbarians (1921):** Former England halfback Adrian Stoop refereed the 1921 East Midlands vs Barbarians match. Somehow he managed to blow the final whistle 14 minutes early. After complaints and protests, the players and referee had to get out of their baths and finish the match.

✔ **All Blacks vs Tahiti (1976):** When international teams play the after-match function is usually held well after the match. Not so when the All Blacks decided to play a friendly game against a Tahitian XV. The Tahitians decided to have their function *before* kick-off. They offered the New Zealanders a sumptuous feast including copious amounts of wine and champagne. The tactic backfired when the Tahitian team decided to join in and have a few drinks, too. They ran onto the field somewhat the worse for wear and suffering from extremely blurred vision. The All Blacks won by more than 70 points.

✔ **Portsmouth Victoria vs Southampton Trojans (a date in the 1890s):** Numerous matches have been interrupted by stray dogs running onto the pitch, but only one dog has ever been used to score a try. In a game between Portsmouth Victoria and Southampton Trojans, a ball kicked into the Trojans in-goal area rebounded off a dog. One of the Portsmouth players gathered the ball and claimed a try. Although the Trojans protested, the try stood. The Rugby Football Union ruled that the decision was correct, because dogs were not classified as spectators. If the ball had bounced off a spectator, it would not have been allowed.

If It's Going to Happen, It Happens on Tour

Touring teams often like taking the mickey out of local journalists. When the Fijian team toured Britain in 1970, a young scribe asked one of their huge forwards how they celebrated after matches. "The winners eat the losers," was the reply. The gullible scribe thought he was serious and included it in his report.

Strange as it may seem, some of the most memorable things that happen on a rugby tour do not occur on the pitch. And not all things that happen on tour are good – tragedy strikes everywhere.

- **Jonah and the Happy Snapper:** The 1994 Hong Kong Sevens heralded the arrival of a rugby phenomenon named Jonah Lomu. After Lomu had helped New Zealand to win the title, Dave Rogers, a British photographer, was trying to get a picture of the Kiwi giant with his captain, Eric Rush. However, a drunken young fan consistently got in the way, larking about and spoiling the shot. An exasperated Rogers could finally take no more, saying: "Just **** off will you – how old are you anyway?" "Nineteen", responded Jonah.

- **A right royal salute:** During the 1984 Australia tour of the British Isles a royal incident occurred when Queensland back-rower Chris Roche decided to perch himself on an antique hall table on the team's visit to Buckingham Palace. Within a few seconds, the table, unused to heavy weights like Roche, crashed to the floor. As Roche looked for somewhere to hide, Prince Philip turned around and casually said, "Don't worry. There are plenty more of them in the storeroom."

- **War stops play:** The award for the saddest tour of all goes to the 1939 Wallabies, who arrived in the United Kingdom just before World War Two was declared. The tour was immediately abandoned. After spending several days filling sandbags to protect their hotel in Torquay, the players returned home without a game being played. But they still endured a hazardous trip, with their boat forced to zigzag to throw off submarine attacks.

- **A tragedy in Australia:** The worst tragedy on a rugby tour occurred in Australia in 1888 when British captain R L (Bob) Seddon drowned while sculling on the Hunter River near Maitland. Just over a century later, when the 1989 British Lions toured Australia, there was a scare when several players found themselves in trouble during a rafting expedition.

Brothers Like to Battle It Out Together

Rugby seems to run in the blood of some families. Brothers frequently wind up playing side by side – usually on the same team. The following list names some of the "firsts" in sibling players:

- The first brothers to appear together in a rugby international were John and Francis Luscombe, who played for England in 1871.

- The first instance of three brothers in an international match occurred in 1875 when Scotland's NJ, AB and JF Finlay played in a scoreless draw against England.

✔ The first time that brothers appeared on both international teams was in 1885 when George and Richard Maitland played for Scotland and Bob and Arthur Gould appeared for Wales.

✔ Stewart and Jim Boyce became the first twins to play in an international, when they played for Australia against New Zealand in 1964.

✔ Gordon Brown of Scotland was the first brother to replace a brother when he replaced his injured brother Peter in a match against Wales in 1970.

The Unlikeliest Lads Can Make It to the Top

As a clear reminder that in rugby you should never give up, we offer the stories of three players who came out of nowhere to achieve great things:

✔ **Which cocky player?** After the main England trial for the international team against the first Springboks tour in 1906, it seemed a certainty that Liverpool and Lancashire representative Noel Slocock, a forward, would be selected. Slocock was a formidable lineout jumper, something desperately required against the touring South Africans. Although the national selectors put Slocock's name on the Test list, an administrative bungle led to the name of Arnold Alcock appearing on the list instead. Alcock was a little-known medical student who had played in a hospital cup team. Somehow, Alcock played for England and managed to help his country to a 3-all draw.

✔ **Whose autograph?** One man who did all he could to get noticed was England international Carston Catcheside, a winger. After his first international game, Catcheside made certain that the people who mattered knew who he was. He wrote his name all over the bald head of one of the selectors.

✔ **Deserves a Merrick increase?** One player who wasn't expected to get there, but did anyway, was Australian international scrum-half Steve Merrick who emerged from the small New South Wales country town of Singleton to play in the two-Test series against New Zealand in 1995.

When rugby turned professional later the same year, the salaries that could be earned turned the heads of a number of Australian players. Merrick was different: He didn't want to be a well-paid, high-profile sportsman. He simply didn't want to move from peaceful Singleton to be part of the Sydney rat-race, and so turned his back on lucrative player contracts and the chance of holding a long-standing mortgage on both the New South Wales and Australian halfback positions.

Part VI
Appendixes

"That's why we call him 'The Mole'."

In this part . . .

Appendixes are not usually the first part of the book that readers head for. For most people, the first and only time they notice a book's appendix is when they are standing in the bookstore flipping through the book to see if it meets their requirements. In the case of this book, though, the three appendixes are collections of vital information.

The first appendix gives details of the winners of major rugby tournaments – the kind of information you need if you enjoy statistics. The second appendix, the glossary, is one you find yourself turning to time and again when you want to refresh your memory about the meaning of certain words and phrases. And the third appendix helps you to get in touch with the organisations, teams and clubs that make up the world of rugby.

Appendix A

Honour Boards

●●

*W*ith international fixtures stretching back 132 years, we would need a new whole *For Dummies* book to log them all here, but we are able to provide you with a recent form guide by providing the results of major international tournaments and fixtures over the last decade.

Rugby World Cup

This has become the biggest event in the international rugby calendar since its inception in 1987. The tournament is held every four years with the winners earning the right to be called world champions.

World Cup winners 1987–1999			
Year	Winner	Result	Location
1987	New Zealand	New Zealand 29 France 9	Eden Park, Auckland
1991	Australia	Australia 12 England 6	Twickenham
1995	South Africa	South Africa 15 New Zealand 12	Ellis Park, Johannesburg
1999	Australia	Australia 35 France 12	Millennium Stadium, Cardiff

Six Nations

The "Daddy" of annual international competitions, and still the most compelling. It is effectively a European championship, and as competitive as they come.

Previous winners 1993–2003

Year	Country
1993	France
1994	Wales
1995	England
1996	England
1997	France
1998	France
1999	Scotland
2000	England
2001	England
2002	France
2003	England

Grand Slam winners 1992–2003

Year	Country
1992	England
1995	England
1997	France
1998	France
2002	France
2003	England

Grand slam winners history

Country	Year
England (11times)	1913, 1914, 1921,1923, 1924, 1928, 1957, 1980, 1991, 1992, 1995, 2003
Wales (8 times)	1908, 1909, 1911, 1950, 1952, 1971, 1976, 1978

Country	Year
France (7 times)	1968, 1977, 1981, 1987, 1997, 1998, 2002
Scotland (3 times)	1925, 1984, 1990
Ireland (Once)	1948

Triple crown winners 1992–2003

Year	Country
1992	England
1995	England
1996	England
1997	England
1998	England
2003	England

Triple crown winners history

Country	Year
England (23 times)	1883, 1884, 1892, 1913, 1914, 1921, 1923, 1924, 1928, 1934, 1937, 1954, 1957, 1960, 1980, 1991, 1992, 1995, 1996, 1997, 1998, 2002, 2003
Wales (17 times)	1893, 1900, 1902, 1905, 1908, 1909, 1911, 1950, 1952, 1965, 1969, 1971, 1976, 1977, 1978, 1979, 1988
Scotland (10 times)	1891, 1895, 1901, 1903, 1907, 1925, 1933, 1938, 1984, 1990
Ireland (6 times)	1894, 1899, 1948, 1949, 1982, 1985

England versus Scotland

This is the oldest international fixture of the lot, with the first game between the old enemies played in 1871. Even though it is now played as part of the Six Nations, it has its own special trophy, the Calcutta Cup.

England v Scotland international match results 1993–2003			
Year	*England*	*Scotland*	*Location*
1993	26	12	Twickenham
1994	15	14	Murrayfield
1995	24	12	Twickenham
1996	18	9	Murrayfield
1997	41	13	Twickenham
1998	34	20	Murrayfield
1999	24	21	Twickenham
2000	13	19	Murrayfield
2001	43	3	Twickenham
2002	29	3	Murrayfield
2003	40	9	Twickenham

England versus Ireland

England may be well ahead on the overall ledger of games dating back to 1875, but the Irish have always proved themselves capable of springing a few surprises.

England v Ireland international match results 1993–2003			
Year	*England*	*Ireland*	*Location*
1993	3	17	Dublin
1994	12	13	Twickenham
1995	20	8	Dublin
1996	28	15	Twickenham
1997	46	6	Dublin
1998	35	17	Twickenham
1999	27	15	Dublin

Year	England	Ireland	Location
2000	50	18	Twickenham
2001	14	20	Dublin
2002	45	11	Twickenham
2003	42	6	Dublin

England versus Wales

This is the most keenly contested rivalry in the Championship, although the Welsh have not had much to sing about recently. In 2003, after 109 matches, they were separated by just one win with Wales on 49, England on 48, and 12 draws.

England v Wales international match results 1993–2003			
Year	England	Wales	Location
1993	9	10	Cardiff
1994	15	8	Twickenham
1995	23	9	Cardiff
1996	21	15	Twickenham
1997	34	13	Cardiff
1998	60	26	Twickenham
1999	31	32	Wembley
2000	46	12	Twickenham
2001	44	15	Cardiff
2002	50	10	Twickenham
2003	26	9	Cardiff

England versus France

In overall results England are well ahead because France won very few of the early encounters. But France are now a European rugby superpower to rank alongside England, as the parity in recent results shows.

England v France international match results 1993–2003

Year	England	France	Location
1993	16	15	Twickenham
1994	18	14	Paris
1995	31	10	Twickenham
1995	9	19	Pretoria
1996	12	15	Paris
1997	20	23	Twickenham
1998	17	24	Paris
1999	21	10	Twickenham
2000	15	9	Paris
2001	48	19	Twickenham
2002	15	20	Paris
2003	25	17	Twickenham

England versus Italy

The new kids on the block, Italy were only admitted into the Six Nations in 2000. Since then they have struggled – just as the French did at the start of the previous century – but are improving steadily.

England v Italy international match results 2000–2003

Year	England	Italy	Location
2000	59	12	Rome
2001	80	23	Twickenham

Year	England	Italy	Location
2002	45	9	Twickenham
2003	40	5	Twickenham

England against the Tri Nations

Since 1997 England have sought annual fixtures against top southern hemisphere opposition, resulting in an autumn series with regular matches against Australia, South Africa and New Zealand.

England versus Australia

There's not much in it, although England have traditionally found it hard to win on Aussie soil, having to wait until 2003 for their first success. However, Twickenham has also become a stumbling block for the Wallabies.

England v Australia international match results since 1995			
Year	England	Australia	Location
1995	25	22	Cape Town*
1997	6	25	Sydney
1997	15	15	Twickenham
1998	0	76	Brisbane
1998	11	12	Twickenham
1999	15	22	Sydney
2000	22	19	Twickenham
2001	21	15	Twickenham
2002	32	31	Twickenham
2003	25	14	Melbourne

* match played during the World Cup

England versus New Zealand

England's record against the New Zealand All Blacks is nothing to shout about, but two consecutive victories in 2002 and 2003 made inroads into redressing the balance.

Year	England	New Zealand	Location
England v New Zealand international match results since 1993			
1993	15	9	Twickenham
1995	29	45	Cape Town*
1997	8	25	Manchester
1997	26	26	Twickenham
1998	22	64	New Zealand
1998	10	40	New Zealand
1999	16	30	Twickenham*
2002	31	28	Twickenham
2003	15	13	Wellington

* match played during the World Cup

England versus South Africa

England and the Springboks share one trait: they are historically bruising, uncompromising opponents. Nothing has altered over the last decade, as these statistics show

Year	England	South Africa	Location
England v South Africa international match results since 1994			
1994	32	15	Pretoria
1994	9	27	Cape Town

Year	England	South Africa	Location
1995	14	24	Twickenham
1997	11	29	Twickenham
1998	0	18	Cape Town
1998	13	7	Twickenham
1999	21	44	Paris
2000	13	18	Pretoria
2000	27	22	Bloemfontein
2000	25	17	Twickenham
2001	29	9	Twickenham
2002	53	3	Twickenham

Tri Nations previous winners

This annual competition among the big southern hemisphere nations, New Zealand, South Africa and Australia, began in 1996.

Previous winners 1996–2002	
Year	**Country**
1996	New Zealand
1997	New Zealand
1998	South Africa
1999	New Zealand
2000	Australia
2001	Australia
2002	New Zealand

Tri Nations Grand Slam winners

With each nation playing the others home and away each season, Grand Slams are hard earned in the Tri Nations.

Grand Slam winners	
Year	**Country**
1996	New Zealand
1997	New Zealand
1998	South Africa

Club and Provincial tournaments

Since professional rugby began in 1995 there has been a growth in cross-border competitions at provincial and club level, with the Heineken European Cup in the northern hemisphere and the Super 12 in the southern hemisphere as the standard bearers.

Heineken Cup

Clubs and provinces from England, France, Ireland, Wales, Scotland and Italy compete to become the champions of Europe.

Previous Heineken Cup finals 1996–2003			
Year	**Winner**	**Results**	**Location**
1996	Toulouse	Toulouse 21, Cardiff 18	Cardiff Arms Park
1997	Brive	Brive 28, Leicester 9	Cardiff Arms Park
1998	Bath	Bath 19, Brive 18	Stade Lescure, Bordeaux
1999	Ulster	Ulster 21, Colomiers 6	Lansdowne Road, Dublin
2000	Northampton	Northampton 9, Munster 8	Twickenham
2001	Leicester	Leicester 34, Stade Francais 30	Parc Des Princes, Paris

Year	Winner	Results	Location
2002	Leicester	Leicester 15, Munster 9	Millennium Stadium, Cardiff
2003	Toulouse	Toulouse 22, Perpignan 17	Lansdowne Road, Dublin

Zurich Premiership

The English Premiership, sponsored by Zurich, has become recognised as one of the toughest domestic competitions in the game.

Previous league champions 1988–2003

Year	Winners
1988	Leicester
1989	Bath
1990	Wasps
1991	Bath
1992	Bath
1993	Bath
1994	Bath
1995	Leicester
1996	Bath
1997	Wasps
1998	Newcastle
1999	Leicester
2000	Leicester
2001	Leicester
2002	Leicester
2003	Wasps

Zurich Premiership Championship finals

The first two finals did not decide the champions, because that honour went to the side that finished top of the Premiership table. But in 2003 a winner-takes-all Premiership final between the side at the top of the table and the team finishing second was introduced.

Previous Zurich Premiership Championship finals 2001–2003

Year	Results	Location
2001	Leicester 22, Bath 10	Twickenham
2002	Gloucester 28, Bristol 23	Twickenham
2003	Wasps 39, Gloucester 3	Twickenham

Celtic League

Revamped in 2003, this competition features 12 provincial and regional sides from Wales, Ireland and Scotland. There is no promotion or relegation.

Celtic league final results 2001–2003

Year	Results	
2002	Leinster 24, Munster 20	Lansdowne Road
2003	Munster 37, Neath 17	The Millennium Stadium

Super 12

This is the southern hemisphere's premium tournament below international level, with 12 provincial sides from New Zealand, South Africa and Australia competing against each other. There is no promotion or relegation.

Previous Super 12 finals 1996–2003

Year	Results
1996	Blues 45, Sharks 21
1997	Blues 23, Brumbies 7
1998	Crusaders 20, Blues 13
1999	Crusaders 24, Highlanders 19
2000	Crusaders 20, Brumbies 19
2001	Brumbies 36, Sharks 6
2002	Crusaders 31, Brumbies 13
2003	Blues 21, Crusaders 17

Appendix B

Glossary

10 metre law: When the team-mate of an offside player has kicked ahead, the offside player is considered to be taking part in the game if the player is in front of an imaginary line across the field which is ten metres from the opponent waiting to play the ball, or from where the ball lands. The offside player must immediately move behind the imaginary ten metre line.

10 metre line: The imaginary line behind which an offside player must move in order to take part in the game.

22 metre line: The line marked on the ground between the halfway line and a team's goal line or tryline.

advantage: Nothing to do with tennis. Occurs when a referee allows play to continue, even if there has been an infringement. The referee gives the team that has been fouled the chance to do something positive with the ball. If the team is unable to do this, the referee takes play back to the site of the original infringement and awards the aggrieved team a penalty. Advantage basically gives the innocent team two chances.

Age Grade rugby: The term for all rugby from ages six to eighteen.

Alickadoos: Members of the unpaid army of secretaries, sponge men, bar staff and all purpose workers who are the backbone of amateur rugby clubs.

ankle tap: Where a defender attempts to stop an attacking player by tapping him on the ankles. The defender strikes the ball carrier on the ankle from behind, causing him to lose balance. Not to be confused with a tap on the shoulder, or water on the brain.

back row: The third line of the scrum, comprising one number 8 and two flankers. Players are known as back-rowers.

back three: The fullback and the two wingers.

backs: Players who stand behind the scrum and are not involved in the lineouts.

ball carrier: The player carrying the ball.

binding: Firmly grasping another player's body from the shoulder to the hips with the whole arm from hand to shoulder.

Bledisloe Cup: The annual competition between Australia and New Zealand, staged since 1931.

blindside: The area between the ball and the closest sideline.

blindside flanker: The flanker who binds onto the scrum on the blindside or the short side. Usually wears the no.6 jersey.

blood bin: If a player is bleeding, he must leave the field of play until the wound is covered or dressed. While he is being treated, he is said to be in the blood bin.

bomb: A high kick generally aimed at the opposition fullback in the hope that under pressure he drops it and loses possession. Also called an *up and under*.

box kick: A high kick aimed to land in front of the opposition winger.

breakaway: The two forwards in the team, wearing jersey numbers 6 and 7. Also known as flankers, they bind on the side of the scrum, with their prime pursuit being to win the ball at the rucks and mauls. They are also important linkmen between the forwards and the backs.

breakdown: Occurs when play has been halted temporarily and possession (especially possession of the ball) is being contested by both teams. A tackle is the prime reason for a breakdown to occur. Also used to describe what a coach has when his team doesn't follow his orders.

Calcutta Cup: A trophy crafted from melted Indian silver rupees played for annually by England and Scotland as part of the Six Nations.

caps: A term used to denote the number of times a player has represented his national team. When someone is said to have 22 caps for Australia, it means that he has played 22 Tests for the Wallabies.

Celtic Cup: A newly-created cup competition for the Celtic League sides.

Celtic League: An Irish, Welsh and Scottish 22-game competition to rival the Zurich Premiership. There are 12 teams, playing in a home and away format.

centre: The players wearing the number 12 (inside centre) and number 13 (outside centre) jerseys. They are the heart and soul of a team's attack. The inside centre is sometimes called the *second five-eighth*.

channel: The path a ball takes when coming back through the scrum between the legs of the forwards.

charge down: The blocking of a kick by an opposing player.

chip kick: A short kick, usually directed over the top of the opposition's defensive line, hopefully to be retrieved by the kicker or a team-mate.

clearing kick: A kick aimed for the touchline as a way of relieving pressure.

Colts rugby: The under-19 age group level before adult rugby.

conversion: After a try is scored, the attacking team is allowed a free shot at goal. If successful, 2 points are added to the score. As a try is worth 5 points, a converted try is naturally worth 7 points.

corner flag: The flag situated at each corner of the playing field.

counter attack: An attacking move in response to an opposition attack, where the ball has passed from one team to the other.

County Championship: Once the most prestigious competition in English rugby, now a second tier tournament played by club players.

crossbar: The bar joining the two uprights of the goalposts. For a conversion or penalty goal to be successful, it must go over the crossbar.

cross kick: A kick across the ground aimed towards the attacking team's openside winger, who plans to run through the defence and re-gather the ball.

cut-out pass: A pass that deliberately misses one or more players and goes to the next player in the attacking line.

dead: The ball is out of play. This occurs when the ball has gone outside the playing area and remained there, or when the referee has blown the whistle to indicate a stoppage, or when a conversion kick is being taken.

dead ball line: The far end lines of the field.

decoy: A player who makes out that he is about to receive the ball in a bid to deceive the opposition's defensive line. Hence the phrase *decoy runner*.

defence: Used by one team to stop the other team when it is attacking. Also, the wooden barrier found around smaller grounds.

dive pass: Passing the ball while diving towards the person to whom the pass is intended for.

dodge: To move quickly to one side to avoid being tackled.

Dragons Rugby Trust: The Welsh version of age grade rugby.

drawing the man: Committing an opponent into tackling you just before passing the ball to a team-mate.

dressing room: The place where players get changed.

drift defence: A defensive system which sees the defending players drift sideways across the field.

driving maul: A maul where the opposition is driven back through sheer force.

driving tackle: When the tackler pushes the ball carrier backwards.

drop goal: When a player drop kicks the ball from general play over the crossbar of the opposition's goalposts. It is worth three points.

drop kick: The type of kick used to kick a field goal.

drop out: The kick used to restart play from a team's 22 metre line.

drop punt: An accurate form of punt kick, where the ball is dropped onto the boot and the ball spirals backwards from end to end.

Ellis, William Webb: The alleged creator of rugby. In 1823, Ellis reportedly picked up a ball and ran with it, thus inspiring a new form of football called rugby. Many historians dispute this story.

European Challenge Cup: Europe's second tier competition, but with a great knockout format, and often featuring form teams.

European Cup: The most compelling competition between club and provincial sides played in the world, featuring 24 teams from England, France, Wales, Ireland, Scotland, and Italy.

European Shield: Knockout shield for the first round losers in The European Challenge Cup.

feed: The placing of the ball into the scrum by the scrum-half.

fend off: When an attacking player uses an arm to push away a defender. Also called a *hand off*.

field goal: antipodean version of a drop goal.

five-eighth: The antipodean term for a *fly-half*.

five-metre scrum: A scrum that is set 5 metres from the defending team's tryline.

flick pass: A quick pass to a team-mate. The player throwing the ball flicks his wrists to quicken the ball's trajectory.

fly-half: The back who wears jersey number 10. The fly-half is one of the most important players in the team, often deciding how a side bases its attack. In Australia and New Zealand he is called the *five-eighth*.

forward pass: An illegal pass to a player who is ahead of the ball.

foul play: Play deemed by the referee as being dangerous. The offending player is penalised, possibly sent to the sin bin or even sent off.

free kick: A kick awarded to a team for a minor penalty.

front row: Forward players comprising of the loose-head prop, hooker, and tight-head prop. These players are called the *front-rowers*.

fullback: The back who wears the number 15 jersey and who plays behind the team's backline.

fulltime: The end of the game, usually after 80 minutes (two 40-minute halves).

Garryowen: A high kick, up and under, or bomb. Named after the Irish club renowned for using the kick.

goal: A successful kick between the goalposts.

goal kicker: The designated player in the team who has the task of kicking conversions and penalty goals.

goal line: The line that has to be crossed for a team to score a try. For this reason, the goal line is often called the *tryline*.

goose-step: Nothing to do with Nazis. A move made famous by Wallaby winger David Campese, involving a quickstep where the knees are locked and the legs are straight.

Grand Slam: The term used in the Six Nations when one side beats all its opponents during the tournament. (Also applies to touring sides if they beat all the Home Unions).

grubber kick: A kick that rolls along the ground and bounces unpredictably.

haka: A cultural display performed by numerous Southern Pacific teams, in particular, New Zealand, to intimidate the opposition. Usually performed before kick-off.

halfback: The antipodean term for a *scrum-half*.

halfback pass: A fast, accurate and often deceptive pass thrown by the halfback.

halves: Term used to describe the team's halfback and five-eighth.

halfway line: Marks the centre of the field where the game is started and also re-started after successful tries or penalty goals.

hand-off: pushing off an attacking player with a flat hand, palm-first.

Heineken Cup: Named after its sponsors, beer company Heineken, this is another name for the European Cup.

high tackle: A dangerous tackle, which hits the opponent above the armpits. Often sees offending players either given a yellow card or sent off.

hit and spin: When the ball carrier commits himself to being tackled, and then spins himself out of the tackle.

Home Nations: England, Wales, Ireland and Scotland.

hooker: The forward wearing the number 2 jersey and who is the central figure of the scrum. In the front row, he is supported in the scrum by the two props. Also throws the ball into the lineout.

hospital pass: A badly timed pass which puts the person catching the ball in great danger as it arrives exactly at the same time he is about to be smashed by an opponent.

infringement: Occurs when a team is guilty of breaking a law and prompts the referee to award a penalty to the non-offending side.

injury time: During a match, the referee stops the clock whenever there is an injury. After normal time has finished (40 minutes each half), play continues for the amount of time lost for the injury stoppages.

inside centre: The player who wears jersey number 12.

interchange: The reserve bench and the system by which coaches are allowed to swap players during a match, using players on the interchange to replace those on the field.

International Rugby Board: The body which controls the world game, runs the World Cup and determines the laws of the game.

judiciary committee: A group of officials (usually three) who determine whether a player who has been sent off should be suspended or not. They usually meet the day after the match.

kick-off: Used to start a game. One team kicks the ball from the centre line to the opposition. The kick is required to go 10 metres.

knock-on: When a player drops the ball to the ground and it goes forward.

ladders: A competition table showing how each team is performing in a competition, and setting out the number of wins and losses.

lifting: When a lineout jumper is lifted in the air to catch a throw from his hooker or intercept the throw from the opposition hooker.

lineout: How play is restarted when the ball has been taken out over the sideline or kicked into touch. The two sets of forwards line up in a row beside each other. The side with the ball decides how many players are in the lineout and where the throw is to be directed. The throw must be straight down the middle of the two lines.

lob pass: A high looping pass, aimed to go over the heads of the opposition.

lock: The two forwards who wear jerseys number 4 and 5. Usually the biggest players in the team, the locks are charged with providing the strength in the scrum and winning the ball in the lineouts. Also known as the *second row*.

loitering: Refers to someone who is standing in an offside position and preventing the opposing team from playing the ball as they wish.

loop: When a player runs around a team-mate to whom he has just passed in the hope of receiving the ball back from him.

loose-head prop: The prop packing in on the left-hand side of the scrum, closest to his halfback when his team is putting the ball in the scrum.

loosie: A term often used in New Zealand for the three members of the back-row: number 8 and the two breakaways. So called because they are supposed to be the first to the loose ball.

man-on-man defence: A form of defence where the tackler takes on the man directly opposite him.

mark: A player who catches the ball while standing behind his own quarter line and calls "Mark" is allowed to take a free kick.

match ball: The (hopefully) high quality rugby ball used in a match.

maul: When a player carrying the ball is held by one or more opponents and several of his team-mates also bind onto the ball carrier. A maul basically becomes a struggle for possession when the players are on their feet and the ball is in someone's hands. The big difference from a ruck is that the ball is not on the ground.

Midi rugby: The form of rugby played from ages 9 to 13, before full contact.

Mini rugby: The form of rugby played by children aged 6 to 9.

muddied oafs: Rudyard Kipling's opinion of the type of people who play rugby.

national divisions: The English professional/semi-professional tier of three divisions immediately underneath the Zurich Premiership.

number eight: The forward in the team who binds the scrum together. He is the central figure in a team's back row, working with the two breakaways.

obstruction: Unfairly getting in the way of an opposing player. Usually penalised.

offside: A player who is in front of his team-mates and is not allowed to be involved in the play. In general play, a player is offside if the player is in front of a team-mate who is carrying the ball, or in front of a team-mate who last played the ball.

onside: A player who is the right position to play the ball, usually being behind his team-mates.

open side: The area between the ball and the furthest sideline.

openside flanker: The flanker who binds onto the scrum on the openside.

out of play: When the ball or ball carrier has gone over the sideline or the dead ball line.

outside centre: The player who wears jersey number 13.

overlap: When a team has one or more players in the attack, compared to the opposition defence.

pack: A term used for the forwards when they are about to scrummage.

palm-off: see *hand-off*.

pass: When a player throws the ball to a team-mate.

peel: When a forward runs round the front or back of the lineout to drive the ball on from a tap or catch.

penalty: When a referee rules that a team is guilty of an indiscretion or has contravened the laws of the game. The innocent team is allowed to kick for goal, with a successful penalty goal worth 3 points.

penalty kick: A kick awarded to a team because of an illegality by the opposition. The kick is taken at the goalposts and if successful is worth 3 points.

penalty try: When a referee fervently believes a team would have scored if not for the opposition's illegal play.

pick-and-go: A forward charge where the ball is placed on the ground at the tackle and a forward quickly picks it up and runs with it to continue the attack.

place kick: The ball sits on the ground and is kicked by a designated player. Place kicks are used to start play, for conversions after tries have been scored, or for penalty kicks.

Pool system: Not something you swim in, but instead the groups of four into which teams are divided in the European Cup.

Powergen Cup: The English knockout cup which dates back to 1972.

prop: The two forwards who wear jerseys number 1 (loose-head) and number 3 (tight-head). They support the hooker in the scrums and the chief jumpers in the lineout.

protective vest: see *shoulder pads*.

punt kick: The most popular form of kick used during a match.

pushover try: A try scored by the forward pack. Happens during a scrum when the pack is able to push the opposition scrum across the tryline, while dragging the ball with them. Often scored when a five-metre scrum has been set.

quick throw-in: When a lineout throw is taken quickly, either precisely when the lineout has been formed or just before.

red card: The card shown to a player when the referee is sending him off for foul play. A player who is sent off takes no further part in the match and must appear before a judiciary committee.

referee: Person appointed or mutually agreed to officiate at a match. Called "Sir" by the players, but also known as the whistleblower, for obvious reasons!

reserve bench: The name given to the place where the reserves sit during a match.

restart: The kick that restarts play at each half and after points have been scored by a team.

rolling maul: A maul where the attacking team moves forward up the field by transferring the ball from player to player within the maul.

ruck: When one or more players from each team, who are on their feet, close around the ball on the ground. They usually attempt to use their feet to win possession of the ball. Once a ruck has been formed, players cannot use their hands to get the ball. The big difference to a maul is that the ball is on the ground.

scissors pass: Passing to a team-mate who cuts back in the opposite direction in a bid to disorientate the opposition.

screw punt: A form of punt kick where the ball spirals in the air, which increases its distance.

scrum: Players from each team come together in a formation, where eight forwards bind in against eight opposing forwards, with the aim of winning the ball which is thrown in between the front rows of the two packs.

scrum feed: When the halfback throws the ball into a scrum.

scrum half: The player wearing jersey number 9 who feeds the ball into the scrum and re-gathers the ball from the scrums, rucks, mauls and lineouts. Is also called a *halfback*.

scrum machine: An apparatus used at training where teams practise their scrummaging skills.

second row: Another name for *lock*.

set piece: A set way of restarting play, such as a scrum or a lineout.

sevens: A form of abbreviated rugby, where seven players, involving three forwards and four backs, play a quick game of seven minutes each half.

shortened lineout: When the team throwing the ball into the lineout calls for fewer than seven of their players to be part of the lineout.

shove: When the players in an attacking scrum push in unison.

sideline: See *touch line*.

side-on tackle: A tackle used when a ball carrier is trying to run in between defending players.

side-step: A way to avoid a tackler by stepping to one side.

sin bin: The referee can send players to the sin bin for ten minutes if they are guilty of a minor offence, including repeated obstruction of an opponent. The sin bin is usually a seat on the sideline, which the player must sit on before being allowed back onto the field.

Six Nations: The biggest annual tournament in international rugby, involving England, Ireland, Wales, Scotland, France, and Italy.

smother tackle: When a ball carrier is running straight at the tackler, the tackler aims high and tries to stop the attacking player by throwing himself at his opponent.

spiral pass: A pass where the player imparts spin on the ball to improve its trajectory.

squad: A group of players who make up a rugby team. A rugby squad usually involves 22 players.

stationary tackle: Usually a front-on tackle.

stiff arm tackle: A dangerous tackle where the tackler uses a straight arm to stop his opponent.

Super 12: The annual tournament involving the 12 best provincial teams of Australia, New Zealand, and South Africa.

support: Backing up the ball carrier.

swerve: A form of run where the attacking player attempts to swerve past his opponent.

tackle: Where a player brings an opponent carrying the ball down to the ground.

tackle area: The general area in which a tackle has been made, usually defined as several metres around where the player has fallen to the ground with the ball.

three quarters: Term used for the two quarters, two centres and two wingers, who are stationed between the five-eighth and the fullback.

throw-in: When the ball is thrown into a lineout.

tight five: The term given to the three front-rowers and two second-rowers.

tight-head: The prop on the right-hand side of the scrum, who packs in on the opposite side of where his halfback puts in the ball. The basic anchor of the scrum. "Winning a tight-head" happens when the team wins the ball from the scrum when the ball has been thrown in by the opposition.

touch judges: Assist the referee during the course of the game. The two touch judges who patrol either sideline have numerous duties, including deciding the exact position where lineout throws are taken, checking whether teams are offside, watching for foul play and determining whether penalty goals and conversions are successful.

touch line: The two lines situated on either side of the field. A ball is described as going "into touch" when it crosses either of those two lines and goes out of the field of play.

training ball: The type of rugby ball used for training purposes.

Tri-Nations: The annual tournament involving Australia, New Zealand and South Africa.

Triple Crown: The term used in the Six Nations if one of the Home Unions (England, Scotland, Ireland or Wales) beats all the others during a season.

try: The grounding of the ball by an attacking player in the opposition's in-goal area. It is worth 5 points and for many is the *raison d'être* of rugby.

tryline: The line marked on the field at either end near the goalposts that must be crossed to score a try. The attacking team must ground the ball over the tryline.

TV Match Commissioner: During international matches the commissioner is there to study video evidence of misdemeanours by players which have gone undetected, and to cite them for disciplinary action.

up and under: see *bomb*.

uprights: The two large posts which are part of the goalposts.

wheel: When a scrum moves more than 90 degrees.

Willie away: A New Zealand term used when a player peels from the lineout. Former All Black captain Wilson Whineray was one of the first to use this move.

wingers: The two attacking players who play closest to the sidelines and are usually renowned for their speed.

Wooden Spoon: The term used in the Six Nations when one side loses all its matches during the tournament. (No actual spoon is awarded!)

yellow card: A card shown to a player by the referee if the referee considers him guilty of foul play. The referee produces the card from the pocket of his shorts when cautioning the player and suspends him for ten minutes. The player goes to the sin bin which is situated on the sideline.

Zurich Premiership: The English Premiership, a highly competitive 12-team, 22-match competition, played home and away, which currently finishes in a Premiership Final, and involves a series of play-offs.

Appendix C

Key Rugby Organisations

● ●

*T*his appendix provides contact details, email addresses and Web site addresses for the organisations referred to earlier in this book. Please note that if certain details, such as an email address, are missing, that organisation has not made them available.

International Rugby Unions

The International Rugby Board (IRB) is the World Governing body for Rugby Union, runs the World Cup and determines the laws of the game. The IRB's website is www.irb.org

The following Web addresses enable you to keep in touch with or contact national rugby unions.

English Rugby Football Union, Rugby House, Rugby Road, Twickenham, TW1 1DS, England; phone, +44 (0) 208 892 2000; website www.rfu.com; email reception@rfu.com

Irish Rugby Football Union, 62 Lansdowne Road, Ballsbridge, Dublin 4, Ireland; phone +353 (0) 1 647 3800; website www.irishrugby.ie; email manager@irishrugby.ie

Scottish Rugby Union, Murrayfield, Edinburgh, EH12 5PJ, Scotland; phone, +44 (0)131 346 5000; website www.sru.org.uk; email feedback@sru.org.uk

Welsh Rugby Union, Millennium Stadium Group, 1st Floor, Golate House, 101 St Marys Street, Cardiff, CF10 1GE, Wales; phone +44 (0) 870 013 8600; website www.wru.co.uk

If you're outside of the UK, or wish to contact an international rugby union, here are the contact details.

Australian Rugby Union, Level 7, 181 Miller Street, North Sydney, NSW2060, Australia; phone +61 299 563444; website `www.rugby.com.au`; email `rugby@rugby.com.au`

French Rugby Union, Fédération Française De Rugby, 9 Rue de Liège, Paris 75009, France; phone +33 153 211515; website `www.ffr.fr`; email `secretairegeneral@ffr.fr`

Italian Rugby Union, Federazion Italiana Rugby, Stadio Olimpico, Foro Italico, Roma 194, Italy; phone +39 636 85730; website `www.federugby.it`; email `federugby@atleticom.it`

New Zealand Rugby Football Union, 1 Hinemoa Street, Centre Port, Wellington, PO Box 2172, New Zealand; phone +64 449 94995; website `www.nzrugby.co.nz`; email `mediacentre@nzrugby.co.nz`

South African Rugby Football Union, Boundary Road, PO Box 99, Newlands, Cape Town 7725, South Africa; phone +27 216 596700; website `www.sarugby.net`; email `sarfu@icon.co.za`

Zurich Premiership

For those of you who want to track the progress of your favourite team in England's Zurich Premiership, or find out about the team's players, what they have for breakfast, and loads of other details ... you can check up on them on their Web sites.

Bath Rugby, 11 Argyle Street, Bath, BA2 4BQ; phone 01225 325200; website `www.bathrugby.com`; email `info@bathrugby.com`

Bristol Rugby, Unit 4, Eastgate Office Centre, Eastgate Road, Bristol, BS5 6XX; phone 0117 311 1461; website `www.bristolshoguns.co.uk`; email `lcoles@bristolshoguns.co.uk`

Gloucester Rugby, Kingsholm, Kingsholm Road, Gloucester, GL1 3AX; phone 0871 871 87 81; website `www.gloucesterrugbyclub.com`; email `postbox@gloucesterrugbyclub.com`

Leeds Tykes, St Michael's Lane, Headingley, Leeds, LS6 3BR; phone 0113 278 6181; website `www.leedsrugby.com`; email `info@leedsrugby.com`

Leicester Tigers, Ayelstone Road, Leicester, LE2 7TR; phone 08701 28 34 30; website `www.leicestertigers.com`; email `tigers@tigers.co.uk`

London Irish, The Avenue, Sunbury on Thames, Middlesex TW16 5EQ; phone 0118 987 9730; website www.london-irish.com; email info@london-irish.org

London Wasps, Twyford Avenue Sports Ground, Twyford Avenue, Acton, London, W3 9QA; phone 0208 993 8298; website www.wasps.co.uk

NEC Harlequins, Stoop Memorial Ground, Langhorn Drive, Twickenham, Middlesex, TW2 7SX; phone 020 8410 6000; website www.quins.co.uk

Newcastle Falcons, Kingston Park Ground, Brunton Rd, Kenton Bank, Newcastle Upon Tyne, Tyne And Wear, NE13 8AF; phone 0191 214 5588; website www.newcastle-falcons.co.uk

Northampton Saints, Franklin's Gardens, Weedon Road, Northampton, NN5 5BG; phone 01604 751543; website www.northamptonsaints.co.uk; email clubinfo@northamptonsaints.co.uk

Saracens, Rigby House, 34 The Parade, High Street, Watford, Herts, WD17 4AB; phone 01923 475222; website www.saracens.com

The Sharks, Heywood Road, Sale, Cheshire, M33 3WB; phone 0161 283 1861; website www.salesharks.com; email dave.swanton@salesharks.co.uk

Celtic League

If your loyalty lies with a Celtic League team, you can find out the comings and goings at your favourite club, the date of birth of your favourite player, the details of forthcoming fixtures, and many more things by heading off to their Web site.

Bridgend, The Brewer Field, Tondu Road, Bridgend, CF31 4JE; phone 01656 65 27 07; website www.bridgendrfc.co.uk

Cardiff Blues, Cardiff Arms Park, Westgate Street, Cardiff, CF10 1JA; phone 029 20 30 2000; website www.cardiffrfc.com

Connacht, Galway Sportsground, College Road, Galway, Ireland; phone +353 (0) 91 561568; website www.connachtrugby.ie

Ebbw Vale, Eugene Cross Park, Ebbw Vale, Gwent, NP23 5AZ; phone 01495 30 59 99; website www.ebbwvalerfc.co.uk

Edinburgh, Murrayfield, Edinburgh, EH12 5PJ; phone 0131 346 5252; website www.edinburghrugby.com

Glasgow, 5 Somerset Place, Glasgow, G3 7JT; phone 0141 353 3468; website www.glasgowrugby.com

Leinster Lions, Donnybrook, Dublin 4, Ireland; phone +353 (0) 1 2693224; website www.leinsterrugby.ie

Llanelli, Stradey Park, Llanelli, Carmarthenshire, SA15 4BT; phone 01554 783900; website www.scarlets.co.uk

Munster, Musgrove Park, Pearse Road, Cork, Ireland; phone +353 (0) 21 4323563; website www.munsterrugby.ie

Neath, The John Smiths Gnoll, Gnoll Park Road, Neath, SA11 3BU; phone +44 (0)1639 769660; website www.neathrfc.co.uk

Newport, Rodney Road, Newport, NP19 0UU; phone 01633 670690; website www.newport-rfc.co.uk

Pontypridd, The Clubhouse, Sardis Road, Pontypridd, CF37 1HA; phone 01443 405006; website www.pontypriddrfc.co.uk

Swansea, St Helens, Bryn Road, Swansea, SA2 0AR; phone 01792 424242; website www.swansearfc.co.uk

The Borders, Coach House, Nether Road, Galashiels, TD1 3HE; phone 01896 750045; website www.sru.org.uk/proteam/borders

Ulster, 85 Ravenhill Park, Belfast, BT6 0DG; phone 028 9064 9141; website www.ulsterrugby.ie

Heineken Cup

If your team isn't in the Zurich Premiership or the Celtic League, but takes part in the Heineken Cup, never fear, you can still read all about your team and favourite players on the Web.

AS Beziers Herault, Rond point Pierre Lacans, BP 23, 34501 Béziers Cedex, France; phone +33 4 67 11 80 90; website www.asbh.net; email asbh@asbh.net

Amatori & Calvisano, via San Michele, 10225012 Calvisano (BS), Italy; phone +39 030 96 80 12; website www.calvisanorugby.it; email staff@calvisanorugby.it

Biarritz Olympique, Parc des Sports Aguiléra, Rue Cino Del Ducam, 64200 Biarritz, France; phone +33 4 67 11 80 90; website www.bo-pb.; email bo@bo-pb.com

Bourgoin, Club Sportif de Bourgoin-Jallieu, 28 Rue de la Liberté BP 141 38304, Bourgoin, France; phone +33 4 74 19 0810; website www.csbj-ugby.fr; email csbj@wanadoo.fr

Montferrand, Association Sportive Montferrandaise, 84 Bd Léon Jouhaux, 63021, Clermont-Ferrand, France; phone +33 4 73 30 48 66; website www.asm-rugby.com; email contact@asm-rugby.com

Perpignan, Union Sportive Arlequins Perpignan, Stade Aimé Giral, Alleé Aimé Giral, 66000 Perpignan, France; phone +33 4 68 61 18 18; website www.usap.fr; email b.faytre@usap.fr

Toulouse, Stade Toulousain, 114 Rue des Troenes, 31200 Toulouse, France phone +33 4 68 61 18 18; website www.stadetoulousain.fr; email jl.brumont@wanadoo.fr

Viadana, Rugby Viadana SRL, Via L Guerra, 12 46019 Viadana (MN), Italy phone +33 4 67 11 80 90; website www.rugbyviadana.it; email info@rugbyviadana.it.net

Index

• C •

• D •

Notes

Notes

Notes

Notes

Notes

FOR DUMMIES®

The easy way to get more done and have more fun

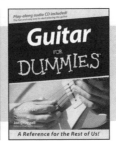

FOR DUMMIES

A world of resources to help you grow

TRAVEL

0-7645-5453-0

0-7645-5438-7

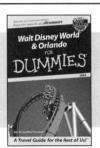
0-7645-5444-1

Also available:

America's National Parks For Dummies
(0-7645-6204-5)

Caribbean For Dummies
(0-7645-5445-X)

Cruise Vacations For Dummies 2003
(0-7645-5459-X)

Europe For Dummies
(0-7645-5456-5)

Ireland For Dummies
(0-7645-6199-5)

France For Dummies
(0-7645-6292-4)

Las Vegas For Dummies
(0-7645-5448-4)

London For Dummies
(0-7645-5416-6)

Mexico's Beach Resorts For Dummies
(0-7645-6262-2)

Paris For Dummies
(0-7645-5494-8)

RV Vacations For Dummie
(0-7645-5443-3)

EDUCATION & TEST PREPARATION

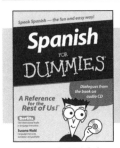
0-7645-5194-9

0-7645-5325-9

0-7645-5249-X

Also available:

The ACT For Dummies
(0-7645-5210-4)

Chemistry For Dummies
(0-7645-5430-1)

English Grammar For Dummies
(0-7645-5322-4)

French For Dummies
(0-7645-5193-0)

GMAT For Dummies
(0-7645-5251-1)

Inglés Para Dummies
(0-7645-5427-1)

Italian For Dummies
(0-7645-5196-5)

Research Papers For Dumr
(0-7645-5426-3)

SAT I For Dummies
(0-7645-5472-7)

U.S. History For Dummies
(0-7645-5249-X)

World History For Dummi
(0-7645-5242-2)

HEALTH, SELF-HELP & SPIRITUALITY

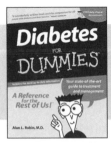
0-7645-5154-X

0-7645-5302-X

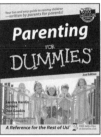
0-7645-5418-2

Also available:

The Bible For Dummies
(0-7645-5296-1)

Controlling Cholesterol For Dummies
(0-7645-5440-9)

Dating For Dummies
(0-7645-5072-1)

Dieting For Dummies
(0-7645-5126-4)

High Blood Pressure For Dummies
(0-7645-5424-7)

Judaism For Dummies
(0-7645-5299-6)

Menopause For Dummies
(0-7645-5458-1)

Nutrition For Dummies
(0-7645-5180-9)

Potty Training For Dummi
(0-7645-5417-4)

Pregnancy For Dummies
(0-7645-5074-8)

Rekindling Romance For Dummies
(0-7645-5303-8)

Religion For Dummies
(0-7645-5264-3)